SRI RAMAKRISHNA

Sri Ramakrishna Paramahamsa

SRI RAMAKRISHNA
A Prophet for the New Age

⇛ RICHARD SCHIFFMAN ⇚

PARAGON HOUSE
New York

First edition, 1989

Published in the United States by

Paragon House
90 Fifth Avenue
New York, NY 10011

Copyright © 1989 by Paragon House

Photograph of Sri Ramakrishna Paramahamsa courtesy of Ramakrishna–
Vivekananda Center, New York.

Manufactured in the United States of America.

Library of Congress Cataloging-in-Publication Data

Schiffman, Richard.
Sri Ramakrishna Paramahamsa.

Bibliography: p.
Includes index.
1. Ramakrishna, 1836–1886.   2. Ramakrishna Mission—
Biography.   3. Hindus—India—Biography.   I. Title.

BL1280.292.R36S35   1989   294.5′55′0924   [B]   88-25408

ISBN 1-55778-120-6
1-55778-208-3(pbk)

*Dedicated to Mata Amritanandamayi,
in whom the ecstatic spirituality of Sri Ramakrishna
is alive today.*

Contents

Acknowledgments

THE AUTHOR GRATEFULLY ACKNOWLEDGES THE FOLLOWING sources for granting permission to reprint material. (Citations are given parenthetically, in the text.)

Advaita Ashrama, Calcutta, for *The Life of Sri Ramakrishna*.

Sri Ramakrishna Math, Madras, for *Sayings of Sri Ramakrishna, Sri Ramakrishna as Swamiji Saw Him*, and *Thus Spake Sri Ramakrishna*.

Ramakrishna-Vivekananda Center, New York, for *The Gospel of Sri Ramakrishna*, as translated into English by Swami Nikhilananda and published by the Ramakrishna-Vivekananda Center of New York, Copyright 1942 by Swami Nikhilananda, and for *Holy Mother:* Being the Life of Sri Sarada Devi, Wife of Sri Ramakrishna and Helpmate in His Mission, by Swami Nikhilananda, published by The Ramakrishna-Vivekananda Center of New York, Copyright 1962 by Swami Nikhilananda.

→⟩⟩ *Chapter 1* ⟨⟨←

Boyhood

Sri Ramakrishna seems a singularly unlikely hero for this feverish city. And yet, as we pass through the madly teeming streets of Calcutta at dusk, his image is everywhere we look. Thin-boned and intense, wrapped like a peasant in a single plain cotton cloth tied loosely around his waist, he gazes, eyes half closed in ecstasy, out of sari emporiums piled high with colorful reams of cloth, out of bright medical stores named after Lakshmi and Durga and Shiva and crowded with a dazzling assortment of packets and vials, out of bicycle repair stalls huddled at curbsides under torn canvas awnings.

The pictures of Ramakrishna come in countless variations: Ramakrishna with his arms upraised, dancing in rapture; Ramakrishna standing devotedly by the side of the Divine Mother, Kali, Her crimson tongue lolling, holding in one of Her hands a sword and in the other a severed head; Ramakrishna placing flowers at the feet of his saintly wife, Sarada Devi; Ramakrishna seated in profound meditation under a spreading banyan tree.

Gazing out from our ancient bus, as it lurches painfully towards Dakshineswar, we are struck by inexpensive but colorful calendar images blazing like brilliant visions out of the hallucinogenic maelstrom of Calcutta at dusk. The Kali temple at Dakshineswar, Sri Ramakrishna's peaceful retreat on the outskirts of

Calcutta for over three decades, has long since been swallowed up by the city which has made him its patron saint.

Even before we catch our first glimpse of the imposing towers of the temple of Kali at Dakshineswar, it is clear that the great Master is no longer there. Now he is everywhere. The flower and incense merchant proudly displays his subtly smiling countenance amid mountains of marigolds and fragrant jasmine; the tea *wallah* keeps Sri Ramakrishna's garlanded image poised just above his clay oven to look down with divine favor upon his worldly affairs. At the center of the broad avenue, on a thin raised island precariously afloat a sea of rickshaws, sacred cows, motorcycles, ox carts, and wooden lorries painted over with bright visions of paradise, a family of lepers, having claimed as home the only unoccupied plot of ground for blocks around, cooks rice in a blackened pot and burns a single stick of incense before their only nonfunctional possession, a framed and gaily decorated picture of Sri Ramakrishna Paramahamsa praying before the black Kali of Dakshineswar.

Across the river, under the spreading dome of one of the most distinctive buildings in all Calcutta, the Belur Math (an inspired amalgam of mosque, cathedral, and Hindu temple), a congregation of ochre-clad monks accompanied by lay devotees are conducting their evening services. The invocatory hymn which they render passionately before the life-size white marble statue of Ramakrishna is, like the temple—indeed, like the great Master himself—a strange mixture of religious and devotional moods. Now measured and tranquil as a gregorian chant, now hypnotic and expansive like a *raga*, now soaring dizzily, it rises a dervish chant to the great dome and beyond.

Yes, the chant spreads beyond the temple, through the darkening air, rising silent on the wings of devotion, rising like the faint wisps of smoke even now curling serenely from half a dozen funeral pyres on the far bank of the Ganges. Twisting upward through a maroon sky, the lofty chant ascends and expands like a thin mist of light until it covers the sacred river, Calcutta, Bengal, India herself. For that indeed is what has happened. The spirit of Ramakrishna has expanded beyond all the conventional limits of caste and class, of dogma and religious affiliation—and

2

finally beyond the last and most intractable barrier of all, the egoistic bounds of "I" and "mine," to embrace the Infinite. Ramakrishna's spirit has gone on to spread its radiance over spiritual India, and beyond.

Over a century since his passing, the great prophet Sri Ramakrishna Paramahamsa remains one of the most profoundly beloved figures in India. Of all the nations of the world, India alone seems to possess the ripened wisdom to honor him above all other men. And what exactly did India see in this unformed son of a peasant and heedless madman of God? In our efforts to understand Sri Ramakrishna, we must first try to understand India.

India, however, is not so easy to take in with one sweeping glance. Far from being a homogeneous unity, India is a crazy quilt of bright colors, each region as distinct in language, culture, and temperament as the nations of Europe, each with a special genius, playing out its *raga* to a *sruti* note all its own. This dominant chord may be hard to define precisely, but the rough popular stereotypes are not difficult to come by—martial spirit in the Punjab, business acumen in Gujarat, the orthodoxy of the Tamil south. But of all the Indian peoples—indeed of all the world's peoples—few have a national character quite so distinctive, quite so sharply etched, as that of Sri Ramakrishna's homeland, the state of Bengal.

The passionate intensity of the Bengalis is legendary. For untold centuries, this easternmost of the Indian nations, where the Ganges fans out and ends her long journey to the sea, has been a haven for poets and revolutionaries, iconoclasts and free thinkers, and the fervent legions of the God-mad, like the celebrated Bauls. In Bengal, two great streams converge that seem at first glance incompatible; the fathomless, eternal stream of yearning for the Infinite that is India joins with swift-flowing liquid fire. From out of this anomalous union, a very special strain of ecstatic devotion is conceived, peculiar to Bengal. It may lie uneasily dormant, coiled just beneath the soil, for generations at a stretch. Then, in a spasm of sheer joy, it bursts forth, scattering glowing missiles in all directions, setting great trees ablaze, igniting the air.

When Bengal erupts, all of India basks in the heat.

Sri Chaitanya danced in rapture down the dusty cow lanes of rural Bengal in the Middle Ages and set into motion an incendiary wave of spiritual fervor that surged unhindered from the Himalayas to the cape of Kanyakumari at the southernmost tip of the subcontinent. But in the ensuing centuries, the flame of *bhakti* died away. By the dawn of our modern era, only a few faintly glowing embers remained. The living heart of Hinduism was once again becoming choked in the ash of ritualistic piety and dry philosophical speculation. But now the challenge of a new order, coming this time from the outside, threatened to extinguish for good the oldest surviving way of life and wisdom on the planet.

In the past, the Hindu spiritual culture had always shown a remarkable resiliency. Each period of decay set the stage for a renewed flowering forth. A long line of reformers and Divine Avatars—Buddha, Shankaracharya, Sri Chaitanya—had passed down the torch of vision lit by the original *rishis,* the sages of prehistory, and kept it aflame for succeeding generations. Time and again the phoenix arose from out of its own ashes.

India watched while the Egypt of the Pharaohs, Classical Greece, Persia, and Chaldea—civilizations that had been her contemporaries—flared their brilliant arcs through the centuries like so many shooting stars. And still her beacon light from the dawn of history shone brightly. Alexander would conquer and Hellenize the known world. But when he reached the valley of the Indus, his fearful juggernaut was stopped cold. His troops, ragged and tired, refuse to fight, and for the first time the conqueror of the world was forced to turn back. Centuries later, the Koran and the sword of Islam seemed invincible in their triumphant sweep eastward. Everywhere they went, nations turned away from the old Gods and embraced the strict monotheism of the religion of Allah. India, too, fell under Muslim sway. And yet, remarkably, when the last Moghul emperor left the Red Fort at Delhi after three centuries of political domination, the people of India were as firmly committed to the *Sanatana Dharma,* the Eternal Way of their sages, as ever before.

Greeks, Mongols, Moghuls—wave upon wave of outward

challenges had broken ineffectually on Hindu shores. India rarely felt the need to repel her invaders; she was satisfied to accommodate them within her immensity. In the end, all those who had come to conquer were themselves conquered, absorbed into a culture that remained stable because it remained flexible, instead of standing rigidly against incursions of the new. Like a palm tree that bends with each passing storm, India endured.

On the spiritual front, the internal menace of factionalism, dogmatism, and all of the debilitating corruptions that come with time had been successfully conquered by Hinduism's genius at integrating the novel into the intricate tapestry of tradition. India rarely threw anything away—not a line from its ancient scriptures, not a ritual, not a minor deity. Most importantly, she never employed the old as a bulwark against the new. She was not afraid of adding new revelations to the established wisdom of the ages. She saw no contradiction between the two. However different in appearance, she recognized in each new revelation a natural development of all that had come before. Just as the tree develops from the seed, so the expressions of spiritual life evolve endlessly out of the unitary seed of Truth.

And so, like a great banyan tree, Hinduism spread in all possible directions—its roots groping for the soil, its branches reaching ever outward, upward, adding tier upon tier—until its scriptures filled great libraries, and its temple towers seethed with an incredible hierarchy of divine beings, and its rituals required an army of *brahmins* to interpret and perform correctly. No religion has venerated its holy Avatars more than Hinduism. And yet no religion has been so liberal in adding fresh names to the hallowed list. Perhaps more than any other factor, the remarkable vitality of Hinduism through the ages flowed from the life-giving springs of Light and Truth emanating from these great souls, whose presence at critical junctures seemed a fulfillment of Sri Krishna's immortal promise in the Bhagavad Gita: "When righteousness is weak and faints and unrighteousness exults in pride, then My spirit arises on earth."

But by the start of our modern age, a threat of a completely new order had come to the land of the sages. By the mid-nineteenth century, when we take up our narrative, the massed black-

ness of an unprecedented storm of the spirit loomed just ahead,
throwing its spreading shadows over the landscape of the mind.
It had been brewing for centuries in Western lands—a maelstrom
of skepticism and rationalistic dogma that rejected as myth anything too subtle to be grasped in its heavy and inflexible instruments of thought. It had effectively gutted its own spiritual traditions and left them hollow caricatures of themselves. Now it
turned like some dark avenging angel, poised ominously above
the world's remaining traditional cultures, ready to cleanse them
of the accumulated "superstition" of millennia.

And India seemed to be the most vulnerable of all. For what
was the culture of India but an arrangement of delicate sky flowers with roots far above, in the invisible, unthinkable reaches of
the Spirit? How could these rare blooms of intuition, whose
unearthly fragrance permeated every single act and thought of a
people, survive the cold rain of a materialism that respects hard
facts and crushes subtle truths? Would the practical new order so
swiftly approaching make room for a race whose greatest men
had never been its kings, its generals, or its scientists—a people
who regarded as its highest heroes the solitary spirits in caves, on
the banks of jungle rivers, and in mountain fastnesses on glacial
summits, men who had abandoned the consensual dream of
earthly life to embrace the far greater dream of God?

In 1836, the year Gadadhar, later to be known as Ramakrishna Paramahamsa, was born the people of India were almost
totally unaware that these questions needed to be asked. Though
nominally subjects of the British Empire, the great masses in the
villages knew nothing of the ways of the British. Outside of the
large towns, perhaps not a single man in a hundred had so much
as set eyes on one of the curious white-skinned sahibs who ruled
his land. Rural India persevered in its age-old rhythms, blissfully
undisturbed by time and history.

In the big cities, however, the currents of change had begun
to stir. Calcutta, that most volatile of cities in the heart of India's
most extroverted and passionate province, Bengal, already
seethed restlessly in a vortex of new ideas. The brightest young
men, the ones who in a quieter age would have turned their
genius to the study and practice of orthodox religion, were reel-

ing under the first intoxicating draft of European thought. A few of the more impressionable among them vied with the British masters in heaping scorn on the traditions of their ancestors. India, backward India—hopelessly mired in superstition, scratching the earth, unsuited to the new age of machines—would have to change. If caste was at fault, let it go; if the multitude of the Gods were to blame, then let them go; if religion held India back, abandon religion. Nothing could be simpler. Science laughed at such things. They were pleasant dreams of an age gone by. But the time for sleep had long since passed. The morning light was streaming through the cracks in a thousand huts of mud, and still their inhabitants slept. India must awaken and enter the brave new world in step with the rest of humanity!

Heady, impatient thoughts to be sure, but who could doubt that they represented the wave of the future? Meanwhile, sixty miles northwest of Calcutta, unknown to the world, in the mud and thatch hamlet of Kamarpukur, the spiritual soul of India was preparing its response.

To place Kamarpukur sixty miles—some three jolting days journey by bullock cart—from Calcutta is to put too much store in the truths of the mapmaker. For it was not the physical distance, measurable in miles, so much as a temporal distance of centuries that separated the village from the city. Calcutta, an artificial appendage of the British East India Company, its port and commercial hub, was worldly, seething, ambitious—an outpost of India's uncertain future. Kamarpukur, sleepy, indrawn, at peace with itself, was a living embodiment of the fathomless past. Yet within the boundaries of the village was one who would span in his ample being the chasm between the two worlds, embodying what was most distinctive in each—the restless probing of an awakened Bengal alongside the eternal values of village India.

From out of Kamarpukur would come perhaps the greatest explorer of the inner realm of the Spirit that the world has known, a man who would chart in his own soul, one after another, all of the ancient *sadhanas,* the traditional paths that India had devised in its single-minded quest for God, until he had traced each one to its goal and carefully mapped out every obstacle, every ford and bend along the way. When his investigations were complete, he would share with his countrymen this hard-won knowledge and reveal to them the hidden purpose behind each of their major lines of ritual, mythology, and philosophy in a way that even the skeptical could appreciate.

He would not quote the scriptures; he would not fall back on the mute authority of tradition, or retreat into the safety of dogma. He would speak from experience—his own experience. And India would listen, not least of all the idealistic, reform-minded, Western-educated sons of Calcutta, who would flock around this boyish son of a peasant to drink in the artless and inspired words of one who so obviously knew what he was talk-ing about. By the beginning of the twentieth century, he would be regarded by millions in his native land as the savior who had preserved a precious spiritual heritage from the clutches of the beast.

Who could have predicted such a fate for the young Gadad-har? Charm he had in excess from the very beginning, an endear-ing guilelessness, but seemingly none of the aggressive drive and self-assured brilliance that mark out in advance the ambitious ones who are destined to forge a name for themselves in the world. He was a mediocre student at best, intelligent enough, gifted in so many ways, but stubbornly set against giving in to the demands of abstractions, like mathematics, which held no appeal to his poet's soul. Instinctively, he rebelled against the regimentation, the wearisome parade of facts and rote memoriza-tion of the classroom. Even as a child, he understood the differ-ence between the conventional knowledge of the schoolmaster and the vital wisdom of the soul. There had never been any question in his mind as to which of the two his inner being thirsted for!

In all respects, we are told, Gadadhar was normal and cheer-ful, full of mischief and a contagious good humor. His lively nature made him the favorite of his playmates, and a pet of the village mothers who relished his liquid, feminine grace of move-ment, and recognized in his ingenious pranks a beguiling reflec-tion of their beloved child-God, Krishna. Gadadhar was well mannered and obedient, to a point. He could also be strong willed, and he clearly had a mind of his own. The only way to get him to behave was by appealing to his reason. He was indifferent to threats. It wasn't enough to say, "Do it, because that's the way it is done." You had to explain why it was done that way, in a manner that touched his keenly honed sense of right and wrong.

All the while, during these calm and idyllic years, his body and mind were preparing themselves from within for the awesome change that was to propel the boy into unknown worlds. Concealed darkly in the vast interior spaces of the soul, the process was largely invisible to all around him, as it must have been to Gadadhar himself. But now and again a glimpse of something tremendous broke momentarily like a great whale, smashing with impetuous force through the outward personality of a child.

Such glimpses surfaced, paradoxically, during the most ordinary activities. Gadadhar, six years old, strolling absentmindedly down a narrow path between the fields, munching on a hoard of puffed rice tucked away in a fold of his dhoti, the thin cotton garment wrapped around his waist, glanced up at the swiftly spreading blackness of a monsoon storm. Suddenly, a sharp arrow of cranes—snow white, silent, immaculate—pierced the darkening cloud. The magnificence of the contrast overwhelmed the young boy. His spirit soared to encompass it. He fell down unconscious. The puffed rice was scattered. His limp body had to be carried home.

This was only the smallest harbinger of all that lay ahead. For even then, the stormy years of awakening lay just over the visible horizon. It would not be long before Ramakrishna, priest of Kali, would spend his days and nights balanced precariously on the very borderline of ecstasy, and the least pretext—a strain of music, a Divine Name, a familiar face—would serve as a window through which his trembling spirit would pass into the radiance of the other world.

For the time being, however, the demands and joys of this world were sufficiently binding. He was a free spirit busily exploring the village and the fields, at home everywhere, intensely curious about everything. Wide-eyed, a keen observer of the realms of nature and of men, he watched intently as a potter molded the image of a God; he then returned home and made his own technically flawless model filled with a subtle inward life that set it far above the uninspired craftsmanship of the professionals. He heard the sweet strains of a devotional song rendered by a passing *sadhu,* and, when he returned to his companions, sang it so feelingly that it brings tears to their eyes. A sacred book inspired him with its exalted music. He painstakingly copied the whole of it into his school exercise book like some medieval scribe.

But the singular love of Gadadhar's childhood was for the colorful rustic dramas which, to this day, form the cultural staple of village India. Aside from their palpable charms—the bright costumes and songs, the flashing mirrors, feathers, and lacquered masks—these ancient morality plays opened up before him a whole undiscovered world of history, philosophy, and spiritual lore. And what is most important, they gave Gadadhar a unique entrée into the minds and hearts of India's saintly heroes; as an actor and a vicarious participant, he came to understand his characters from the inside, and to identify himself with them. His young heart thrilled to the epic themes of heroic love, renunciation, and virtue.

Gadadhar was a sponge greedily sucking up all of his favorite dramas and characters, assimilating them into himself. He possessed seemingly limitless powers of memorization. And, once he had learned a play by heart, he couldn't wait to steal away from school and stage it with his friends in the open fields at the edge of Kamarpukur. It was always a delight for the village folk to watch these unaffected performances. In time, Krishna and Rama, Sita and Hanuman, came to appear as intensely real to Gadadhar as his own flesh and blood companions. When he acted a part, the onlookers were invariably struck by how seamlessly he entered into the role. He appeared to forget himself as he strutted back and forth, gesturing expansively. And his wiry frame took on a regal dignity of bearing that was as convincing as it was uncanny in one so young.

Just how far this identification with a character might take him can be seen by what happened when Gadadhar was cast as the great God, Shiva. Made up with an ascetic's thickly matted hair, a rosary of sacred Himalayan *rudraksha* beads strung around his neck, his body smeared with the ashes of renunciation, he walked out onto the makeshift stage with slow and measured steps. Suddenly, to no apparent cause, Gadadhar stood riveted, tears of rapture pouring freely down his cheeks. He could not speak a single word of his part. He just stood there and wept out a flood of tears. A murmur of astounded admiration rippled through the audience as they realized what had happened. Indeed, there could be no mistaking it; Gadadhar's countenance was eloquent with bliss. He was possessed of the God. The play was over before it had even begun. The boy had to be carried off the stage on the shoulders of some of the village men. For the rest of the night, he was lost in a strange and exalted realm where none could follow.

Thereafter, such spontaneous flights of the spirit became more frequent. The divinity struggling to be born within Gadadhar stirred fitfully, and each time it stirred the umbilical chord that tied him to the world of appearances loosened its hold. The passing of his father, Khudiram, when Gadadhar was only seven years old, added a powerful impetus to the boy's growing mood of dispassion. The experience was not frittered away in barren trauma. Where other children might have retreated into dumb, unreasoning woe, Gadadhar became thoughtful. It was as if a veil of illusion had been lifted, and for a moment he saw clearly what had been hidden; he saw life stripped of its pretensions, bare boned and starkly real.

This vision transformed Gadadhar subtly, yet profoundly. He turned more serious, not somber—never in his life would he be capable of somberness. But the games and play of childhood lost their relish. And he began to pass his time with the monks in a nearby rest house for pilgrims. All day long, he absorbed their silent influence, and sometimes he spent the night with them as well, singing, meditating, chanting, and hearing their wanderers' tales. Gadadhar gladly helped the venerable ascetics with their chores—gathering firewood, hauling water, preparing their pipes—and they, in turn, adopted him as one of their own, sharing with him the alms they collected and painting his body with the holy emblems of their fraternity. One day Gadadhar returned

11

home all smeared with sacred ash, his dhoti in shreds and fitted loosely as an ascetic's loin cloth. The moment she saw him, his mother, Chandra Devi, panicked. She forbade her son to visit the *sadhus* ever again. Heartbroken, Gadadhar had no choice but to obey. Only after the holy men formed a delegation to reassure the frightened mother that they wouldn't take her boy away, did she finally relent.

In a certain sense, though, the promise of the *sadhus* had come too late. Gadadhar's restless spirit had already taken flight. Having thrilled to the siren song of a God-dedicated life, there was no longer any question of turning back. Chandra Devi didn't know it at the time, but in imagination—if not yet in fact—her youngest son had already slipped irrevocably from the restraining net of hearth and home.

→→→ *Chapter 2* ←←←

Calcutta

In the serene years of Gadadhar's childhood, no member of his family had properly assessed the passion for renunciation burning within him; their anxious plans for him had effectively blinded them. In badly straitened circumstances, as they were since the death of Khudiram, the family looked hopefully to Gadadhar to waste no more time in equipping himself for a wage-earning life in the world. Their expectation was that the bright and talented boy might be groomed for a lucrative position in government service. With this end in mind, Gadadhar was sent in 1852 to Calcutta, where his elder brother, Ramkumar, had opened a small Sanskrit school.

Not surprisingly, Ramkumar's well-intentioned designs to make a scholar of his young brother miscarried badly. If Gadadhar remained something of a mystery to others, he was, nevertheless, perfectly clear in his own mind. He knew exactly what he wanted out of life. And he knew what was required to achieve it. A worldly education of the sort that had been planned for him clearly did not enter into the equation. Moreover, to Gadadhar's intensely principled way of thinking, school was not merely an irrelevancy, it was something vaguely shameful—a prostitution of the mind, which was created for better things. Having set his mind on the pure gold of God-realization, the thought of turning it toward the skills needed to accumulate the baubles of wealth and worldly honors made him shudder with revulsion.

Gadadhar clung tenaciously to his ideals. While he dutifully helped Ramkumar with the practical chores at the school, he held himself aloof from the classroom like a chaste wife.

In short order, the school, which had been on a shaky financial basis from the start, was compelled to close its doors. Sorely pressed for employment, Ramkumar accepted the position of last resort for poor but learned *brahmins* by becoming a priest at the newly consecrated temple of Kali at Dakshineswar some four miles north of Calcutta and fronting the sacred Ganges. Gadadhar accompanied his brother somewhat reluctantly. At first he felt ill at ease there. Ironically, when we consider his radical abandonment of caste distinctions a few years later, Gadadhar was uncomfortable because the Kali temple had been constructed by the noble-spirited widow Rani Rasmani, a member of the *sudra* caste. Technically, it was a violation of caste rules for a *brahmin* like Ramkumar to officiate at a temple belonging to a member of a lower caste.

In order to understand something of Gadadhar's feelings in this matter, it will be useful to take a brief look at the caste system. In order to understand caste, we must go back through the millennia to the ancient sages who are said to have uncovered the laws of caste in the first place. These sages started from the fundamental perception that all men are *not* created equal. This wasn't a value judgment on their part, as it might seem, but simply a recognition of the fact that mankind was not a homogeneous mass, that individuals had not all been stamped out in the same mold—indeed, that they had been created with vastly different aptitudes. So if God had made men different, they reasoned, He must have had His reasons. And if men were to live in harmony with God, then they had better learn to respect those differences. Each man individually had to live according to his own *dharma*, the God-given law of his nature. And society as a whole had to organize itself in accordance with the various *dharmas* of its members. Caste, in its purest form, was just such an attempt to group men harmoniously in keeping with their natural endowments, their individual *dharmas*.

The four main divisions that the ancient philosophers saw reflected in the society of their own age were the basic caste groups that have existed in India to this day. In the original conception, they were believed to represent the fundamental psychospiritual categories into which all men naturally fall. These were *brahmin, kshatriya, vaisya,* and *sudra,* roughly corresponding to priests, warriors, merchants, and laborers. In time these main castes were further subdivided into different occupation groups; the caste of metalworkers, the caste of barbers, and so forth. But the basic divisions remained.

At the dawn of Indian civilization, it is likely that the caste a man belonged to was determined by his occupation. As the system hardened into its mold, however, the opposite came to be true; a man's occupation was determined by his caste, and not the other way around. Caste had come full circle. What had started as a philosophical framework for describing human differences had been transmuted into a system for preserving them in a particular form. Caste was now a rigid and complex web of relationships, rights, and duties regulating all facets of life from cradle to grave. Every function in society was carefully meted out, and every man knew exactly what was expected of him. It was a complete social universe, at once limiting and reassuring. A man knew exactly where he stood; he also knew that he had to stay there.

To our modern democratic way of thinking, caste is an unmitigated evil. We think of it (if we think of it at all) as being just another ingenious system that the rich and powerful have devised to lord it over their less fortunate neighbors. Without glossing over all of the painfully obvious failings of the caste system, it should be pointed out that simplistic criticism does not take into account the complex reality of caste. Caste divisions differ from class distinctions as we understand them in the West in a number of significant respects. For one thing, the political power of society did not reside with the so-called highest caste, the *brahmins,* but with the warrior caste, the *kshatriyas,* from which the maharaja himself was born. Furthermore, aside from the maharaja, who was very rich indeed, the wealth of society was concentrated neither in the hands of the *brahmins* nor the *ksha-*

triyas, but in those of the *vaisyas,* the merchants—a caste whose prosperous members, to this day, can be immediately identified in any Indian crowd by their sumptuously well-padded forms. And even the *vaisyas* had no monopoly on worldly goods. Rani Rasmani, the wealthiest figure in the Calcutta of her day and a philanthropist of legendary proportions, was, as we have already seen, a *sudra,* a member of the lowest caste.

In talking about caste, we are compelled to use the terms higher and lower. In fact, these concepts are not accurate to the intentions of the framers of the caste system. They are not even accurate to the much degraded system of caste that came into being in the centuries that followed. Just why these words are a subtle barrier to a fuller understanding of caste will be made clearer by an analogy.

We might speak of higher and lower organs in the body, but is it really meaningful to do so? The body is an inseparable unity of its parts. A brain that thinks itself more important than the lungs would soon enough be disabused of its superiority complex if the lungs should withhold from it a supply of oxygen for any period of time. And what is true for the body was thought to be equally true for society at large. From ancient times, Hindu society has been regarded as a vast body with arms and legs and a head and a heart and so on—every organ crucial to the whole, but every organ distinct. To expect the *brahmins* to do the work of the *sudras* was like asking the stomach to do the work of the kidneys, or the arms to act in place of the legs. To the architects of caste this seemed not only foolhardy, but contrary to God's plan. Just as in the body, the health of society was thought to depend on every man fulfilling his proper role in the greater scheme of things.

This, at any rate, is the theory. To what extent practice followed theory and questions of the justice of the system as it actually worked itself out in the world are beyond the scope of our present discussion. It is enough that we have had a small glimpse of caste as Gadadhar might have seen it—not as a repressive hierarchy of superior and inferior beings, but as a divinely ordained division of function. In the orthodox world of his father's household, the laws of caste were as little questioned as the coming of the monsoon rains or the blossoming of a flower. They were not matters for discussion and debate. They were facts of nature.

However, in the larger world outside Kamarpukur, many of the unwieldy prohibitions of caste were even then losing their grip on the Western-educated class. The new mercantile order of urban India had made them seem anachronistic. In accepting employment with Rani Rasmani as a practical matter of convenience, Ramkumar was certainly doing no more than others before him had also done. Nevertheless, it deeply challenged his younger brother's sense of propriety. Ramkumar's action was, in Gadadhar's eyes, something incomprehensible—a violation of the natural order of things for the sake of temporary worldly gain. And he could have nothing whatever to do with that. So, while his more adaptable brother went about his priestly duties and sustained himself with the temple *prasada* (the blessed food which had been offered to Kali) Gadadhar prepared his own meals and kept aloof from the daily routine of the temple.

It was, of course, a separation that could never last. To expect a spiritual prodigy like Gadadhar to remain at a distance from the overflowing life of a full-blown Hindu temple is a bit like expecting a bumblebee to boycott the clover patch. However hard he tried to resist, the vibrant spirituality of the place—the endless rounds of ritual worship called *poojas,* the scholarly religious discourses, half-sung and half-chanted in a melodious Sanskrit, the frequent and colorful temple festivals, the continual stream of inspired pilgrims, practitioners in all of spiritual India's kaleidoscopic traditions of God-realization—wove its inevitable spell on the boy's emotions. Equally importantly, the extensive temple grounds with their ample groves and overgrown jungle spaces provided Gadadhar with a solitude which nurtured his spirit. At odd hours during the day, but especially in the tranquility of early morning and at dusk, he would wander off to meditate or to sit in awed silence on the banks of the Ganges. More than anything else in those early days, it was the Ganges that enthralled the young devotee and tied his spiritual imagination to Dakshineswar with a celestial bond.

For Gadadhar, the mythic Ganges—river of light and life—

was, in the most literal sense, a dream come true. The full impact of the Ganges on his young spirit is difficult for those of us bred in colder, more sober climes, where men have all but lost their sense of the magic of place, to gauge fully. Even to picture the Ganges, in terms of our own cultural experience, as a kind of Statue of Liberty, Mount Rushmore, and Yosemite Valley all rolled into one evocative bundle can't help but fall short of its timeless resonance in the Indian psyche. It falls short because the Ganges is not special because of its historical associations, however glorious, its length or breadth, its innate beauty, its economic importance, or any other earthly cause. The Ganges is special because in some undefined, indefinable, every-mysterious way it is a physical incarnation of the metaphysical; its actual waters, gliding serenely across the north Indian plains, lapping on common banks of clay, flow simultaneously through the crystalline Mind of God.

In other words, the Ganges is special because the Ganges is *sacred.*

And it is precisely at this point that we become rather puzzled. Hardly surprising, given our background! We live, after all, in a culture that has not had a working sense of sacred geography any time recently (not since the great age of European pilgrimage during the Middle Ages, in any event). If we have any idea at all about the sacred, it is probably an abstract one. But in traditional cultures, sanctity is never abstract. It is a palpable energy, concrete as a mountain is concrete, as an idol is concrete, as a grotto is concrete, or as a river.

When the youth Gadadhar sat by the Ganges at Dakshineswar, he would have felt that the river was something exalted beyond measure. He would surely have known how it had descended to the earth from out of the matted locks of Shiva Himself; he would be aware that to bathe in its waters with sincere repentance was instantly to be cleansed of the most terrible sins. Moreover, he would recognize in the flowing waters a symbol for life itself—life which like a river is ever changing and ever the same, a noun and a verb, a state of being and a process of becoming. And more than just a symbol, the Ganges actually would have been an embodiment of life to Gadadhar. It would have been life in the precise and literal sense that the wine in the chalice actually *is* the blood of Christ to the communicant before the altar. In the liquid murmuring of the river, Gadadhar would have heard *Aum*, the seed syllable of creation forever renewing itself, the infinitely mysterious humming transformer between Pure Being and its material reflection in time and space—the physical world.

Of course, these are things that every Hindu absorbs with his mother's milk; they come with the territory. And yet it is undeniably true that Gadadhar's territory was altogether more vivid and expansive than the everyday turf of others. For if Gadadhar was not yet fully the saint that he would become, he was already entirely a poet when he took up residence at Dakshineswar. As a poet, he perceived the world through the sensibility of an awakened heart. And his heart whispered to him continually that the world was alive to the core, full of a Divine Life. The Ganges, river of mystery and of life, beneficent Mother of all creation, was the supreme symbol of that divinely animate nature. For young Gadadhar at Dakshineswar, with his limitless resources of childlike wonder, the proximity of the Ganges was truly electrifying. Its spiritual potency was so real to him that every breeze wafting off the turbid waters seemed to carry a bracing charge of purity. Moreover, it was an awareness that would not fade. His sense of the sanctity of the Ganges deepened and intensified with time. The sacred river, whose banks he would never leave again for any extended period, was to be one of the two great physical incarnations of the Divine to greet him every day. The other was Kali, the Divine Mother.

As we have seen, Gadadhar gradually became reconciled to life at Dakshineswar. In the congenial atmosphere of the temple, his initial reservations faded away, and soon he was gladly assisting his brother in the performance of the daily ritual worship of the Divine Mother. Then, in 1856, barely a year after assuming the priesthood of Kali, Ramkumar died suddenly and without warning.

It was a tragic loss for Gadadhar. The elder brother had been like a father to him ever since the passing of Khudiram. Despite their philosophical differences, Gadadhar had looked up to Ramkumar and loved him dearly. Now, for the second time in as many decades, Gadadhar felt on his skin the chill breeze of death. The effect was immediate and sobering. It reminded the young devotee that behind the shimmering mirage of life something permanent and infinitely worth finding was concealed. And it also reminded him, urgently, that he had not yet found it.

As in a silent shifting of gears, the steel of an unshakable resolve was falling into place within Gadadhar. Outwardly it was still invisible. It would not remain so for long.

Chapter 3

Kali

GADADHAR'S BUDDING DEVOTION HAD, FOR THE MOST PART, GONE
unnoticed. It was not yet unavoidable. It was not yet spectacular
and flamboyant, as it would soon become. For most men of the
world, it would have been all but invisible. Perhaps only those
who themselves wore the magic glasses of devotion could recognize in Gadadhar the Vesuvius, glowing with an inner fire, which
was ready at any moment to erupt in spiritual splendor. Mathur
Mohan, the son-in-law of Rani Rasmani, was such a man.

Mathur was hardly the sort one would have expected to
show such a remarkable spiritual sensitivity. A rich landowner
and an associate in the affairs of the temple, he appeared every bit
the swaggering dandy, bejeweled in costly silks, with a fine han-
dlebar moustache waxed and glistening. But beneath the facade
of the proud man of the world, the heart of a sincere and childlike
devotee of the Divine Mother lay concealed—a devotee as capable
as Gadadhar himself of weeping plaintively before Kali. The eyes
of that hidden devotee had been strangely drawn to Gadadhar
from the very beginning. And what Mathur saw was at once awe
inspiring, unsettling, and immensely attractive. He had observed
the boy's spiritual moods. Moreover, he had the intuitive gifts to
realize their import. Mathur found himself irresistibly attracted
by the natural grace and the unstudied, kingly aloofness that set

Gadadhar so clearly apart. He felt a subtle power emanating from the youth—a power which he could no more understand than ignore. Gradually, Mathur became possessed with the idea of involving Gadadhar fully in the life of the temple.

At first, sensing the elder's friendly interest, Gadadhar reacted with a winged creature's instinctive mistrust of the snares of earthbound responsibility. That the responsibilities, in this case, would involve a temple and worship rendered them hardly less onerous in his eyes. In a sense, it made them even more so. For the principled Gadadhar, devotion was exclusively an affair of the heart between himself and his Maker, not a service for hire or something to be performed mechanically according to a rigid liturgical schedule. Furthermore, he shrank from taking responsibility for the worldly goods of the temple. But the wealthy and powerful Mathur was not accustomed to being refused; and the son of a peasant from Kamarpukur, for his part, was respectfully uncomfortable about refusing him directly. So rather than confront Mathur, Gadadhar decided to avoid him. Even his casual strolls around the temple grounds were planned accordingly. Mathur, however, could not be evaded indefinitely. And when their paths inevitably did cross, the elder was ready with his offer. Gadadhar, perhaps out of boyish good manners, felt reluctantly compelled to give in.

Gadadhar agreed to perform a certain portion of the worship of Kali, on the condition that his nephew, Hriday, be given responsibility for the valuable ornaments of the deity. That is where things stood when Ramkumar died. At that time, with one foot already caught in the door, as it were, Gadadhar did not resist stepping in completely. When Mathur offered him the position of head priest, with full ritual duties, Gadadhar accepted.

In making the appointment, Mathur predicted with uncanny foresight that the new priest would awaken the dormant image of Kali to spiritual life by the sheer vitality of his devotion. He might have added with equal truth that Kali would awaken the sleeping divinity in her young devotee. For the eternally childlike and trusting Gadadhar, the conception of God as a loving Mother of the universe had a galvanizing effect, as we shall see. It should be mentioned here that, aside from being an enthusiastic sponsor for his young priest, and the first to gauge something of his inward potential, Mathur was (as legend has it) the one who gave him the name by which he would be known henceforth. It is by that name of his mature years—Ramakrishna—that we will refer to him from this point onward.

In every possible sense, Ramakrishna's assumption of the priesthood of Kali was the watershed event in his life. The resolve to dedicate himself to God had remained, until then, essentially formless and unfocused. Now, virtually overnight, that devotion had coalesced. The figure of Kali around which his priestly day revolved acted as a powerful lens concentrating the scattered rays of yearning to a point of flame. And burn Ramakrishna did, with a ferocious intensity of devotion that has hardly been equaled in the history of religion!

In retrospect, we can see that the tinder of ego had been well dried out in advance by an extraordinary purity of character and spirit of renunciation. Is it any wonder then that the mild and unassuming young man sprouted wings of fire? But to Ramakrishna's contemporaries, the metamorphosis of caterpillar into fiery butterfly was pure, incomprehensible sorcery. His soaring, erratic flights of the spirit seemed to many the deranged dance of a madman, to others the symptoms of possession. A sympathetic few like Mathur and Rani Rasmani reserved judgment and watched in hypnotic fascination. But before plunging ahead with our young hero into that firestorm of devotion in which he was to be consumed for the better part of a decade, we would do well to take a brief detour, lest the reader be even more puzzled than were Ramakrishna's contemporaries by the startling events which are about to follow. We will find it useful to pause for a moment to ask two fundamental questions: Who exactly is this Kali? And what tremendous impulse drove Ramakrishna headlong toward Her?

Up until this point, our young priest's passions have been recognizable on a human scale. We can empathize with Gadadhar the poet, sympathize with Gadadhar the truant, dream with Gadadhar the dreamer. We have had no difficulty following him thus far. But Ramakrishna's road was about to turn precipitously, to incline steeply upward and out of the gentle, forested realm of our experience. What inspires a boy to reject hypocrisy and to forge his own way in the world is clear enough and requires no explanation. What causes him to emulate the mythic heroes of his land and romantically identify with them should also be familiar to anyone who has been a child! On the other hand, what drives a mature young man to conduct a frenzied pursuit of a stone Goddess for years at a time is not so clear—not, at any rate, in this day and age when only sex, money, and worldly status are deemed worthy of our adult frenzy, and the Gods and Goddesses and God Himself receive, at best, only our collective lip service and the occasional patronizing nod of Sunday sentiment while we busy ourselves with more practical matters.

So we would do well to pause and remind ourselves that Ramakrishna's devotion also sprang from a universal fount of human experience. And, however foreign, however intense, and however bizarre its expression, the basic impulse remains familiar.

Kali, we just might discover, is but another name for our own deepest yearnings.

It is curious that we even need to ask Who is Kali and what caused Sri Ramakrishna to pursue Her so recklessly? For most of human history, the answers to these questions would have been self-evident. Traditional cultures have called Her by many different names and have worshiped Her in countless different ways. But it never would have occurred to any of them to doubt Her existence. Neither would it have occurred to our ancestors to question the wisdom of dedicating the best energy of a lifetime to Her pursuit. Man is a child of the Universe, an infant tied by the umbilical cord of space and time to that great nurturing Mystery out of which he has (from no impulse of his own) been born, and to which he will (without his volition) inevitably return. Our dependency on that Mystery is absolute; our intimacy is also absolute. No human relationship can compare with it. Is it any wonder that we humans have propitiated and worshiped this Maternal Mystery at the very heart of our lives? Is it any wonder that we have personified Her, prayed to Her, whispered our deepest secrets to Her, cried out to Her in our pain and our joy, danced before Her, and wept before Her? The real puzzle is why we have all but ceased to do these things—why in our day and age Sri Ramakrishna's burning love for Kali needs to be justified or explained.

But it *does* need to be explained. The fact is that man has become a stranger to his Divine Mother, a stranger to himself. He has rendered the universe and his own being into objects for analysis and manipulation, all but losing the integrating sense of unity with the Great Matrix of Life in the process. In his spiritual teachings, Sri Ramakrishna would frequently refer to our present era as *kali yuga*, the dark age when an exclusive concern with the body and the purely physical side of existence has eclipsed from view our metaphysical roots. He recognized that modern man is becoming increasingly alienated from the living waters of the spirit which have nurtured past generations and given them a sense of the high purpose of life.

Fundamentalists in various religions blame science for this collective fall from grace. However, for Ramakrishna and the Hindu tradition, the *yugas*—the divinely ordained cycle of the ages ranging from the enlightened spirituality of the *satya yuga*, the golden age of Truth, to the gross materialism of our own *kali yuga*—are not caused by mankind's scientific explorations or by anything else we have done, but, rather, follow each other as naturally and as inevitably as one season the next. From this cosmic perspective, the rampant secularism of our present day is just one phase in the vast turning wheel of consciousness which, when it reaches the low point of alienation, will spontaneously begin again the long journey back to Unity.

In fact, the all-too-familiar dualism between science on the one hand and spirituality on the other would strike Sri Ramakrishna as false and misleading. Science is neutral; it only describes the world as it is perceived by our sense organs and their technological extensions. It is not science, as such, but the superstitious deification of the material world which science describes, that is a source of so much confusion. Sri Ramakrishna regarded the sensory world as a thin shell concealing the depths of Reality. By concentrating exclusively on the shell and ignoring the great spiritual treasure which underlies it, we cheapen life and distort its transcendent meaning. In truth, no accumulation of statistics on blood and bones and amino acids can make the sheer wonder of our existence any less a miracle. No possible technological development can make us less dependent on that sublime power which made possible the airplane, the atom bomb, and the human mind which devised them in the first place. This is the great discovery of mystics like Ramakrishna; it remains as vital in our age of science as it ever was.

Science does not inherently oppose mysticism or render it obsolete; the greatest scientists and mystics have recognized this instinctively. Indeed, both the scientist and his mystic brother share a common devotion to truth. While the one pursues that truth by analysis, separating out the continuum of being into its component threads and chronicling their outward variety, the other pursues it through synthesis, seeking the shared essence of all beings, objects, and processes of the world, the unifying Divinity at the core of life itself. These two aspects of Truth—the analytic and the synthetic, the outer and the inner, multiplicity and oneness—are complementary rather than contradictory.

Ironically, by pursuing either science or spirituality to its logical conclusion, the practitioner inevitably comes upon its opposite. At the very end of his path the mystic discovers that the diversity of objects and forces (the world of science) is not separate from the Unity which he has all along adored, but is indeed the concrete expression of that Unity ("*samsara* is *nirvana*," as the Buddhist tradition frames this ultimate realization, or, "the world is God," as Sri Ramakrishna might have expressed it in theistic terms.)

Similarly, the scientist who pursues the implications of his own discipline deeply enough discovers at the end of his road that the multiplicity of objects and laws, which he has been attempting to study in isolation from one another, can only be properly understood when they are perceived in a larger context as harmonious elements of a vast Unity. It is not by accident that Albert Einstein sounds most like a mystic when he is writing of his own profound reactions to the scientific process. Barring differences in diction and style, the great physicist's words could as easily have been spoken by Sri Ramakrishna himself: "The individual feels the nothingness of human desires and aims and the sublimity and marvelous order which reveal themselves both in nature and in the world of thought. He looks upon individual existence as a sort of prison and wants to experience the universe as a single significant whole."

While the spiritual yearning central to Einstein's life and scientific quest is present in all, it is, like any other human capacity, not equally developed in all. For many, the urge toward self-transcendence remains primarily latent and unconscious. Such individuals can be compared to trekkers through fog-bound mountains who rarely if ever catch sight of the radiant peaks all around them. They are completely lost in the mists of ignorance. If you try to tell them about the wonders that surround them, they will laugh and call you a dreamer. They plod doggedly through the world of the senses without even the shadow of a suspicion that there might be anything beyond what is a yard in front of their noses at the moment. Only after many lifetimes of often bitter experience and disillusionment, according to Hindu belief, will such immature "young souls" finally feel goaded to search beyond the instinctual bounds of the sensory world for a more enduring reality.

There are others, though, who are no longer capable of such innocent obliviousness, having gazed up and caught fleeting glimpses of shapes looming through the fog. We might try to ignore or even, perversely, to deny these glimpses of the spiritual peaks around us, but some gnawing doubt always remains and prevents us from settling back too comfortably into an easy complacency. A faint yet haunting nostalgia for the dazzling heights that exist just beyond our accustomed range of vision makes us restless for a goal which remains poorly defined, though oddly compelling. These are the spiritual seekers—including readers and writers of books such as this one—suspended somewhere in the vast, shadowy no-man's-land between obscurity and vision.

Then there is a third category of pilgrim, by far the rarest of all. Sri Ramakrishna is a perfect example of this group. These "eternally free" souls are blessed with sunny weather from the start. Virtually from birth itself, the fog of delusion can never mar their view. In peerless clarity, every feature of the surrounding slopes shimmers and beckons. They gaze up at the awesome beauty of the snow-clad peak in whose lofty purity they perceive the very image of their own transcendent nature. The sight is entrancing beyond words, but it is not enough. In their inmost hearts, the ever-free will never be fully satisfied until the peak is won, that is to say, not just seen externally, but experienced at all times as indivisibly united with their own eternal Being. They cannot rest content with the vision of God. They must become one with Him. But even a natural-born spiritual genius like Sri Ramakrishna can't just wish himself up to the divine summit. So the problem—or, better, the ruling obsession of the lives of the spiritually illumined—is how to get there, what route to take, how to equip for the ordeal.

This analogy is not flawless. The summit of consciousness, unlike a peak of rock and snow, is formless and without dimensions. But if the goal remains ultimately indefinable, the route to the summit and the techniques employed to reach it must of necessity take a particular form. Just what the "proper" route is has not been mandated from above like some rock-hewn commandment made to last throughout eternity. God is not (however much we might, in our zealous sectarianism, want to picture Him so) the scheming owner of a toll road concerned that all the traffic be funneled down one and the same thoroughfare while He sits at His gatehouse and exacts the identical three farthings from all. Those who claim that there is only one path to God insult His all-encompassing wideness. Ramakrishna, for whom all creedal exclusivity was anathema, was to emphasize time and again in his teachings that there is not a single "correct" way up the divine mountain. There are many possibilities. Each individual, after carefully considering the lay of the land, his own conditioning, and his strengths and weaknesses as a climber, has to choose the path that suits him best.

This decision is not as formidable as it might at first appear. And we don't need to have the goal perfectly in view from the very start, as Sri Ramakrishna and the other eternally free souls were blessed to have it. Fortunately for us, a wide variety of routes have been carefully charted in advance by the generations of aspirants that have preceded us. So it is possible for anyone with a reasonable knowledge of his or her own capacities to find an appropriate way.

There are three basic paths which correspond to the broad divisions in human nature between active, intellectual, and devotional personalities. These three core yogas are perhaps not so narrow as the term "path" might imply, but are generalized modes of approach, within each of which exists a whole range of possibilities. Later on in our story, we will have a chance to take a look at some of the more specialized forms of spiritual practice that Sri Ramakrishna himself performed. For now, however, we would do well to briefly examine the broad outlines of the three yogas as they have been been taught and practiced for ages in Hindu India.

For those in whom discriminating intelligence predominates, the way of *jnana* yoga, the path of wisdom, is enjoined. The *jnani* uses his mental powers to evaluate everything that comes his way in terms of its ultimate reality. He meticulously scrutinizes all of the things that other men take for granted or pass over without awareness, asking basic questions: Will this speed my journey to the Absolute, or will it slow me down? Is this real, or is it a mere appearance like the thin bridge of snow-covered ice over a crevasse that only seems solid, but will collapse under the least pressure? For the *jnani*, the world itself is like that treacherous ice-bridge—a realm that seems to promise security, but delivers up all who depend on it to danger and, ultimately, to destruction. By inquiring at all times into the true nature of his experience, the *jnani* keeps to the solid ground of the Real, systematically avoiding everything that is relative and therefore unstable, trimming away all the excess baggage of sentiment and prejudice until, lean and hard, he makes it to the summit of his own unaided efforts. The heroic path of *jnana* yoga in its various modes was practiced by the great Upanishadic sages, by Shankaracharya, and by Sakyamuni Buddha.

The second of the great paths is *karma* yoga, the way of dedicated work. Unlike the inner-directed *jnani*, the *karma* yogi, the man who thrives on action, is encouraged to climb the peak with the awareness that it is not he himself, but God, who animates his muscles and directs his mind to make the right choices along the way. By perceiving himself as a servant of God, the egoism of the *karma* yogi is effaced, and he learns to recognize and to act in accordance with a will greater than his own. He is like a porter who is led to the top of the mountain by a trustworthy master climber. He uses his own energy, but allows it to be directed by the Divine Guide. This path of service is best exemplified in the Hindu tradition by the monkey Hanuman, the tireless servant of the Lord Rama. Hanuman's faith in Rama's power was so great that by uttering His Divine Name he was able to jump over the sea, carry mountains on the palm of his hand, and perform other great miracles, culminating in his freeing Sita, Rama's consort, from her bondage to demons.

The last of the three paths—and the one that Sri Ramakrishna himself followed—is *bhakti* yoga, the way of devoted surrender. The *bhakta* is a man of the heart who feels toward the universe what a lover feels toward the beloved. Everything that the *bhakta* perceives brings to mind the Divine Beloved. Unlike the *jnani*, he does not reject the world as illusory. On the contrary, he rejoices in creation and makes good use of its wonders as potent reminders of the bewitching attractiveness of his God. Nevertheless, he doesn't allow himself to forget that the world is just the outward costume that the Supreme has put on—precious to be sure, but only in so much as it adorns the person of the Beloved. Since he has surrendered himself body, mind, and soul to God, the *bhakta* does not think to scale the peak of vision on his own two feet. Instead, to use one of Ramakrishna's favorite analogies, he allows himself to be carried up by the Divine Beloved as a kitten allows its mother to carry it about without the least worry or personal effort.

In Ramakrishna's view, *bhakti* is by far the easiest, the most direct, and the most practical spiritual path for men in our age. "Pure knowledge and pure love are one and the same thing," he claimed. "Both lead the aspirant to the same goal. But the path of love is much the easier."[1]

In the expansive capacity to love that we all share in common, Sri Ramakrishna recognized an unequaled power to rise above human limitations and to know God, the illimitable source of love and Lover for all His creation. Love directed toward an infinite goal becomes itself infinite, bursting the ephemeral bubble of personality, merging Lover and Beloved in an indissoluble divine union. No special talents or esoteric knowledge are required of the devotee on the path of love, only a sincere yearning and integrity of purpose. As Ramakrishna often insisted, when our love for God reaches a high level of purity and intensity, then we must inevitably find Him: "Men shed streams of tears because sons are not born to them. Others wear away their hearts in sorrow when they cannot get wealth. But how many are there who sorrow and weep because they haven't seen God? Very few indeed! One thing is for certain—the person who seeks Him, who weeps for Him, attains Him." (T.S., p. 18)*

For the great majority of us, however, God (unlike wealth, position, children, and creature comforts) remains a vague and elusive entity. If we do not weep for Him, it is because we do not feel His existence concretely in the same way we do a wife, a job, or a loaf of bread. Part of our difficulty stems from the utterly transcendent nature of the Divine. Even those gifted ones who sense the existence of a radiant principle at the core of life find themselves unable to visualize or to conceive of it directly. The best that they can hope for at this stage is to catch an occasional oblique glimpse out of the corner of the eye as of the noonday sun. To attempt to look straight at the Divine is self-defeating. It is to be blinded by an amorphous brilliance without scale or shape, to be forced to look away. And this is where Mother Kali comes in—and Christ, and Buddha, and Shiva, and Kuan Yin, and all of the myriad other forms in which men have conceived the Absolute. Because we cannot hope, as we set out on the spiritual path, to look directly at the Divine, we must devise a way to look at it obliquely. The Gods, the Avatars (divine incarnations), and the Messiahs are so many vehicles for looking obliquely at the sun of Truth.

So who is Mother Kali? We might say that She is a catalyst, a way station between us and the inconceivable Godhead, between the limited and the illimitable. However, if we were to stop there, Kali would remain an abstraction at best. And Kali is not an abstraction—least of all was She an abstraction to Ramakrishna. On the other hand, there is the opposite danger that we will take Her too literally and look only at the external form that

---

*Here and throughout, second reference to previously cited work will be listed thusly. Abbreviations of works appear in Endnotes.

31

She displays to the world. Many Western critics have done just that. Overwhelmed by Her fearsome aspect—by her lolling tongue and her sword and her chain of severed heads for a necklace—they have labeled Kali "the Goddess of destruction." Nothing could be further from the playful, loving Mother Ramakrishna knew and worshiped.

So how did this misapprehension of the Divine Mother come about? An analogy may be helpful. A tribesman from New Guinea might wander into a Catholic church and conclude from the bloody figure nailed to two logs up front that he had unwittingly stumbled upon the temple of some sort of death cult. If he had the nerve to stay for the eucharistic service, he would discover that it was not only a death cult, but a cannibalistic one at that! Should our hapless native "anthropologist" not immediately flee in terror, he might eventually find out from the participants themselves that the crucifix, far from symbolizing death, actually stands for the resurrection—the victory of Spirit over death. He would also learn, to his great relief, that the "body and blood of Christ" are really tokens of the worshiper's spiritual participation in the Divinity of their God and not the menu of some macabre feast. To expect that he would stay (or bother to ask the right questions if he did) is, of course, to ask a lot.

Many of the early orientalists never did stay long enough to ask the proper questions about Kali. If they had, they would have found out that first impressions can be deceiving. For one thing, they would have learned that Kali's swords and severed heads symbolize precisely the same thing that the cross symbolizes for Christians—the victory of Spirit over matter.

But we are getting ahead of ourselves. We have penetrated too quickly to the core of the mystery. Kali is not to be understood exclusively on one level alone. She is best revealed a layer at a time. And, as with an onion, we must start with Her glossy outermost covering, Her visible mask—that of Mother *Maya*. Here She is nature bringing forth all beings from Her womb, feeding them at Her breast, then devouring and assimilating them back into Herself. In this incarnation, we can say that She is the material cosmos as it is known to science, a superficially purposeless chaos of opposing qualities—creation and destruction, cause and effect, light and darkness, good and evil. She appears here as a randomly willful despot, elusive and distantly aloof. This is Her public mask.

The face that Kali shows to Her friends, to those who value intimacy with Her above the evanescent charms of Her creation, is altogether different. To these fortunate ones, the untamable Mother Nature becomes a doting spiritual Mother whose sole concern is their ultimate well-being. The dynamics of this transformation are nicely captured in a suggestive analogy by the twentieth-century yogi, Swami Ram Tirtha. So long as we pursue the things of the creation for their own sake, the Swami avers, they will ever remain frustratingly elusive like a shadow that is always ahead and just out of reach. At this stage, the world seems alien and unfriendly. However, the moment we wake up from our folly of trying to grasp the ungraspable and turn around to face the sun of the Creator, rather than the shadow of the creation, the shadow itself follows dutifully along like the tail of a dog.

This metaphor captures the experience of devotees in many traditions who affirm that nature itself becomes a vehicle of grace, a friend and collaborator working vigorously to clear the path and speed the progress toward spiritual fulfillment the moment a person sincerely turns toward God, the Master of nature. This principle of spiritual life is suggested in Christ's enigmatic saying from the book of Mathew: "To him that hath much, much shall be given. But verily from him that hath little, that little shall be taken away."

So Kali, as an embodiment of universal energy, or *shakti*, has two very distinct faces. The first, a horrific one, is perceived by those who insist on swimming against the stream of Her laws, who spurn Her and seek a false security in the things which She has created; to these She manifests as death, because everything that they cling to so desperately, both in the world and in themselves, will inevitably be swallowed up by Her and disappear. The other face, the one She shows to those who strive to unite with Her, is a benevolent one. Because such devotees do not cling to what must change, because they consent to flow with the current of the world and not to struggle against it, they recognize Kali as life eternal, an unfailing guide to that quintessential aspect of being which shall not pass away with the body.

The black basalt statue at Dakshineswar that Ramakrishna

worshiped symbolizes for the initiate the powers of spiritual guidance and protection of the Divine Mother. Each of the idol's four arms has a very precise esoteric meaning and function, at odds with its more literal significance. The arm on the upper left hand side holds a sword. On the exoteric level of Kali as Mother Nature, this sword stands for the destructive half of the world process. For the person who sees no deeper than this symbolism, the weapon is naturally frightening. The worldly man senses—and quite rightly so in his case—that the sword is ultimately directed at him personally and at all that he holds dear. His sole interest is in staving it off as long as possible. If he approaches Kali at all, it is only when he feels himself or a loved one to be in some immediate danger. At that time, he comes with an exaggerated, groveling subservience. Full of a dark fear that effectively deadens the nerve of genuine devotion, he pleads and bargains like a bazaar cloth merchant offering all he has to offer—vows full of hypocrisy, goats, piles of shining coins.

The devotee, on the other hand, who is familiar with the esoteric purpose of Kali's sword, does not react with fear at all. Where the ignorant man sees the sword hanging above his own neck, his enlightened counterpart finds it pointed at the deadly enemies on the road to spiritual development—lust, greed, pride, and the rest of the demonic brood. The severed head that Kali holds in Her lower left hand is a token of Her invincible success in defeating the demons of our egoism.

The arms on Kali's right side represent the positive correlates of the negative functions on the left. On the exoteric level, they precisely counterbalance terror with hope, and thus complete the circle of the world as we know it, a chaos of contradictory qualities, creation and destruction, light and darkness, cause and effect, good and evil. To the initiate, however, they have a deeper meaning. The raised hand, palm facing outward, on the upper right side is an ancient gesture, the *abhaya mudra*, signifying the divine protection given all sincere aspirants to spiritual knowledge. The lower right hand offers boons, assuring the devotee that anything lacking in his personality that is necessary for spiritual unfoldment will be granted unasked, as a gift of grace.

Yet even this figure of Kali the maternal liberator, as She

appears to devotees, is not Her innermost reality. When ignorance is finally slain, the aspirant turned *jnani* realizes that the one
who appeared to him at first as frightful and incomprehensible
maya and then, closer up, as a succoring and benevolent Mother,
was all along a manifestation of his own hidden identity. He
himself is the Mother—and not only himself, but all things, are
the forms that She has assumed in Her magical play of the one
as the many.

Sri Ramakrishna was to describe this realization in the most
vivid terms: "Do you know what I see? Trees, plants, animals,
grass—these and all other things I see as different coverings, like
pillow cases. Some are made of fine cotton, and others of coarser
stuff, some round in shape and others square. But within all of
these pillow cases is one and the same substance, cotton. Just so,
all of the objects in the world are stuffed with unconditioned *Sat
Chit Ananda* (Being, Consciousness, Bliss). I feel as if the Mother
has wrapped Herself in many different cloths and is peeping
furtively from each of them."[2]

And yet, when Ramakrishna took over as temple priest at
Dakshineswar, this final realization was still many years in the
future. From the start, he approached Kali not as a convenient
symbol of the omnipresent Divine, still less as being identical
with his own inner self, but with the simple faith that She was
Mother. "Why does the God-lover find such ecstatic delight in
addressing the deity as Mother?" Ramakrishna once asked
rhetorically. "Because the child is more free with the Mother than
with anybody else, and for that reason She is the dearest of all."
(S.R., p. 198) This striking intimacy and playfulness characterized
Ramakrishna's relationship to the Divine throughout his life.

This attitude might appear to us charmingly naive, but is it
really so? Or is the naivete our own in thinking the Creator
immeasurably distant, off in some high heaven, or existing only
as a kind of metaphysical abstraction—eternal, infinite, forever
aloof and unreachable by the products of His own creation? What
has always set the great mystics apart from the merely religious
is not the belief in God, or even the emotional intensity of that
belief, but the belief in God as a *personal fact*.

Christ and Saint Francis, Chaitanya and Ramakrishna, were

alike in treating the Divine as the nearest and dearest of the soul. They walked with God and talked with Him/Her; they pleaded, argued, wept, and cajoled. To others, the intimacy often seemed blasphemous. The respectable and religious men of the world were greatly scandalized by it. Possibly it struck them as a dangerously democratic idea that any man off the streets might go above their heads and converse directly with the King of Kings! Out of fear, they beheaded, they threw to the lions, they crucified. And when they didn't crucify, they suppressed. And when they felt secure enough in their ignorance not to suppress, they laughed derisively. But it made no difference to our heroes. Only one thing mattered to them—to remain in the good graces of their Friend. All else was vanity.

Here we must note that the situation has always been somewhat different in India. As a rule, mystics have been suffered tolerantly there—even while they were doing and saying all of the inconvenient things to which mystics are prone. The idea that God and man should be on intimate terms, moreover, has a very long tradition in India, and is mostly taken for granted. Even today, most Indians can tell you of an aunt who talks with Krishna or a neighbor who falls into trance during the singing of devotional songs. In moderation, such harmless manifestations are quite acceptable, even admirable. But Ramakrishna, never one for moderation where devotion to God was involved, stepped over the invisible boundaries of propriety time and again. More than a few eyebrows arched at his unconventional worship of Kali.

Those who came to the temple to take part in the daily service would watch incredulously as the young priest, having completed the formalities of worship, staggered over to the idol like a drunkard, his chest and eyes flushed crimson from emotion, and caressed Kali endearingly on the chin, sang to Her, held a morsel of food up to the cold stone lips and pleaded with Her to eat, and then caught hold of Her stiff black arms to dance in ecstasy. There seemed to be no end to the eccentricities of this mad devotee. His worship became progressively less predictable, more bizarre. At times Ramakrishna would sit like a catatonic, insensible, lost in tears or plaintive moans. Again, he would drift off into reverie in the midst of some ritual act and remain for hours on end mechanically waving a camphor lamp before the idol, or going through the motions of an offering long after the flame had gone cold and the pile of flowers and leaves to be offered had dwindled to nothing. Gradually, Ramakrishna's obsession became so intense that every last vestige of normal routine in sleep, food, and personal hygiene was torn from its moorings and carried away in the frenzied whirlwind of his devotion. It was as if the world and all the things men cherish simply vanished. Day and night he could think of nothing but God.

Sri Ramakrishna himself described his extraordinary state at that time as follows:

> As I was perfectly unmindful of the cleaning of the body at that time, the hairs grew long and got matted of themselves, being smeared with dirt and dust. When I would sit in meditation, the body would become stiff and motionless like a stork, through intense concentration of mind, and birds, taking it to be an inert substance, came and freely perched on the head, and pecked into the matted hair in search of food. Sometimes I used to weep so intensely the pangs of separation from God, that in great bitterness I rubbed my face in the earth; often I used to get cut and bleed. In meditation, prayer and other devotional practices, the day used to fly by so quickly that I was not conscious of it. At dusk, when the approach of night was announced by the ringing of bells and the blowing of the conch from the temple, I used to be reminded that the day had passed and the evening had set in. With this consciousness a frenzy of despair would seize my soul and I would throw myself on the ground and rub my face on it, crying out loudly, "Mother, another day has passed and still you have not appeared before me!" (S.R., p. 304)

Always it was the same refrain: "Mother, come to me. Show Yourself. I have abandoned everything—money, friends, family, sensual pleasure—and still You keep aloof!" The same anguished cry one day to the next. The holy scriptures, the testimony of the sages and saints, and the ancient legends were all agreed that if you shunned everything for the sake of God, the Divine Mother, then She was bound to take you gently into Her infinite arms, even appear in flesh and blood concreteness, if need be, to brand you with the deathless signet of Her love. But so far, She had failed to do so. She had come maddeningly close, to be sure. Ramakrishna had felt Her warm breath passing through the hollows of his being, and he had trembled in resonance with Her soulful voice within. Time and again, Her veiled smile had touched with rapture every cell of his body. If he had not yet seen Her face, Her shadow had already fallen upon him countless times. And yet in his moments of anguish, it seemed to have availed him nothing. For all the unmistakable signs of Her presence—the perfume on the wind, the gentle tinkling of anklets, things he had actually perceived with his physical senses—She had remained always just out of reach. Finally, Ramakrishna had to admit that nothing he had said or sung or whispered or wept had melted the Mother's heart of stone. It was a realization that caused him the most acute agony of spirit.

At tortured intervals, the priest of Kali was driven to think the unthinkable: "Are You for real Mother, or is it all a pleasant fiction, mere poetry without substance? If You exist, then why can't I see You *now*? Is all religion just a fantasy, a castle in the air? Are you merely a figment of man's imagination?"[3] Ramakrishna, who cherished Truth above a merely comfortable faith, could not fail to ask even these questions.

The moments of doubt, however, were necessarily fleeting; he had seen far too much at that point to entertain them seriously. The young man, who had already gazed more than once upon the unearthly radiance beyond the horizon of the known, was like a hound on the chase. With the scent strong in his nostrils, there was no longer any question of holding back.

Ramakrishna would offer an amusing analogy for this state of mind to his great disciple Vivekananda:

> My child, suppose there is a bag of gold in one room and a robber in the next. Do you think that the thief can sleep? Not at all. His mind will always be mulling over how to enter the room and get hold of the gold. Do you think that a man who is firmly persuaded that there is a reality beyond all these sensations, that there is a God, that there is One who never dies, One who is the infinite sum of all bliss, a bliss compared to which the pleasures of the senses are mere

trinkets, can he rest contented without struggling to attain
it? Can he cease his efforts for one single moment? Not a
chance! He will become crazed with longing.[4]

To a nature as passionate as Ramakrishna's, the pain of
separation was unacceptable and unbearable. His emotions,
which had been festering for so long without relief, were a powder keg waiting for the match. For the dramatic scene when they
flashed swiftly to a climax, we turn again to the Master's own
description:

> One day I was torn by intolerable anguish. My heart
> seemed wrung as a damp cloth might be wrung. I was
> wracked with pain. A terrible frenzy seized me at the
> thought that I might never be blessed with the divine vision.
> I thought if that were so then enough of this life! A sword
> was hanging in the sanctuary of Kali. My eyes seized upon
> it and the thought raced through my brain like a flash of
> lightning—"The sword it will help me put an end to it." I
> rushed up to it and seized it like a madman. . . . And lo! The
> whole scene, doors, windows, the temple itself simply van-
> ished. It seemed as if nothing existed anymore. Instead I saw
> an ocean of the spirit, boundless, dazzling. In whatever di-
> rection I turned, great luminous waves were rising. They
> bore down upon me with a loud roar, as if to swallow me
> up. In an instant they were upon me. They broke over me,
> they engulfed me, I was suffocated. I lost all normal con-
> sciousness and fell to the ground. . . . How I passed that day
> and the next I know not. Round me rolled an ocean of
> unspeakable joy such as I had never experienced before. And
> inside me was an immediate knowledge of the light that is
> the Mother.[5]

It was a major breakthrough, a miraculous solar burst at
midnight of the dark night of the soul. But it is characteristic of
Ramakrishna that he could not rest content with this unearthly
radiance, which was destined to fade with time. He had not yet
reached the end of his journey. He had been granted a vision of
the destination. But where a lesser soul would have basked comfortably in the mellow afterglow of that wondrous light, Rama-

krishna's restless spirit could derive no satisfaction from what came for a charmed interlude and then vanished. The madman of God could not stop short of the utter union with the Beloved that he so desperately desired.

Instead of dampening the fires of his discontent, the vision fueled them still further. Now that he had feasted on the nectar bliss of the spirit, the coarse pleasures of the world seemed doubly gross and unpalatable. Day and night, Ramakrishna burned without relief—and not just metaphorically, but physically, bodily. His flesh was being consumed by merciless psychic fires, and the pores of his skin oozed droplets of blood. Shaken by spasms, he would roll on the ground groaning and weeping inconsolably like some grief-stricken elephant. Crowds of the curious gathered around him to gape at the bizarre spectacle without comprehension. But to the priest in his agony, they seemed unreal, like shadows, or figures painted on a canvas. Devoid of inhibitions and the least shadow of self-consciousness, Ramakrishna had vanished and some mighty power flowed through the hollow marionette of his body, making it speak and act in ways that amazed him quite as much as those who had gathered to stand and stare.

At one point, even Mathur Babu, his staunch ally and protector, pleaded with Ramakrishna to keep his feelings under control and heed the conventions of society. Even God, he argued, followed rules of his own making—He never made flowers of two different colors, red and white for instance, to bloom on one and the same stalk. Ramakrishna was defenseless against such an argument. As we have seen, he was quite as puzzled as everyone else, and humble enough to question his own impulses. Was it possible that he had really gone too far? Had he trespassed the Mother's own boundaries in his blind and headlong pursuit of Her? The more he pondered Mathur's words, the less he could dismiss them from mind. Tortured by these nagging doubts, the following morning he was gathering hibiscus flowers for his worship of Kali when to his amazement there were two blooms, one blood red and the other white, side by side on the same stem. He eagerly picked the branch and brought it to Mathur.

The message was immediately clear to both of them; God indeed has His own laws. In creating Ramakrishna, He had broken all of them.

→》》 *Chapter 4* 《《←

The Pursuit

RAMAKRISHNA HAD A BEAUTIFUL IMAGE OF MANKIND. ANYONE who has been in an Indian city in season and seen the multitude of kites soaring and darting in the wind from a thousand rooftops will appreciate it. Souls are like those kites, the Master was fond of saying, yearning for the freedom of the air, but held fast to the earth by invisible strands of illusion. The Divine Mother watches this tremendous spectacle of Hers from behind the scenes. Now and again, like a playful girl, She cuts one of the kites loose from its moorings and laughs merrily as it floats free.

Ramakrishna must have been reflecting on his own experience when he pictured the divinely gifted spirit as a free-floating kite. For he had made the dizzying flight himself, and he was intimately familiar with the vertigo of a soul torn asunder from familiar social landmarks, soaring giddy and alone in the limitless radiance of the air. He alone knew the thrill of it, and the terrible fear of it—the exhilaration of the billowing spaces, and the horror of the abyss yawning in very real menace below. On occasion, weary and trembling, even he must have yearned wistfully for the secure, dull, and predictable life of the earthbound. When Chandra Devi called her son back to Kamarpukur, it is not hard to imagine that Ramakrishna himself heaved a thankful sigh of relief.

41

Chandra had come to know about her son's erratic behavior, and she summoned him home in the simple faith that the familiar surroundings of his childhood would soothe him back to his senses. Her maternal instincts proved sound. Almost from the moment he arrived, the anguish of Dakshineswar melted gently away. Even the physical symptoms, the burning and trembling of the flesh, vanished. For the moment, Ramakrishna was at peace. It was a blessed interlude in which to assimilate all that had been shown him in the storm of revelation, a time to recover a lost balance and regroup the battered forces of personality in preparation for yet another assault on the bastion of the Divine Mother. Indeed, Chandra Devi had the sure intuition to know that the apparent serenity was unlikely to last when her son returned again, as he must, to the Kali temple in Calcutta. Only after he was married, she reasoned, would the weight of worldly responsibilities, the ballast of the senses, keep him safely tied to the earth. So, with a keen sense of urgency, the search began in earnest for a worthy bride.

In India, the very thought of marriage has, for ages, been anathema to those drawn to a life of holiness. The reasons for this aversion are obvious enough. All too often, the self-centered pre-occupations and innate conservatism of married life exact a chilling toll on the spiritual idealism of youth. Tightly shuttered, shielded behind four walls of attachment and worldly cares, all wider dreams and more universal aspirations tend to wither and die with the result that, tied to nest and brood, the spirit ventures outward no more. The winged freedom of the air is exchanged for the narrow security of the earth.

This process is not completely inevitable. India, like the West, has had its share of married saints. But these have been regarded as the heroic exceptions that prove the rule. In practice, the life of the householder has been so closely associated in the popular imagination with the restriction and bondage of the spirit that a single word, *samsara*, has come to mean both "family life" and "bondage."

Given this atmosphere of thought and Ramakrishna's own intense yearning for freedom, it is remarkable that he made no objection when his mother suggested marriage. He even seemed to take an innocent delight in the idea. Nevertheless, when the search began for a suitable match, it was perversely frustrated at every turn. Unmarried girls of the right age, disposition, and family background proved very hard to find. And when a prospective match was located, the exorbitant demands for the dowry invariably fell beyond the range of the family's meager means.

Just as all was beginning to appear hopeless, Ramakrishna gave the clue to his bewildered mother: "It is useless to search here and there. Go and look in the family of Ram Mukhopadhyaya of the village of Jayrambati. The bride has been marked by a straw and kept reserved there." (No place, no date.)* In Bengal, it was customary to mark the finest fruits and vegetables, the ones set aside to be offered to God, with a straw tied around the stem. This was to prevent them from being consumed or sent off to market. The metaphor is a telling one. For, truly, Sarada Devi was being set aside for a higher end than the marketplace of the world. Ramakrishna's union with Ram Mukhopadhyaya's daughter was not destined to be a marriage in the conventional sense at all, but rather a mutual offering up to the Lord in the person of the spouse.

For Sarada, Sri Ramakrishna was to be no mere husband, but God in human form, her guru and spiritual guide. For Ramakrishna, Sarada would be none other than the living form of the Mother he worshiped in the temple.

The marriage ceremony was arranged at once. For all practical purposes, it amounted to a betrothal; because of her youth (Sarada was only five years old at the time), she would not join her husband until after attaining puberty. Reflecting on his marriage many years later, Ramakrishna insisted that the families were merely instruments in fulfilling a divine edict. In spirit and in truth, the matchmaker was the Divine Mother Herself.

The Divine Mother had chosen very well indeed, as it turns out. In Saradamani, Sri Ramakrishna would discover a spirit as refined and pure-hearted as his own. Sarada's lofty aspiration is beautifully captured in a spontaneous childhood prayer that she

*From here on, this will be abbreviated N.p., n.d.

43

repeated again and again like a saving charm: "Oh Lord, there are dark spots even on the bright moon. But make my character stainless!" (G.S., p. 17). It was a singularly appropriate, even a prophetic, prayer. Under the demanding guidance of her husband, she would grow radiant indeed with a moonlike purity—cool, liquid and soothing—the perfect complement of the radiant solar orb of Ramakrishna. If ever there actually was a "match made in heaven," it was this partnership between equals in the realm of the spirit. But whereas Ramakrishna's growth to consciousness was destined to be fiery and tempestuous, Sarada's would be a gradual flowering, in keeping with her gentle nature.

The girl of five would have to wait nearly a decade, however, before she would enjoy any sustained contact with her husband, or feel the force of his exalted spirituality. Ramakrishna did not stay for long in his homeland. Chandra's intuition had been exactly right. The irresistible call of Kali sounded all too quickly. And no sooner had her son returned to Calcutta, then he forgot all about the marriage. The brief idyll of restful peace was shattered in a moment. The God-madness, with all its terrible physical symptoms, returned—only more intensely. One day to the next, one hour to the next, Sri Ramakrishna was tossed mercilessly from vision to despair and back again.

As he was to recall:

> An ordinary man couldn't have borne a quarter of that tremendous fervor; it would have burned him up. I had no sleep at all for six long years. My eyes lost the power of winking. I stood in front of a mirror and tried to close my eyelids with my finger—and I couldn't! I got frightened and said to Mother: "Mother, is this what happens to those who call on You? I surrender myself to You, and You give me this terrible disease!" I used to shed tears—but then, suddenly, I'd be filled with ecstasy. I saw that my body didn't matter—it was of no importance, a mere trifle. Mother appeared to me and comforted me and freed me from my fear.[1]

During the daytime, the priest would pursue his eccentric dialogues with Kali in the temple. "Sometimes I'd open my mouth and it would be as if my jaws reached from heaven to the underworld. 'Mother!' I'd cry desperately. I felt I had to pull Her in as a fisherman pulls in fish with his dragnet" (R.D., p. 85). With the coming of night, Ramakrishna would enter a jungle-infested cemetery and, casting off into the dust his thin cotton dhoti, and the sacred thread, which no *brahmin* may remove, he communed with the Divine as he knew one must—naked to the world, without shame, without pride, without fear, without memory, without hope. Straining he prayed, opening his heart wider and still wider until it burst like a bubble on the waves merging freely once more into the blissful ocean of the Mother's Being. In a thousand subtle nuances and tones of love, he would cry out to Her, and in as many ways She responded, appearing in vision now as a young girl, now as a prostitute, now as light, now as consciousness itself. The parochial boundaries of form were dissolving, as a morning fog before the radiant sun of Truth. And the Truth proclaimed at every turn: The Mother is not restricted to an image, a ritual, a particular line of thought or action; She is in all—She *is* all.

Intoxicated with this liberating vision of the Mother's immanence, the orthodox superstructure of Ramakrishna's thought and action came crashing down like a bamboo shed in a typhoon. The *brahmin* who a few years earlier wouldn't touch the temple offerings in dread of caste pollution, now gathered together half-eaten scraps of *chapati* and curry from the discarded leaf plates of untouchables, relishing them as the most holy *prasad*. He took in hand the rough, matted tangle of his own hair and used it to mop clean the huts of the poorest of the poor. If he was preparing to offer some food ritually to the idol in the temple and a cat slinked by, he would hold it out to the cat instead, imploring, "Won't You take it, Mother?" He didn't act this way to be provocative, to flaunt the petty rules of men, or to proclaim his own liberated spirituality to the world. He did it because the old and familiar universe was disintegrating before his eyes. The borderline between God and the world, Spirit and matter, himself and others, was, to use his own evocative analogy, revealed to be shifting precariously at every moment like a board afloat the Ganges—insubstantial, a line drawn on water, separating water from water. And Ramakrishna found himself afloat a trackless ocean of God.

Many years later the Master would reminisce: "I used to worship the deity in the Kali temple with flowers. It was suddenly revealed to me that everything is Pure Spirit—the utensils of worship, the altar, the doorframe—all Pure Spirit. Then like a madman I began to shower flowers in all directions. Whatever I saw, I worshiped."[2]

As a result of this overwhelming sense of Her universal presence in all beings, including himself, the priest's intimacy with Kali, which had always been shocking, became now thoroughly scandalous. He would enter the sanctum without prostrating and lie down on the ceremonial couch reserved for Kali, nibbling freely of Her offerings. He would rub the cooling and fragrant sandal paste prepared for Her worship on his own feet, and playfully toss the Mother's flowers into his long, matted hair. He did all of this perfectly innocently, without the least taint of personal pride. If he acted at times as an equal of the deity, then it was the equality of an infant incapable of distinguishing its own body and self from those of its mother. But to others who lacked insight into his true motives, these actions often seemed insufferable and outrageous. They complained bitterly to Rani Rasmani. And she would ignore them. Her faith in Ramakrishna was absolute. At times, she would steal away unseen to the temple and secretly watch his worship, enthralled. Most of all, the hauntingly beautiful hymns Ramakrishna sang to Kali enchanted the Rani and filled her with a strange bliss.

One day, as she was seated by Ramakrishna's side listening to his ecstatic singing, he abruptly broke off and slapped her twice on the cheeks, exclaiming, "Those thoughts even here!" The Rani remained silent, but her attendants were scandalized and ranted shrilly calling for the immediate dismissal of the insolent priest. The Rani, who had been mulling absentmindedly over a pending lawsuit at the precise moment of Ramakrishna's timely rebuke, answered them quietly, "You don't understand. It was the Divine Mother Herself who punished me and thereby illumined my heart." (R.D., p. 68) She forbade them to so much as mention the incident again.

The Pursuit

On numerous occasions, the advocacy of Rani Rasmani and her son-in-law, Mathur, had shielded their eccentric priest from the ill will of the ignorant. And while they protected him from others, it was given to Ramakrishna's nephew, Hriday, to protect his absentminded uncle from himself and to maintain his health. Together, these three were the helmsmen deputized by the Mother to navigate the storm-wracked vessel through troubled waters. But even they were forced to scratch their heads in sheer bafflement at times, wondering if the ship wasn't headed for some disaster and if it would not be the better part of wisdom to ease it into the nearest safe harbor, rather than allow it to plunge still farther, blindly, into the crashing waves of the open sea. With the purest of good intentions, Mathur and Rani hit upon an ingenious plan to lure their battered mariner to the security of the quay.

Convinced that Ramakrishna's rigid observance of continence was to blame for some of his more troubling excesses, they decided to provide a safety valve for his high-strung energies. Being careful not to reveal anything in advance, Mathur brought Ramakrishna by hackney carriage to a rented flat in Calcutta where several carefully chosen accomplices waited to overcome the unsuspecting priest with their undeniable charms. And overcome he was. But not, as it turns out, in the way Mathur had expected. Seeing the prostitutes, Ramakrishna, who had long since come to regard all women as living embodiments of his beloved Mother, repeated Her Divine Name a few times out loud, and then fell effortlessly into an ecstatic trance.

The women were not slow to smell the rat. Becoming suddenly mindful of the grave consequences that lie in wait for those who would tempt a saint, they started loudly and tearfully imploring the holy man for his forgiveness. Hearing the ruckus from afar and wondering what it was all about, Mathur hastened to the scene, only to discover with amazement how dramatically his plan had backfired. The final shot in this marvelous farce worthy of the Marx brothers would show the hapless Mathur beating a hasty retreat, showered by the infuriated agents of his scheme with the choicest epithets of their age-old profession.

Well, Mathur can hardly be faulted for trying! He was neither the first nor the last to have misjudged Ramakrishna.

Indeed, at times the Master himself was no more certain about the true nature of his state, and could not have said with any degree of confidence whether it was pathological or providential. If he clung stubbornly to his path, it was not out of a smug self-assurance or easy piety. He did what he had to do, what he was made to do. Some demon, some deity—he wasn't sure which—drove him blindly on. And therein was his greatest suffering (one shared by mystics of all ages and traditions)—simply not being sure; does it come from God or the devil, is it true or false, reality or sheer imagination?

Of course, these questions do not arise—cannot arise—during the heat of the rapture. It would be easier to doubt one's own existence. But when the fires have cooled and all that remains is a fading memory and a gnawing pain of emptiness, and the whole world proclaims with a single voice that it is sheer madness and delusion, then how can one say for certain that they are dead wrong? Can one cling to what has already passed and reject the clear verdict of common sense with an imperious shrug? It was not given to Ramakrishna to be able to do so. Hypersensitive by nature, he could be cruelly tortured by the views of others, especially if they were men of scholarship, whose judgments he would continue naively to revere for many years to come.

One of those who caused the Master endless troubles with his learned sophistry was an elder cousin of Sri Ramakrishna, Haladhari. Haladhari's attitude toward his young relation teetered erratically between genuine reverence on the one hand and erudite condescension on the other. Witnessing the riveting spectacle of his nephew absorbed in Kali worship, Haladhari invariably felt overwhelmed, so much so that he would prostrate himself on the ground before Ramakrishna. But in no time, the haughty scholar would recover his accustomed pride and ridicule the very actions that had seemed so compelling while he was witnessing them. One day, feeling especially piqued at Ramakrishna's naive devotions, Haladhari set out to demonstrate by quotations from the holy scriptures that Ramakrishna's visions and spiritual states could be nothing but delusions. God is transcendent, beyond being and nonbeing, he insisted. Anything apprehended through the senses or experienced by the emotions must, of necessity, not be God, since God, by definition, remains out of reach of all human organs of perception and feeling.

Confused and unsettled by these arguments, the Master wandered off, finally taking refuge in the Kali temple, where he wept in an agony of wounded love. "Do You have the heart to deceive me, Mother, because I am an unlettered fool and don't know any better?" (G.S., p. 17) he cried out bitterly. Suddenly, a luminous haze appeared, within which was the figure of a white bearded sage of dignified mien and golden complexion. "My child, remain on the threshold of relative consciousness," (G.S., p. 17) the sage intoned solemnly and, after repeating the words thrice, dissolved gently into the encircling radiance.

Thus reassured that his experiences were of a very high order of reality, Ramakrishna's mind was set at ease, if only temporarily. The experience by its very nature, however, was powerless to offer any permanent and unimpeachable consolation. Indeed, from a certain point of view, the vision itself was a part of the unsolved problem. So far, Ramakrishna only had such visions, only had the internal evidence of his own spiritual experiences in support of their genuineness. It was a bit like having to rely on the testimony of the defendant at his own trial. Maybe true, maybe false—but certainly not disinterested.

What the young priest really needed was the independent judgment of an outsider, someone with the breadth of vision and experience to verify what he was going through first hand. But where was such an enlightened soul to be found? Up until this point, the Master had always been surrounded by people to whom he was essentially a mystery—including both those who spurned him and those who admired him. For Rani, Mathur, and a few others, to be sure, he was a wondrous, an undeniably holy mystery. But for all of their sympathy and encouragement, they were in no position to fathom the great forces that clashed within him or to offer a genuine spiritual consolation or understanding. At the deep levels of his being, Ramakrishna was alone and exposed, fated to plow blindly ahead out of sheer instinct, without either chart or help. But the period of his spiritual isolation was coming to a close.

A timeless principle of Indian spirituality is that the Divine must send a guru when the disciple is in genuine need of support on the spiritual path. Sri Ramakrishna was to be no exception. The guru assigned to him by the Mother had already been granted a vision of her spiritual child. She knew only that he lived somewhere by the banks of the Ganges and that she would meet him when the time was ripe. For three expectant years, she had searched in vain.

Ramakrishna must have sensed that help had finally arrived almost from the moment he first caught sight of her disembarking onto a landing on the Ganges just below the temple terrace. The woman's bearing and the subtle glow of her inwardness spoke of a dignified and refined spirituality. Physically, she was arresting; tall and stately, in her late thirties, she was draped in the faded saffron robes of a renunciate and crowned by a disheveled profusion of hair. Carrying a bundle of well-worn sacred books and a small idol of Rama, her sole possessions, she looked half a wild woman, half a queen. The dramatic scene of their first meeting marks the beginning of a new phase in Ramakrishna's journey to God.

Hardly able to conceal his excitement, the Master urged Hriday to bring the woman to him at once. At first Hriday hesitated to fulfill such an odd request, but Ramakrishna reassured him, "Don't worry. Just go and tell her about me and she will surely come."

She did come, and the moment the tall ascetic set her eyes on Ramakrishna, they filled spontaneously with tears of pure delight. "My son, I have been looking for you for such a long time!" she exclaimed. Nestling up to her like a small child with its mother, Ramakrishna proceeded to pour out the long tale of his spiritual trials—the visions, the erratic impulses, the physical symptoms, the strange moods. Finally, he gazed up at her with a pleading look: "Mother, what are these things that are happening to me? Am I really going mad?" (R.D., p. 92)

The woman's eyes melted with infinite tenderness, and she replied, "My son, everyone in the world is mad. Some are mad for money, some for physical comforts, some for name and fame. And you are mad for God!" (G.S., p. 18)

She then proceeded to explain how all that Sri Ramakrishna

had related, down to the spontaneous trembling and burning sensations of his body, were long ago singled out by the Hindu devotional scriptures as signs of the extremely rare state of *mahab-hava*, the most exalted rapture of love for God. With her treasured books spread out before her, she went on to cite chapter and verse in support of her contention. It was all an unspeakable revelation; that centuries-old texts should catalog Ramakrishna's most idiosyncratic spiritual experiences as precisely and matter-of-factly as a merchant's list of his wares was something so extraordinary and unexpected, beyond anything he might have hoped for. It was at the same time a wonderful vindication, and proof that he was on the right path, a well-traveled and ancient way that would lead inevitably to the blessed consummation of union with God.

There was a touching sequel to this first meeting with the woman whose name Ramakrishna would never know, whom he would call simply the *Bhairavi Brahmani*, the *brahmin* nun. After their meeting, she went to the Ganges and prepared food, as was her habit, as an offering to the stone idol of Rama, her *Ishta Daiva* (chosen deity), before consuming it herself. Setting this meal reverently before the image, she closed her eyes and entered into profound meditation. At about this time, Sri Ramakrishna, in a semiconscious divine state, wandered over to where the Brahmani was seated and compulsively started to eat the food set out before the deity. When the Brahmani opened her eyes onto this scene, Sri Ramakrishna felt acutely embarrassed, like a sleep-walker suddenly awakened from deep trance.

He apologized profusely: "Really, I don't know why I do this sort of thing in a state of unconsciousness." (L.R., p. 117)

But, far from being offended, the Brahmani was thrilled. Ramakrishna's innocent behavior vividly confirmed what had just been revealed to her in meditation—within the childlike vessel of the priest of Kali was a Divine Being, an Avatar of God, whose spiritual power would soon be manifest to the world. By eating the food set aside for Lord Rama, if only unconsciously, Ramakrishna was actually accepting his rightful due and revealing his hidden identity, the Brahmani realized.

It was an omen and a confirmation for her. A few hours

later, the Brahmani consigned the idol of Rama, which she had worshiped so lovingly and for so long, to the waves of the Ganges. It had fulfilled its purpose; the fruit had come, the flower could be discarded. As a result of years of devoted worship, the very Divinity which she had visualized tirelessly in the stone was now before her in flesh and blood. From now on, the only worship that would be required of her was to bring all of the accumulated motherly powers and spiritual knowledge of a lifetime to bear on one task—that of nurturing the high destiny which she has glimpsed in Sri Ramakrishna. The attitude she spontaneously adopted toward the young priest was the maternal devotion of mother Yashoda for her child, Krishna. Like Yashoda, the Brahmani delighted in feeding the youthful Ramakrishna with sweets and dainty preparations. Tenderly, she comforted and reassured him at every turn, building up his self-confidence, patiently instilling in him the certainty of his latent powers.

Just as importantly, the Brahmani guided Ramakrishna methodically through a full course of Tantric *sadhana*, a method of practice which endeavors, through ritualistic means, to reveal the divinity inherent in the ordinary objects and energies of the physical world. Through these Tantric practices, she guided Ramakrishna consciously and by a new route to the same peak of spiritual vision he had previously stumbled upon blindly through his own unaided efforts. As a result, he developed abilities and awarenesses previously unknown to him. He experienced the volcanic upwelling of *kundalini*, or serpent power, in the spinal column, and its final explosive merger in the highest psychic center, the *sahasra padma*, or thousand-petaled lotus at the crown of the skull. Along with this mastery of the *kundalini*, an array of awesome supernatural powers were Ramakrishna's for the taking. However, the Divine Mother revealed in vision that these *siddhis*, as they are called in India, are foul and unclean; by fostering pride, they lead the spiritual aspirant astray. Ramakrishna immediately renounced them.

Thereafter, he always cautioned against dabbling in psychic powers in the most graphic terms: "Shun them like filthy excrement. Sometimes they come of themselves when you practice *sadhana*. But if you take any notice of them, you'll stick fast. You won't be able to reach God" (R.D., p. 90).

52

The Pursuit

The period of the Brahmani's guidance was not so much one of breaking radically new spiritual ground or of rising to fresh plateaus of awareness, although this would come shortly, rather, it was a time when Sri Ramakrishna's knowledge widened rather than deepened, and the gains of the past were consolidated and made firm. By methodically leading her pupil through a variety of *sadhanas*, the Brahmani demonstrated the scientific basis of spiritual practice—how certain practices lead, invariably and over time, anyone who performs them with the requisite sincerity and energy to the selfsame results. Moreover, these results are achievable through a variety of means. Devotion, ritual, meditation, the Tantric disciplines for regarding the material creation as the physical body of God—all of these and more besides were the practical methods discovered by the ancient sages for approaching the Ineffable. The esoteric prescriptions scratched onto palm leaves in jungle retreats at the dawn of history remained as potent as on the day they were first recorded. This discovery was breathtaking in its ramifications. Truly, Ramakrishna was not alone! The same irresistible psychic winds that lifted him up to undreamt of spheres of consciousness and experience had blown since the beginning of time.

The detailed knowledge that Ramakrishna gained from the Brahmani of the myriad techniques of spiritual realization would prove of more than academic interest. It would be an invaluable resource in the future when devotees of every possible temperament would flock to Dakshineswar for guidance. Sri Ramakrishna, who would undergo such a dazzling variety of spiritual disciplines himself, always guided his pupils individually, prescribing a different regimen of practice to each one, according to the aspirant's unique capacities.

After successfully completing the course of Tantric discipline, Ramakrishna turned, under the Brahmani's guidance, to the devotional techniques of the Vaishnava sect. According to the Vaishnava scriptures, there are five basic attitudes which a devotee can adopt in his relationship with God. He can look upon the Almighty as a servant looks upon his master (*dasya*), as a friend looks upon his friend (*sakhya*), as a parent looks upon its child or a child its parent (*vatsalya*), as a lover looks upon his beloved (*madhura*), and as a tranquil devotee before the transcendent

53

source of all love *(shanta)*. The various approaches are beautifully embodied in the Hindu scriptures by the great relationships of the mythic past, such as Radha's immortal love for Krishna, the monkey Hanuman's heroic service of Rama, and Krishna's divine friendship with Arjuna.

Ramakrishna, the born lover of God, wished to enjoy the unique thrill of each of these relationships, and threw himself headlong into one after another of them with his usual shocking literalness and singleness of purpose. In his quest for authenticity of feeling, the childhood actor in Ramakrishna really outdid himself! When he identified with Hanuman, for instance, he subsisted on unpeeled jungle roots and fruits, and passed his time jumping and swinging through the canopy of an adjoining forest. His eyes became restless just like those of a monkey, and, incredibly, his coccyx grew of its own accord over an inch in length, forming a kind of impromptu tail. As with the Christian stigmatists, Ramakrishna's concentration on the ideal was so intense that he actually became transfigured into an image of the God he was identified with at the time. In imitation of Radha, the beloved of Krishna, the Master dressed in a gorgeous sari, wore the gold ornaments of a married woman, and developed such realistic and convincing feminine mannerisms that even Mathur could not recognize him, and Hriday was unable to pick his uncle out of a group of women. This remarkable transformation was not the result of playacting, however impeccable. Here, as with his Hanuman persona, Ramakrishna's mental identification was so total that his physical body was compelled to go along—his facial features softening and his breasts swelling noticeably. For several days, the Master called on Krishna plaintively with a lover's bittersweet intensity of longing, with the result that he was finally rewarded with a vision of the incomparably beautiful Lord of the Gopis (the milkmaid devotees, of whom Radha was the loveliest and most beloved).

In this way, Ramakrishna was granted intimate glimpses of many of the legendary figures in the Hindu pantheon. Radha, Krishna, Sita, Bala Rama, and others appeared before him and, when he had satiated himself with their vision, the figures would approach the Master and merge themselves into his body. Sometimes they would leave him with a permanent keepsake, as Sita did when she bequeathed upon him her bewitching smile, a smile the Master is said to have retained until the very end of his life.

In the last chapter, we asked the question: Why do the saints and sages picture God, who is beyond all limitations, in a particular form and with particular qualities? Now the reader may be wondering. Granted, it is necessary to bring the Almighty within the range of our apprehension. Because we are human, our God must be human as well, or at least possessed of attributes we can recognize. Granted, Christ and Jehovah, Shiva and Kali, are useful, even indispensable, bridges between our own frail, time-enslaved separateness and the unthinkable vastness without a name. But why invoke the Absolute endlessly in different names and forms? If Krishna was enough for Mira, and Jesus sufficient for Saint Francis, then why did Ramakrishna feel the need to cry out in turn to Kali, to Krishna, to Rama, to Sita, and even, as we shall soon discover, to Christ and the God of Mohammed? The mystics of the past had gone into the candy shop and made a single selection. Ramakrishna, on the other hand, had exited with hands and mouth and pockets overflowing. Could anything but indigestion result?

In reflecting upon this mystery, Ramakrishna's disciples would probably say that the Master wanted to demonstrate through his actions that all embodiments of God are great, and that devotion to any one of them ultimately reaches the one Ineffable—God beyond all names and forms, God in all names and forms. This seems reasonable enough. But still, we must wonder whether Ramakrishna was being as intentional and premeditated as all that. Or was he simply driven by a hunger that he would not have tried to rationalize or understand? One thing is certain, the spirit of creedal narrowness that seeks to imprison the Infinite within a single approved symbol for worship was completely alien to his nature. And so was the complacency that rests content with what it already knows. Even in the future, when men gathered at his feet, treasuring his every word, Ramakrishna would ask the newcomer to tell *him* about God, and, if he spoke from genuine experience, the Master would listen rapt with wonder. The simple child of God never imagined that he had exhausted the inexhaustible. The true teacher was not afraid to learn from his pupils. And, if he was ready to learn from those who had come to learn from him, how much more was he prepared to learn from the Gods, the Avatars, the prophets who had come to teach mankind.

In India, it is said that God has three hundred million faces and that each face stands for a particular divine attribute, each attribute incarnating a different form of God. The exact number is not important. The meaning is that God's attributes are beyond reckoning and that a lifetime, even a thousand lifetimes, is not sufficient to know Him in all His infinite aspects. The true devotee is not intimidated by these statistics. And he is not impatient either. If the play of his love for God should last for all eternity that would be none too long for him. Who could tire of such an unfathomable lover?

To the rationalist, all of this may smack uncomfortably of polytheism. They will wonder: Why three hundred million Gods? Why so many attributes? Sri Ramakrishna once narrated the story of just such a rationalist, a *sadhu* of the austere Vedanta sect, who used to carry a prism with him at all times. He kept the prism as a reminder. Every time he looked at it he would remember that, just as the myriad colors in the prism are illusions caused by the refraction of white light, so too all of the varied phenomena of the world are illusions caused by the refraction of God's pure white light of Truth. In a figurative sense, we might say that Ramakrishna also carried with him a prism. But Ramakrishna would have looked through his prism from the other end, as it were, and the lesson he would have drawn from it would have been just the opposite from the *sadhu's;* since every rainbow hue derives from the white light of God, the Master would have said, each color is but a form of God Himself.

God the nameless, formless essence is pure radiance. God with name and form—the Avatars, the Gods—reveals Himself in every color of the spectrum. Each point of view is equally valid. Each is equally true.

So, from Ramakrishna's standpoint, the seeming polytheism of Hindu devotional religion is not as it appears at first sight. Yes, God has manifest in many forms. However, each form is understood to derive from, and be an expression of, the One Undifferentiated Source. If the Master showed an enthusiasm to know all of the forms of God, it was for what they revealed to him of the many-faceted divine nature. They were all precious, because they each had something unique to say about God. Krishna showed His supreme beauty and bewitching attractiveness; Rama revealed His righteousness; Shiva embodied His austere purity and power; Kali, His maternal intimacy with creation.

Sri Ramakrishna was the ultimate connoisseur of these Avatars of the Divine. He savored each one with a fresh thrill of discovery, and marveled at all that they revealed to him of the compassion, the power, the inscrutableness, and the whimsical playfulness of the Absolute. He adored God, the Artist of Worlds, and watched Him at work behind the scenes with His palette of many colors. If it had been left to him, he never would have stirred from this privileged and rapturous vantage point at the very threshold of relative consciousness, where the white light of eternity spreads out in all of its marvelous profusion.

And yet, something remained in Ramakrishna's deepest being that would not allow him to rest. Consciously, he was well satisfied. His heart's desire had been fulfilled to excess. God had appeared before him, spoken to him in a multitude of forms, revealed His innermost secrets. The slightest concentration now was all that was necessary to bring Ramakrishna into the highest reverie of *savikalpa samadhi,* where all else vanishes and the Ideal alone, glorious and dazzling, floods the inner sight. What more could be desired now that the key to paradise was in his hand, the Mother's riches spread out before him as his own?

Still, something agitated him and drove him onward, as if he obscurely sensed that his realizations, however wondrous, remained in some way partial and incomplete. What more remained undiscovered Ramakrishna could not have said, and neither could the Brahmani, who was filled with a mother's pride to see her spiritual son at the very pinnacle of devotional love.

But there was someone who would be able to tell him what was still missing. We shall meet him in the next chapter.

Chapter 5

Realization

U<small>NLIKE THE BRAHMANI, THE ASCETIC MONK TOTAPURI DID NOT</small>
recognize Ramakrishna when he first caught sight of him amid
a gathering of pilgrims by the Ganges. Totapuri had been granted
no vision by God or the Gods beforehand. He had not received
the divine edict to search out Ramakrishna and to instruct him.
Indeed, he did not much believe in God or the Gods, still less
would he have felt compelled to follow their commands.
Totapuri was very much his own boss, fiercely independent, even
willful. And if he was no slave of God, he was even less a vassal
of the world.

To Totapuri, both God and the world were essentially illusory. Because he had experienced that ultimate transcendental
state where all phenomena great and small resolve themselves into
an immensity without name or form, everything had come to
seem unreal to him. Because everything had come to seem unreal,
Totapuri no longer searched for anything or expected to find
anything that merited his attention in the world of the senses. If
he still wandered naked over the length and breadth of India, it
was not so much in the hope of discovering something new or
worthy as to remind himself that the ever-shifting landscape of
place and event had nothing new or worthy to offer. The world
demonstrated time and again that it was eternally empty of sub-

stance. The more he saw of it, the less real each of its fleeting images came to appear. The less enduring and substantial the ever-flickering images on the screen of his wanderings appeared, the more firmly convinced he became that all the vaunted goods of the world were just so much smoke and vanity, which no awakened and self-respecting heir of the eternal *Atman*, the indwelling Self of all, could possibly take seriously. And to make absolutely certain that he never did come to take anything of the world seriously, Totapuri was careful not to rest in any one place more than three days at a stretch before continuing again his aimless and incessant wanderings over the surface of the planet.

This was equally true when Totapuri came to Dakshineswar temple; he would halt there briefly on his tireless way from the forests of the sacred Narmada in central India to the plains of the Punjab, his ancestral homeland, or so he thought. But on the bank of the Ganges the day of his arrival, something happened that upset his usual routine. It is true that Totapuri no longer searched for anything. It is also true that, in spite of himself, he had managed to stumble upon something exceedingly strange. Just what he had found would not have been entirely clear, even to him. Not yet. But the very moment his hawk's eyes alighted on the huddled figure of Ramakrishna, rapt with inward joy on the ghat steps, Totapuri's mind froze in its tracks, stunned. Quite against the aloof habits of his *sadhu's* life, he felt compelled to make an unusual offer.

The tall and muscular ascetic strode purposively over to the young man and addressed him with his usual directness: "My son, I see that you have already traveled far along the way to Truth. If you wish it, I can help you reach the next stage. I will teach you Vedanta." (T.L.R., p. 53)

Ramakrishna was filled with an innocent delight. Not that he would have known much about Vedanta, the deep philosophy of oneness which was the province of learned *brahmins* and pundits. At best, he could only have had the vaguest sense of what was being offered to him. But the prospect of fresh spiritual instruction thrilled Ramakrishna, as always, with a joyous expectancy. "I will have to get my Mother's permission first," (N.p., n.d.) he replied, and Totapuri nodded his bemused consent. A few minutes later, the young priest returned from the temple of Kali, a broad smile of acceptance playing on his lips. The Divine Mother had given Her assent, revealing that is was for the purpose of his instruction in nondualism that She had brought Totapuri to Dakshineswar. From that moment onward, Ramakrishna gave himself unreservedly to the holy man's care.

Neither guru nor disciple could have had any idea at the time what an unusual relationship they were embarking upon. Indeed, it would be hard to find anywhere a guru and disciple seemingly less compatible in temperament and philosophy. Totapuri, dry, imperious, and austere, was a monist of the strictest order, whose high spiritual attainments were the fruits of a prodigious intellect and an indomitable will. From earliest youth, his body and mind had been scoured by the most rigorous and unsentimental asceticism, first in a monastery of the *Naga* sect, and afterward in the harsh and lonely discipline of a *sadhu's* life. In obedience to the uncompromising rules of his order, Totapuri never entered a human habitation, sleeping and eating in the open air in fair weather and foul, begging his food, and going about stark naked as an emblem of utter renunciation. Inwardly, he prided himself on his disdain for the world. He mocked the body, whose base animal cravings he had conquered by sheer mental force, mocked society and its manic pursuit of pleasure, mocked creation itself which had come to seem to him insignificant, a paper tiger, an insect afloat in the immensity of his own Spirit.

Totapuri's very being seemed to proclaim haughtily: "I am Brahman. I am the unconditioned, the infinite, the boundless, the nameless, the qualityless—beyond time and space and the farthest reach of thought. The world shall pass away; it is less than a phantom, a fleeting shadow. But *I am* forever the untouched, the self-contained Alpha and Omega of existence, the Eternal Self." For decades he had wandered fearlessly, a lion-hearted warrior doing battle with all that fell short of perfection in his own self, until finally he sat unchallenged in his rightful seat, the egoless summit of all the yogas—the high impersonal throne of *nirvikalpa samadhi,* the formless ecstasy.

When he arrived at Dakshineswar, Totapuri was a true king in beggar's clothing. He had all of a regent's haughty disdain for the cringing submissiveness of his fellow men. The devotional practices of the Indian masses—falling prostrate before the Gods, begging their favors, singing and dancing in the temples—were just so much weakness and idolatry to this saint, whose God dwelt exclusively in the innermost spirit of man and not in some heaven, some image, some ritual born of lamentable hopes and fears. Consequently, he set out with a stern passion to cleanse the promising Ramakrishna of his childish dependence on the Divine Mother.

The Brahmani reacted with a mounting sense of alarm. More than a little jealous of Totapuri's growing influence over her spiritual son and thoroughly out of sympathy with his cold philosophy, she warned Ramakrishna darkly that the life-giving springs of his devotion would go dry if he continued to associate with the passionless and cerebral monk. But her appeal to fear left him cold. It wasn't in Ramakrishna to fear new knowledge; it simply did not occur to him. After all, what was there to protect against? Wasn't he a babe in the Mother's arms? Was it conceivable that She would take him anywhere but precisely where he had to be at the moment? Since it was the Mother Herself who had brought Totapuri to him, there was never any question that Ramakrishna would follow Totapuri till the end. And the end would not be long in coming. Ramakrishna's progress in Vedanta was to be as meteoric, as spectacular, as his progress in devotion had already been.

After he had completed a course of preparatory verbal teachings, Ramakrishna was ready for initiation into the innermost mysteries of Vedanta. On the auspicious morning, the sacred rites took place within a small hut by the Ganges in the chill and lucid predawn silence. It was the *Brahma Muhurta,* the most sacred hour of God, when the stillness of the earth is like the stillness before creation. A small flame danced noiselessly at the center of the mystic circle of the world as Master and disciple sat gravely at its periphery. Since the aspirant cannot embrace Brahman until he has finally and unequivocally thrown off the world, Ramakrishna was guided by Totapuri in the symbolic performance of his own funeral service—first dying to the old self, stripping off his clothing and tossing it into the crematory flame as a token of his abandonment of worldly attachments and desires, then donning the orange robe of the *sannyasi* as a graphic reminder of the flame of renunciation which henceforth would burn steadily within.

These preliminaries over, Ramakrishna was now ready to take the final plunge. Totapuri's manner became solemn. He turned to the initiate and, as his own guru had done decades earlier, he struggled to express in words the inexpressible truths of the soul: "Brahman is the sole Reality, ever pure, ever illumined, ever free, beyond the limits of space and causation. . . . Whatever is within the realm of *maya* is unreal. Give it up. Destroy the prisonhouse of name and form, and rush forth with the strength of a lion. Dive deep in search of the Self and realize it here and now in the beatitude of *samadhi!*" (L.R., p. 189) So Totapuri commanded Ramakrishna to detach his mind from all created things and lift it into the realm of the Ineffable.

The young priest struggled mightily to follow these instructions in meditation, but at the last moment reared back in confusion from the final leap into the unknown. He advanced to the very edge of the precipice of formless consciousness, but he could go no farther. It was no use; the last and most subtle barrier, the golden chain of his devotion, barred the path. The personal God who had lighted his way and guided his steps now stood as a barrier to the realization of the Impersonal Reality. Ramakrishna was faced with the excruciating, the impossible, choice between his heart's Beloved and his love of Truth. He was Abraham, called by God to the incomprehensible sacrifice. Let us turn to the Master's own electrifying description:

> I tried on several occasions to concentrate my mind on the Truth of *Advaita* Vedanta; but each time the form of the Mother intervened. I said to Totapuri in despair, "It's no good. I will never be able to lift my spirit to the unconditioned state and find myself face to face with the *Atman!*" He replied severely, "What do you mean you *can't?* You *must!*" Looking about him, he found a shard of glass. He took it and stuck the point between my eyes, saying, "Concentrate your mind on that point." Then I began to meditate

with all my might, and soon the gracious form of the Divine Mother appeared. I used my discrimination as a sword and clove Her in two. The last barrier vanished and my spirit immediately precipitated itself beyond the plane of the conditioned. I lost myself in *samadhi*. (T.L.R., pp. 54–55)

It is curious that, once again, it was the willingness to put to sword all that was dearest to him that propelled Ramakrishna beyond previous boundaries. Some years before, his feverish impulse to end his life by the ceremonial sword of Kali had effectively rent the veil, and the incomparable form of God as Light in *savikalpa samadhi*, the highest ecstasy in the realm of form, had flooded his consciousness. Now driven again to wield the sword and slay that infinitely blissful *savikalpa* vision of God as Mother, he once more soared beyond the limits of the known. But this time the break with the past was far more radical than before. In putting the Mother to sword, Ramakrishna had really slain himself. It was life's last tenuous thread of striving and desire that he had severed. The old Ramakrishna had died—even clinically. The breath of life had vanished; the vital signs had vanished. And what remained of the priest of Kali sat gazing out without eyes, without thought, without awe. Gazing no longer *at* the face of Truth, but out *from* it.

Let us turn again to Ramakrishna's own description: "The universe was extinguished. Space itself was no more. At first the shadow of ideas floated in the obscure depths of the mind. Monotonously a feeble consciousness of the ego went on ticking. Then that stopped as well. Nothing remained but Existence. The soul was lost in the Self. Dualism was obliterated. Finite and infinite space were as one. Beyond word, beyond thought, he attained Brahman" (T.L.R., p. 55).

For three days and three nights, Sri Ramakrishna sat rigid as an idol of stone, suspended in the incomprehensible still point at the heart of existence. Totapuri could only gaze at his radiant form in wonder. Only he, who had struggled heroically through four decades of the harshest disciplines of mind and body before finally attaining this state, could appreciate what a magnificent achievement this was. For Ramakrishna to have entered *nir-*

vikalpa samadhi with such seeming ease and to have sustained it for so long without being dragged down by the inexorable gravity of the senses was nothing short of miraculous. Finally, by the rhythmic chanting of the sacred formula *Hari Aum*, Totapuri brought his disciple slowly and by degrees back to the world. He gazed on at the awakening priest with an overflowing tenderness and admiration, and Ramakrishna prostrated himself before him. Then guru and disciple locked in an embrace of oneness. Nothing was said. There was nothing to say.

If Totapuri had followed the well-worn patterns of a lifetime, he would now have disappeared tracelessly into the eddying currents of pilgrim India. After all, his purpose had been fulfilled, his pupil had reached the end of knowledge. The habitual fear of worldly attachment should have given wings to his feet. And yet, inexplicably, Totapuri didn't leave; some odd compulsion held him fast at Dakshineswar. More than anything, it was the personality of Ramakrishna himself—so beguiling, so deeply puzzling. One should have expected that the devotional tendencies of the young priest of Kali would have been burnt to ashes in the all-consuming fires of wisdom. Totapuri had taken it for granted that this would happen. But nothing of the sort had taken place. It was almost as if nothing had changed; Ramakrishna continued chanting, singing, and falling into blissful reveries exactly as before.

But even more difficult for Totapuri to fathom were his own reactions to these practices. When Ramakrishna would sing in his wistful, yearning way to the Gods, Totapuri found his own eyes misting over with tears. It was all so inexplicable, even disturbing. How was it possible, having seen through the folly of emotions and realized his own identity with the Impersonal Supreme, that Ramakrishna was still moved by these naive invocations of Rama and Krishna, Shiva and Kali? But while Totapuri's mind was puzzled, his heart was secretly charmed—charmed by the poignant sweetness of the songs and even more charmed by the singer in whom an innocent passion for life existed, incongruously, side by side with the most exalted spirituality. Something in the boyish priest fed and sustained the elder. Imperceptibly, their roles were reversing, the child becoming father to the man, uncovering for him aspects of life silted over by his years of single-minded austerity.

Totapuri's self-contained, wandering existence and the veneration in which he was held by worldly folk must have shielded him to a large extent from the unpleasant, but salutary, tonic of criticism, and from having his cherished ideas challenged openly. Ramakrishna alone felt no reticence in this regard. Ever respectful, he was nevertheless artless enough to say exactly what he felt. A lesser man would have reacted defensively and taken refuge in the guru's divine right to remain unchallenged. Totapuri respected Truth too much for that.

On one occasion, Totapuri and Ramakrishna were seated together before a sacred *dhuni* fire. Totapuri was expounding his philosophy that only Brahman is real, whereas the world is false and trivial, a mere figment of the cosmic illusion—*maya*. Ramakrishna disagreed sharply. The idea that *maya* should be avoided struck him not only as unappealing, but as unattainable. Wasn't it infinitely better to enjoy the breathtaking divine spectacle of the world than to reject it? For even those who rejected *maya* in theory remained under its sway in fact.

In the middle of this discussion, a temple servant came by and tried to light his pipe from the glowing coals of the *dhuni*. Observing this sacrilege, Totapuri became furious, fouly abusing and threatening the terrified servant with his fire tongs. But, incongruously, Ramakrishna fell on the ground, convulsed with laughter.

Red-faced, Totapuri demanded to know what was so funny. "The man was insolent!" he thundered. "Oh yes, he was insolent," Ramakrishna agreed, still quivering with glee. "But you were forgetting your knowledge of Brahman! Weren't you just telling me that there's nothing but Brahman and that a knower of Brahman can't be deceived by *maya?* Yet the very next moment, you forget all that and you are ready to beat one of Brahman's manifestations! You see? *Maya*, which you despise, is stronger than you think. *Maya* is omnipotent" (R.D., p. 121). It is a measure of Totapuri's largeness of spirit that he recognized at once the justice of Ramakrishna's rebuke and became absorbed in thought.

"You're quite right," he reflected after a brief silence. "I forgot Brahman under the influence of anger. Anger is a deadly thing. I shall give it up from this moment onwards" (R.D., p. 121). And it is said that he never went back on this promise.

We must stand in awe of a personality like Totapuri who can so readily admit a defect and then cut it away so cleanly, so surgically. We might wonder if it is really possible that he never gave in to anger again. But the lives of the saints give evidence that it *is* possible. The spiritual traditions of all lands are replete with similar tales of heroic souls who, in a moment of supreme determination, have renounced lust or avarice, hatred or anger, never to succumb again. Pious legend or fact? Perhaps we shall never know for certain until the miracle occurs in our own being. What is certain is that such a thing can only be a miracle. The ordinary human will, as we know it, is incapable of such prodigious feats. If they transpire, it must be on account of some greater power than our own.

Because the testimony of the saints affirms that miracles do happen, because certain things occur in the soul that are beyond the soul's power to bring about, because these things do not follow our own limited plan or timetable, the sages have spoken of Divine grace. Grace is not an explanation; it explains nothing. It merely allows the unexplained to coexist with the explained without getting prematurely swallowed up by it. It admits, in effect, that there is something uncanny, something marvelous, something divine, in our lives that shall never be fully comprehended by the intellect, nor conquered by the will, and that that something, that grace, must be respected and given its due.

Ramakrishna understood this principle from the inside. He knew that the spiritual practitioner must ultimately depend upon a power beyond his personal control. He never felt that he could understand the ways of the Infinite with the limited mind, and he didn't try to do so. But Totapuri thought differently about these things. If Totapuri had one weakness, one spiritual blind spot, it was that he had no concept of grace, of mystery, of *maya*—in short, of the inscrutable. Totapuri lived in a completely ordered and rational world of the spirit. In that world everything could be categorized by the intellect and conquered by the will.

Because his intellect was so sharp and his will so powerful, he was not often brought face-to-face with his own limits. Like other strong souls who have generally gotten their way in life, Totapuri had grown to look upon himself as the sovereign of all that he surveyed.

Totapuri's blind spot is common to many practitioners of *jnana yoga* and to intellectuals in general. It is easy for those who have tasted the strength of the dedicated mind to think of it as omnipotent. The intellect always carries with it a sense of power. "Because I have understood these impulses, emotions, delusions and seen through them, I therefore control them," it seems to assert. But the limitation of the intellect is that it operates in isolation from the objects of its attention. It does have a power of sorts, but it is a power exclusively within its own realm and does not extend beyond it. Seeming to have everything under its control is ultimately to have nothing under its control.

Ramakrishna reflected concretely on this paradox many years later: "You close your eyes and discriminate, 'There is no thorn, there is nothing to prick.' But as soon as your hand is hurt by a thorn you cry out in pain. Similarly, you may reason in your mind that there is no such thing as birth or death, virtue or vice, pain or misery, hunger or thirst—that you are the eternal Brahman, the Existence, Knowledge, Bliss Absolute; but the moment there is some trouble with the body, or temptations overcome the mind, you forget your high philosophy and are overwhelmed with delusion and its painful consequences." (L.R., p. 199)

All of this is not to imply that Totapuri's principles were simply mental constructs without any connection to the real world. From what we know of his remarkable personality, there can be little doubt the monk's spiritual accomplishments were very real and substantial. Still, as evidenced from his anger at the temple servant, Totapuri's mental realizations had outpaced his emotional ones. He could enter the highest state of *samadhi* at will, but when he returned to outward consciousness, it was to a human nature whose failings remained to a significant extent untransformed.

Perhaps in order to point this out, Ramakrishna gently questioned Totapuri once why, if he had fully realized Brahman, he still felt the necessity of meditating every day. Totapuri pointed to his brass water pot. "See how beautifully it sparkles. Won't it lose its luster if I don't polish it daily?" "Yes, that is true of an ordinary vessel," Ramakrishna agreed. "But not if it is made of gold." (N.p., n.d.) And the truth was not lost on Totapuri; for all his attainments in spiritual life, he was still not beyond the tarnishing power of illusion. The lead of his human nature was not yet fully transmuted into the gold of the spirit.

As if conspiring to drive home this very point, a nagging illness, more serious than any the robust wanderer had known before, left Totapuri with a vivid and unaccustomed sense of his own limitations. At first he was able, with difficulty, to lift his mind through meditation above the suffering of the dysentery, but the terrible evening soon arrived when, struggle as he might, he was unable to raise his awareness back to the serene plane of Truth. The inconceivable, the unacceptable, had happened. The dark power of the body had eclipsed the radiant sun of Brahman.

The proud monk reasoned disdainfully: "Because of this wretched body, my mind is out of control today. I know positively that I am not the body, so why should I associate with it and suffer its pains? What is the purpose in dragging it around anymore?" (L.R., p. 201)

Swiftly, he resolved to consign the obstinate flesh to the waves of the Ganges. Totapuri fixed his mind on Brahman and strode without hesitation directly into the glistening black waters of the night. Farther and still farther, he waded through the shallows without reaching the deep current that he sought, until, finally, he was within a stone's throw of the flickering lanterns of a village on the far shore. "How is it possible? Has the mighty Ganges of oceangoing vessels and colorful ancient prows been swallowed up by the sands?" he wondered.

Then suddenly, with the intensity of revelation, the deep significance of what has just happened broke over him, and the stony ascetic burst compulsively into sobs. For the first time, the full knowledge of man's helplessness, of his own helplessness, in the face of the overwhelming forces of the world came flooding in. For how long had he fancied himself captain of destiny! But now it dawned upon him that an invisible hand had been steering the vessel all along. He had not been consulted at the beginning of life; he was not even capable of ending it. Ramakrishna was right! A mysterious Power rules over our living and our dying, our acting and our loving. Saints and sinners, knowers of Brahman and the ignorant—all fall under the Divine Mother's sway. And yet, how few are aware of it! All along Totapuri had been living in Her domain, but fancying himself the sovereign. And now, in a flash, the illusion had been shattered.

He turned around and headed back across the empty waters, feeling neither defeated nor victorious. But, for the first time in memory, Totapuri experienced the exquisite release of surrender—surrender to a force beyond his own, to a Consciousness, to a Living Being whose dominion is the universe, whose special abode is the heart of man. And in his own heart, Totapuri felt the upwelling of gratitude, wave upon wave, engulfing him, drowning him as the Ganges would not. Drowning him in the way the Mother had intended all along—in the tears of *bhakti*, the waters of love.

Arriving back at the Dakshineswar ghat, the *sadhu* built a fire and spent the remainder of the night repeating the holy Name of the Mother. When Ramakrishna came upon him just after dawn, he was amazed to see a changed man, radiant with spiritual joy and once again the very image of vigorous health. "The disease has been a friend to me," the monk explained. "Last night I was blessed with the vision of the Divine Mother and, through Her grace, I was freed from the disease. Oh, how profoundly ignorant I was! Well, get me your Mother's permission to leave. I now understand that it was to teach me this lesson that She kept me here so long. Many times I thought of leaving and actually went to you to say goodbye. But something always held my tongue at such times and diverted me to other topics." (L.R., p. 203)

"Ah, you refused to believe in my Mother and you argued with me to disprove Her," Ramakrishna gently admonished. "Now you see for yourself that She is real. She taught me long ago that Brahman and Shakti [i.e., the formless Absolute and God with form, the Mother] are one, like fire and its burning power." (L.R., p 203) For the first time, Totapuri accompanied Ramakrishna to the temple of Kali. Prostrating together before the deity, both felt at once the Mother's silent blessings for the departure. And so, eleven months after his arrival at Dakshineswar, the elderly ascetic returned once more to the anonymity and the freedom of his wanderer's life.

If Totapuri left broadened and mellowed—vividly aware now that Truth is far greater than any theory or one-sided approach fashioned to contain it—then it is equally true that Ramakrishna's horizons had broadened immeasurably from his contact with the Impersonal. Indeed, the experience of *nirvikalpa samadhi* had stirred him more profoundly than he could know. He lived continually in its shadow now. It was as if some powerful undertow dragged relentlessly, threatening at every moment to carry him directly to the very center of the limitless sea of consciousness. And Ramakrishna was not inclined to resist. After his mentor had left, he resolved to drink deeply of the uninterrupted bliss of *samadhi*. What he had not reckoned on was that once he had entered *samadhi* he would lose all will, all capacity even, to leave it. Indeed, the whole fragile superstructure of Ramakrishna's interest in and desire for earthly life very quickly collapsed. Food, sleep, and ritual, love and hate, light and darkness—everything was gone; for six timeless months, Ramakrishna floated unbridled and alone in the realm of pure consciousness.

By all rights, Ramakrishna should not have survived. Others who had gazed too fixedly from out of the eyes of the Great Mystery had simply vanished from the world of men. Ordinarily a yogi can remain in *nirvikalpa samadhi* for twenty-one days, after which the physical organism falls quietly from Consciousness like a sere leaf, the *jiva* (individual soul) dies, never to be reborn again. In the theology of the East, it is said that the spiraling round of birth, death, and rebirth is broken for such a one. The drop of the ego has merged forever in the ocean of God.

In Ramakrishna's case, it was only the fortuitous ministrations of a passing *sadhu* that kept him from that exalted fate. The monk, recognizing the Master's rare state, took it upon himself to lovingly preserve the body of the holy man for the good of the world. His was an inspired and heroic struggle for which we must be grateful. Whenever Ramakrishna stirred ever so slightly to external awareness, the devoted *sadhu* would immediately thrust food into his mouth. At other times, he would beat his entranced charge vigorously with a stick until he had recovered enough consciousness of the external world to be force-fed. Some days, Ramakrishna would manage to swallow a few bites and gulp down a little Ganges water, other days not. Somehow, miraculously, the tenuous flame of life sputtered on, though barely.

It was not until a severe bout with dysentery forcibly wrenched his attention back to the body and its insistent demands that Ramakrishna finally recovered his foothold in the physical world. As with Totapuri, this disease had come as a friend, as a blessing in disguise. Or perhaps it would be truer to say that the disease came as *our* friend. For Ramakrishna, it was no longer of any account whether he lived or died. Life and death had become equal and unimportant; he had entered that realm where even their shadows had ceased to fall.

But for us, it is crucial that Ramakrishna survived. If Ramakrishna had crossed finally the bridge to the other world, as he no doubt yearned mightily to do, then he would have died just another anonymous Indian holy man. The disciples would never have come; the flood of inspired teachings—one of the greatest legacies of the world's spiritual heritage—would not have materialized; the living example that has nourished and inspired Indians for a century and that revealed the greatness of India's spiritual culture to the world would simply have evaporated without a trace. But the world had need of Ramakrishna, and Ramakrishna survived. Perhaps, in the end, it was that need—the need of generations yet unborn, the need of a world seemingly abandoned by God—that forcibly drew him out of that radiant world without night and back to our own less certain world of shadow and of light.

To return so suddenly, to land with a wrenching jolt back onto the unyielding contours of matter, could only have been traumatic. What a rude shock it must have been for the one who had known himself as the immutable Self to find his spirit the prisoner of a diseased body amid a jostling crowd of phantoms in the shapes of men! And yet, Ramakrishna was far too human, far too compassionate, to have resented it. The Divine Mother had come to him in vision with the command that henceforth he was not to stray beyond the boundaries of the realm of form; for the good of mankind, he was to remain in the world to bring the message of joy and hope to those entangled in the net of the *maya.* And the loving son was content to obey. For the command had not really come from the outside. It is fair to say that Ramakrishna heard his own deepest inclinations of compassion speak with the Mother's voice.

In a parable, the Master reflected upon the motivation that had brought him back—that brought back all the great prophets and Avatars to their fellow men—after the vision of God:

Three men were walking in a field in the middle of which there was an enclosure surrounded by a high wall. From within the enclosure came the gay sounds of music; instruments were playing and voices melodiously sang. The men were charmed and wanted to know what was going on. But there was no opening anywhere to enter by. What was to be done? At length, one of the men found a ladder somewhere and climbed to the top of the wall, while the others waited below. When this fellow reached the top, he gazed within and was so besides himself with joy that he neglected to tell his friends what he saw. He simply uttered a loud cry and jumped right in. The two others exclaimed, "What a fine friend he is! He didn't tell us what is inside. We'll just have to go up there ourselves and find out." So the second man climbed the ladder. And just like the first man, he burst into laughter the moment he peered over the top and jumped in without so much as a word to his friend. The third man became all the more intrigued. He too climbed the wall and saw what was happening inside. It was like a market of happiness given free to all comers. His first impulse was to jump down as the others had and join in the rejoicing. But then he said to himself, "If I do that, then nobody outside will ever know this place exists. Am I to be the only one to find it?" So he forced his mind away from the sight, and he came down the ladder and began telling everyone he met:

72

"In there is a market of happiness. Come with me and we shall enjoy it together!" (R.D., pp. 60–61)

Ironically, when Ramakrishna returned from the top of his own wall of ecstatic knowledge, he found the world largely uninterested in what he had come to reveal. The prospect of unlimited expansion and bliss held less attraction to the great mass of men than their own dreary, shuffling rounds. The sleepwalkers only seemed to be awake. In reality, they were too deeply entranced to respond to the fire which burned within his spirit. It was a profoundly frustrating time for Ramakrishna. He had returned from the summit of consciousness a man with a mission. His larder was stocked to overflowing. More than anything, he longed to distribute the Mother's bounty freely. But those who came to him (and their numbers grew steadily as word spread in Calcutta of the enlightened devotee of Dakshineswar temple) contented themselves with an occasional crumb fallen from the table. Few, if any, hungered to join Ramakrishna in the feast.

Those who came to Dakshineswar came to question, to argue, to compare and contrast, to listen, and perhaps to dream. They came, at best, to warm themselves a moment by the fire of ecstasy and then return to the only world they would ever really know, a world of endless, nagging worries, of small victories and small defeats. For all of Ramakrishna's growing notoriety among the members of the educated middle class (to whom he had been introduced by an admiring Keshab Chandra Sen, the idealistic leader of the reformist Brahmo Samaj, about which we shall hear more later), he experienced in his heart the loneliness of exile.

The same reckless striving that had catapulted him into the lap of the Mother now drove Ramakrishna to yearn mightily for the unencumbered young souls with whom he could share Her. The Mother had revealed that they were to come. She had even granted the Master visions of several of them, his spiritual children and intimate disciples of the future. They were the very limbs of his body. Ramakrishna had no other purpose in life now but to guide them with his love. But where were they? How long would he have to wait?

The Master's state of mind at that time is best conveyed by his own words:

> In those days there was no limit to my yearning. During the daytime, I could just manage to keep it under control, though the talk of worldly people tormented me. I would yearn for the time when my beloved companions would come to me; I kept planning what I would say to this one, and what I would give to that one, and so forth. When evening came, I couldn't master my feelings any longer. I was tortured by the thought that another day had passed and still they hadn't arrived! When the evening worship started and the temple resounded with the ringing of bells and blowing of conch shell horns, I would climb up on the roof of the *kuthi* and cry out at the top of my lungs, with all the anguish of my heart, "Come to me, my boys! Where are you? I can't bear to live without you!." A mother never longed so for the sight of her child, a friend for his friend, or a lover for his sweetheart as I did for them. Oh it was beyond all describing. And soon they did begin to come. (R.D., p. 167)

→→→ *Chapter 6* ←←←

A Pilgrim's Progress

As we have seen in the last chapter, the experience of the Impersonal Absolute in *nirvikalpa samadhi* had not put an end to Ramakrishna's devotional yearnings. But he was not insensible of the dangers. He knew what excessive dwelling on the Infinite could do to a man. He had seen the end products of it at Dakshineswar—strange, desiccated beings with darkly glowing eyes, *sadhus,* ghouls, empty gourds rattling in the cosmic winds—indifferent to man, indifferent to God. Because Ramakrishna had seen all of this with his own eyes, he was wary. He prayed to Kali fervently that She not allow his love to be swallowed up in the fires of an inhuman wisdom: "Oh, Mother, let me remain in contact with men! Do not make me into a dried up ascetic!" (T.L.R., p. 80).

Love was the very oxygen that he breathed—love for God, the Divine Mother of all, and love for man, Her embodiment in flesh and blood. Life without love was inconceivable to Ramakrishna. But love assumes a separateness from its object. Love implies the duality of lover and beloved. And it is precisely this sense of duality, this final illusion of being other than the Cosmic Beloved, that vanishes like a haze before the morning sun in the supreme radiance of *samadhi.* Ramakrishna used to say that the devotee coming back from the nondual state has to consciously

75

reassume a measure of ego, of illusion, just in order to function in the physical world.

In his own case, the Master had reinstated that most sublime and benevolent of all egos, the ego of being a carefree child of God. He accomplished this, however, without losing sight of the deepest levels of his own being at which the Divine Mother was not other than he. Ramakrishna himself was She, and yet, at the same time, he was also her loving son. To cling exclusively to the former would have been to violate Love. To cling only to the latter would violate Truth. So Sri Ramakrishna embraced both at once! It was in the arms of this sublime paradox that he was to live out the rest of his days. A great *bhakta* of our own century has expressed it very beautifully. When asked to reveal his spiritual state, Swami Ramdas of south India replied, "The same as the Ganges which, having reached the sea, flows ever towards it."[1]

Having reached the ocean of Truth, having attained the Vedantic realization under Totapuri's direction, Sri Ramakrishna had completed the last of the major Hindu *sadhanas* that he was destined to undergo. Nevertheless, the river of his devotion flowed on undiminished. And his curiosity about other forms of worship remained keen. When a Sufi holy man took advantage of the Kali temple's liberal policy of offering hospitality to genuine seekers of all faiths, the Master was inspired to seek initiation from him in Muslim practices. Impressed by the evident sincerity of the saintly devotee, Ramakrishna felt intuitively that Islam, too, was one of the great paths to God, and he craved to experience for himself how the Lord blessed devotees who worshiped Him through the forms of Islam.

For three days thereafter, the Master rigorously followed the Sufi's instructions, repeating the name of Allah continually, performing the *namaz* prayer five times daily, and bowing in the Islamic way, facing Mecca. Unsatisfied as always by an exclusively inward devotion, the priest of Kali expressed it outwardly as well with his usual dramatic flair and disregard for public opinion. In his adherence to the manners of the Bengali Muslims, Ramakrishna dressed himself in the Muslim way, ate their food, and faithfully kept their religious laws. Some were amused by this. But the majority of both Hindus and Muslims were scandalized. It was only with the greatest difficulty that Mathur was able to dissuade his priest from the ultimate sacrilege of eating beef!

All of the carefully tended lifelong scruples of a Hindu and a *brahmin* had simply vanished into thin air. Ramakrishna lost all passion for the Gods, all thoughts of them even. He never once entered the temple precincts. Kali had melted tracelessly from view; it was as if She had never existed. The spiritual chameleon had changed colors once more. And not only the skin had changed. In body, mind, and soul, Ramakrishna had actually become a Muslim. The climax of this brief Islamic phase came with the vision of an impressive sage of grave mien and a flowing, white beard (Mohammed?), who approached and finally merged into Ramakrishna's body. This was followed by an absorption in Allah, the Muslim God, whose attributes, in turn, led into the formless Absolute, the Brahman. The river of Sufi devotions had merged with the Hindu stream at the end in the selfsame ocean of the Spirit without either name or form.

The last in the long procession of Ramakrishna's *sadhanas*, his devotion to Christ, took place some eight years later, in 1874. The Master was introduced to Jesus by a wealthy Hindu devotee who had entertained him by reading excerpts from the Christian Bible. The divine teachings and sublime personality of Sri Isa (as Jesus is known in India) easily ignited Ramakrishna's spiritual longing; increasingly in the days that followed, the son of the Mother was given over to fond thoughts of the loving son of the Father.

Then one afternoon, as he was resting casually in the garden house of a Dakshineswar neighbor, Ramakrishna's attention was forcibly drawn to a colorful image of Madonna and child on the wall. Suddenly, the picture blazed forth with an otherworldly radiance. Ramakrishna felt the rays piercing his heart, driving out all Hindu ideas. At first, overwhelmed, he panicked: "Oh Mother, what are you doing? Help me!" (T.L.R., p. 77) But it was too late. For days, Ramakrishna found himself obsessed with thoughts of Christ.

Strolling through a wooded grove by the Ganges shore on the afternoon of the fourth day after his initial vision, the Master saw a radiant figure with a fair complexion, large, subtly luminous eyes, and a flattened Semitic nose. As the serene foreigner approached, he fixed Ramakrishna gently in his fathomless gaze. "Who can this be?" the Master wondered. And then he heard the answer resounding within: "Behold the Christ, who shed his heart's blood for the redemption of the world, who suffered a sea of anguish for the love of men. It is he, the Master Yogi who is in eternal union with God. It is Jesus, love incarnate" (T.L.R., p. 77).

The two supreme lovers of God embraced, and merged into each other. Ramakrishna was propelled into deep rapture, which once again opened into the consciousness of the ineffable Brahman—the true wellspring of spiritual experience known to all the great prophets of mankind, and in which they are eternally united.

From that day onward, Sri Ramakrishna's feeling for Christ remained fresh and vivid. He kept in his room at Dakshineswar a small image of Jesus before which he burned incense mornings and evenings as an act of remembrance. He revered Christ as an Avatar of the divine, in all senses an equal to the great Hindu Avatars like Rama and Krishna. Throughout his life, the Master regarded Jesus as a true son of God and a brother in the Universal Spirit which knows no distinctions of creed or culture, time or space.

Ramakrishna's vision of Christ ended the final phase of what must be considered one of the most remarkable spiritual journeys of our age. Ramakrishna would reflect on it with his disciples:

> I have practiced all religions—Hinduism, Islam, Christianity—and I have also followed the paths of the different Hindu sects. I have found that it is the same God toward whom all are directing their steps, though along different paths. You must try all beliefs and traverse all the different ways once. Wherever I look, I see men quarreling in the name of religion—Hindus, Mohammedans, Brahmos, Vaishnavas, and all the rest. But they never stop to reflect that He who is called Krishna is also called Shiva, and bears the name of the Primal Energy, Jesus and Allah as well.
>
> A lake has several landings. At one the Hindus take water in pitchers and call it "jal"; at another the Muslims

take water in leather bags and call it "pani"; in a third the Christians call it "water." Can we imagine that it is not "jal," but only "pani" or "water"? How ridiculous! The substance is One under different names, and everyone is seeking the same substance; only climate, temperament, and name create differences. Let each man follow his own path. If he sincerely and ardently wishes to know God, peace be unto him. He will surely realize Him! (T.L.R., pp. 79–80)

It is really remarkable when we consider the multitude of paths, the vast landscape of the spirit that Sri Ramakrishna had traversed—and all within sight of the majestic temple towers at Dakshineswar. The adventures that other men seek outwardly, taking to the road, scouring the planet for the novel and the esoteric, the Master had far surpassed by remaining where he was. Whenever Ramakrishna had need of a new spiritual challenge, a teacher had come at precisely the crucial psychological moment to take him in hand and guide him to the next rung of the spirit. Ramakrishna had never needed to search it out himself.

In our Western climate of thought, we often think of spirituality as something external to ourselves, something we need to pursue aggressively; we think we need to seek gurus actively, cultivate mystical experiences actively, enforce morality rigidly. We treat the whole project, often as not, as a complex military campaign. Perhaps we are not altogether wrong in doing this. It is our nature, after all—the nature of our civilization—to try to take heaven by storm. It would be unnatural for us to attempt less. But we are beginning to discover, to our cost, the frightening price of this unbalanced self-assertion in so many realms of our personal and collective lives. Willfulness, determination, and energy certainly have their place in the life of the spirit, as they do in the physical life. What we are only now coming to sense is that they do not occupy the only place, or even the place of honor, and that they need to be well tempered with a healthy dose of surrender, of submission to a power infinitely greater than our own, if we are not to drive the Divine away with the well-meaning but restless gusts of our egoistic resolve to attain Him.

India has known this all along. By comparison to our own

way, Ramakrishna's way—India's ancient way—is remarkably uncalculated. In a certain sense, Ramakrishna never felt that he had to *do* anything. It never occurred to him to impose his view of how things ought to be on how things actually were. He trusted implicitly in the spontaneity and the maternal bounty of nature. He waited patiently, arms open wide, with full faith that whatever was necessary would come to him of its own, uninvited, when the time was right. And come it did, with an exuberant and nurturing abundance. He viewed this principle of universal nurturance in the most intimate terms and called it "Kali."

Ramakrishna had a child's untroubled faith in the Divine Mother, Kali. And the Mother, for Her part, never failed him. How else to explain the long line of protectors, guides, bursars, and friends who came one after the next to look after the needs of body, mind, and spirit of the one who never gave a second thought to those needs himself? Some men go out to conquer the world. Others, like our hero, wait in faith for the world to come to them. Invariably it does come. It comes because it was never really "out there" to begin with. The world was inside all along. But only those who are still enough and patient enough to let the blossom of the world unfold in their own hearts will ever realize it. The rest of us are like that wisely foolish trickster, Nasruddin, of Sufi lore, who is said to have searched frantically under a street lamp one evening.

"Have you lost something out here?" a passerby inquired sympathetically.

"Not at all; I lost a priceless jewel inside my house," the Sufi everyman explained.

"Then why are you looking for it out here?" the passerby wondered.

"I'm looking out here because there is no light in my own house with which to make the search," (N.p., n.d.) Nasruddin responded with the peculiarly twisted logic of our alienation from ourselves.

But Nasruddin was wrong; we are wrong! Our houses—our selves—are full of light, for those with the eyes to see it. Sri Ramakrishna had such eyes.

As we have seen, Ramakrishna never felt the need to leave

Dakshineswar. He was content to wait serenely for things to come to him. In point of fact, aside from two visits to his native village and a few short trips within Bengal, he only left the temple of Kali once for any extended period of travel. This was in 1868, when Mathur convinced him to join in an elaborate pilgrimage to the holy cities of north India. It was a massive and costly undertaking worthy of a maharaja. Three railway cars were hired, and a motley retinue of Mathur's friends, relatives, servants, cooks, priests, pundits, and musicians—well over a hundred people in all—tagged along. While it seemed at times more like a traveling circus than a sacred journey, there was, for Mathur, a serious purpose behind the outward show. In India, making a pilgrimage has traditionally been a favorite method for gaining merit. In sponsoring so many pilgrims, the wealthy landowner was accumulating quite a good store of merit. If it also happened to be the perfect outlet for Mathur's natural gregariousness, his love of pomp, and his rich man's pride, so much the better!

On one occasion, when the party was passing through a backward tribal area in western Bihar, which even today is among the poorest regions in India, the Master felt heartsick at the plight of the famished Shantal villagers. He told Mathur to fulfill his duties as "steward of the Mother's estate" by feeding and clothing them all. But Mathur was reluctant to consent to such a costly undertaking. Weeping bitterly, Ramakrishna crouched in the dust with the peasant folk. "You wretch!" he sobbed. "I'm not going to that Benares of yours! I'm staying right here with my people. They have no one to care for them. I won't leave them" (R.D., p. 132). In the face of this ultimatum, Mathur had no choice but to give in.

The holy caravan then wended its way slowly to Benares and then to the confluence of the Ganges, Jamuna, and the mythic Saraswati at Allahabad, the location of India's famed *kumbha mela* festivals, where the pilgrims bathed in the sacred waters. Finally, the party journeyed on to Mathura and Brindavan in northwest India, the holy places intimately associated with the life of Sri Krishna, which are active centers for Hindu devotionalism to this day.

In making this epic journey, the Master was traversing two distinct landscapes. On the one hand, he was traveling through the literal geography of temples and villages, forests and vast plains, the wheat-growing agricultural heartland of north India. This landscape must have proven endlessly fascinating to Ramakrishna, at once familiar and yet subtly different in many small details of taste and color, dress and language, from all that he had known before. At the same time as he traveled through this literal landscape, however, Ramakrishna also journeyed through the dreamscape of legend, no less real than the landscape of the senses. Indeed, for him, it was much more real, more richly significant and vital.

The landscape of legend was glorious beyond words. The landscape of the senses could be disappointing. The gap between the two was often confusing. Nowhere was it more so than in Benares—Shiva's city, pillar of light, fount of liberation, earthly abode of all the Gods. In Benares, the Master had a vision of the subtle spiritual form of the city bathed in an otherworldly radiance and fashioned out of pure gold. His awareness of the sanctity of this Hindu Jerusalem was so intense that he couldn't bear to relieve himself within the city limits. When nature called, he headed for the outskirts.

Nevertheless, as Ramakrishna quickly discovered, the workaday Benares was a far cry from the celestial abode of the spirit that he had cherished in vision. He had half expected to find the city full of world-renouncing yogis; instead, he found it full of the same pettiness, the same unregenerate worldliness, as everywhere else. It was a world more of Chaucer than of the Hindu Puranas. Pompous pilgrims, scheming priests, avaricious merchants, the baseness of rumor and gossip—in Calcutta, all of this was to be expected; it was almost tolerable there. In Benares, it was painful. On one occasion, Ramakrishna found himself in the drawing room of a wealthy landlord amid talk of finance, real estate, and profit and loss. The worldly chatter was a torment to him. In tears, he cried out, "Mother! Where have you brought me? I was better off in Dakshineswar!" (G.S., p. 119)

But if Benares was depressingly full of the same concerns as elsewhere, there was at least one man in whom the city of legend and the city of the senses appeared to converge. He was the great saint Trailanga Swami, whom Ramakrishna met by the banks of the Ganges. The revered yogi, reputed to be over three hundred years old, was famed throughout India for his miraculous powers. For days at a time, the portly yogi would be seen by untold thousands of pilgrims meditating in lotus posture afloat the Ganges or submerged beneath its waves. He ate almost nothing, but his weight rarely fell below three hundred pounds. On occasion, he would ingest poison with no ill effect, and, as Ramakrishna himself observed, he was capable of lounging upon the searing Ganges sands at midday without any apparent discomfort.

Clearly, through strict ascetic practices, the great yogi had risen above the need to bother with the demands of the body; it would seem he was no longer conscious of having a body! As a result, the shadow of conventional shame had fallen from him. Like Totapuri and like Adam before the fall, Trailanga Swami was accustomed to walking about without so much as a loincloth to cover his nakedness.

For some inscrutable reason, the awesome spectacle of a huge Swami sauntering unself-consciously about Benares completely naked greatly distressed the British colonial authorities. They tried to persuade Trailanga of the error of his ways and, failing that, attempted to forcibly conceal his hulking nakedness behind the bars of their prisons. Twice they locked him up, and twice they found the Swami sprawled in leisurely freedom on the prison roof—his cell door remained inexplicably locked throughout these mysterious episodes! Eventually, the British sagely came to resign themselves to the Swami's nudity.

Trailanga Swami belonged to a class of *sadhus* called *munis* who maintain a habitual silence. Perhaps their silence is a hint to the rest of us, hypnotized by the power of speech as we are, that Truth cannot be conveyed in words, that Truth can be discovered only in the depths of silence. Trailanga Swami, however, was not dogmatic about this. On occasion he would answer, through signs, questions put to him.

When Ramakrishna came to see the yogi, he placed before Trailanga the age-old conundrum of Hindu theology: Is God one or many? It is a question which, like a Zen koan, has no answer, and also many answers. Trailanga Swami signed in reply to Ramakrishna's question that God is one when a man enters into *samadhi;* but so long as any consciousness of "I" and "you" remains, God is perceived as many.

This response dovetailed perfectly with the Master's own realization, and he turned to Hriday saying, "In him you see the condition of a true knower of Brahman" (R.D., p. 133). Later, he said of Trailanga, "I saw that the Universal Lord Himself was using the Swami's body to manifest His presence. All Benares was illumined by his stay there" (R.D., p. 133).

From Benares, the party moved in stages to Brindivan. If Benares with its great turreted shrines and massive ghats is awe inspiring like Shiva, whose incarnation in brick and mortar it is said to be, then Brindivan with its walled gardens and its peacocks and peaceful groves is lovely and seductive as Krishna himself. Brindavan is Krishna's city, the earthly stage for His divine play. In Brindavan, myth and reality, past and present, earth and heaven, meet and embrace. And Krishna is still the reigning king, the invisible monarch of the realm of the heart. What Sri Ramakrishna would have seen in the Brindavan of his day was a city whose life blood was devotion, whose every quarter rang with the chanting of the Divine Names of the Lord of Love and echoed to the vigorous strains of *kirtana,* impassioned devotional singing.

In many respects, Shiva and Krishna—Benares and Brindavan—embody two archetypal pathways to God. Shiva is God as power, God as shining, transcendent purity. He is pictured wielding a trident as emblem of His mastery over the three worlds, the three states of consciousness (waking, dreaming, and dreamless sleep), and the three divisions of time (past, present, and future). Shiva is portrayed as perpetually in *samadhi,* at once beyond creation and the source for all creation. His city, Benares, represents disciplined austerity and yogic practices. Trailanga Swami was the perfect incarnation of that spirit of eternal Benares.

But Krishna's city conveys none of the awe of Benares. Krishna is the God of enchantment, the embodiment of all that is most resplendent and irresistible in the realm of the senses. He is visualized playing a flute, because God is the Pied Piper of souls, luring all who pause long enough to hear His tune out of themselves and their small concerns and into the radiant freedom of His Kingdom. Simultaneously, Krishna is represented as the Divine Lover of all the gopis, a sign that God, though one and undivided, is at the same time the most intimate companion for all beings. His city of Brindavan stands for the path of *bhakti*, the spiritual ascent through love.

Ramakrishna revered Benares. But he adored Brindavan. He felt at home in Brindavan as nowhere else. He was infinitely susceptible to Brindavan's reigning influence. He easily contracted the fever of Krishna *bhakti* and spent his days in a continual whirl of devotional inspiration. He wandered in raptures through the pastoral landscape of meadows, hillocks, gardens, and streams crying out, "Where is my Krishna! Where is Krishna! Why can't I see him? Everything here has been blessed by his presence—but where is he?" (R.D., p. 134).

The Master's love for Krishna drew to him a woman in her sixties, Gangamayi, who was herself a great devotee of Radha and Krishna. Gangamayi intuitively recognized Ramakrishna to be an incarnation of Radha, and the two God-intoxicates became fast friends. Soon Ramakrishna moved into the saint's simple hut. Overwhelmed in the joy of their shared love for Krishna, all thoughts of returning to Bengal had disappeared. Mathur and Hriday became greatly alarmed, but their arguments were to no avail.

Then just as all seemed lost, the thought came to Ramakrishna of his mother Chandra, living all alone at Dakshineswar. What would become of her if he remained in Brindavan?

The path of duty was suddenly clear. He must return to Dakshineswar.

→≫ *Chapter 7* ≪←

Married Life

In the period following Ramakrishna's return to Dakshineswar, several of those with whom he had been closely associated passed away. The Brahmani died in Brindavan, where she had stayed on after accompanying Ramakrishna there from Benares. Some three years later, Mathur took sick from typhoid fever, and at the exact hour that the wealthy benefactor succumbed to the disease in his Calcutta home, Ramakrishna, returning from trance, told his companions at Dakshineswar: "Mathur's soul has ascended to the sphere of the Mother" (R.D., p. 141). It should be mentioned that Rani Rasmani had died of dysentery in the year 1861.

The death of Ramkumar's son, Akshay, about one year after the Master's return to Dakshineswar, deserves to be treated in some detail, because Ramakrishna actually witnessed it. His unorthodox reactions at the time reveal graphically how he looked upon death. Akshay was a priestly colleague at the Dakshineswar temple, and an intimate companion of Ramakrishna. A pure soul, the young man possessed a strongly devotional character and a good-natured boyish simplicity. Of all Ramakrishna's relations, Akshay was the closest to him in temperament. The Master loved his nephew dearly for his sunny disposition and his transparent purity. Then, tragically, just a few months after Ak-

shay was married, he fell seriously ill. For some time, his condition fluctuated; he would gain strength only to lose it again. But
Ramakrishna was not at all hopeful. One day, as he was telling
the family to secure the best medical treatment available, some
power beyond his control caused him to add ominously: "But the
boy won't recover" (R.D., p. 138).

The words were jarring, and Ramakrishna himself was
more shocked than anybody by them. But he could not retract
them. he had uttered them, but he knew very well that they had
issued from the Mother Herself. And the Mother's prediction was
not long in being fulfilled. The Master himself was by his friend's
side at the end. Later, he would recall:

> I felt nothing at the time. I stood there and watched
> how Man dies. It was as if there was a sword in a sheath.
> Then the sword was drawn out of the sheath. The sword
> was still the sword, as before. Nothing had happened to it.
> And the sheath lay there, empty. When I saw that, I felt a
> great joy. I laughed and sang and danced. They took the
> body away and burned it, and came back.
>
> But the next day, I was standing on the porch outside
> my room—and do you know what I felt? I felt as though a
> wet towel was being wrung inside my heart. That was how
> I suffered for Akshay. Oh, Mother, I thought, this body of
> mine has no relation even to the cloth that enfolds it; then
> how can it feel so much for a nephew? And if I feel so much
> pain, what agony must the householders suffer! Is that what
> You are teaching me, Mother? But, you know, those who
> hold on to the Lord, they do not lose themselves in grief."
> (R.D., p. 138)

This incident is so revealing because it shows us two equally
valid, but very different, Ramakrishnas. There is Ramakrishna
the suffering, completely recognizable human figure, weeping for
his friend, feeling the same emotions as anyone else would in
similar circumstances. And there is also the madman of God,
laughing and dancing, soaring beyond the surface appearance of
death to the ecstatic perspective which sees it as a blissful un-
sheathing, a freeing of the inner spirit from the narrow confines

of the flesh. The two Ramakrishnas appear to contradict each other. But are they really incompatible?

One thing is certain, we needn't search far for seeming inconsistencies in the Master's behavior. They are everywhere we turn. A one-dimensional man or a plastic saint can perhaps afford to be consistent. Ramakrishna could not. Ramakrishna, as should be clear by now, was a psychic amphibian, moving freely from the water to the land and back again, from the human to the divine, from earth to heaven and beyond, and then to earth once more. Holiness, for Ramakrishna, was not a one-sided development, but psychic wholeness. He was too human to embrace his divinity at the expense of his humanity, and too divine to act as the common run of *maya*-enslaved men. He could never be satisfied with either one or the other. He demanded both at once.

Nevertheless, if both Ramakrishnas are real enough, there is no question which is the deeper, the more central, of the two. If Ramakrishna could both laugh and cry at the death of a friend, there can be no doubt that he felt more comfortable with the laughter. The tears struck him as strange and out of character. So much so, in fact, that he could only understand them as an object lesson from the Divine Mother on how the rest of the world suffered in the bondage of family life. Of all the things that tie a man to the earth, the bonds of family seemed to him the most intractable.

In Ramakrishna's view, attachment to kith and kin is a delusion, a barrier that keeps man from the recognition of his true nature. By focusing narrowly on the relations of the body, the individual loses sight of his or her true identity as spirit. Ironically, by affirming our kinship, in a special sense, with a few, the Master understood that we sacrifice our more fundamental kinship with the totality of life. That is why *maya's* first line of attack is to foster this false sense of "I" and "mine." Once that soil is in place, every form of illusion easily takes root.

Ramakrishna taught that spiritual life, authentic life, is a solitary affair demanding the most total inward independence and freedom of action. He used to recommend to even his householder devotees that they spend some time out of each year in retreat away from their family members and familiar surroundings, so that they could develop the necessary perspective and detachment to maintain a spiritual consciousness when they returned to the world. Ramakrishna recognized that one who never takes the trouble to separate himself from the values and expectations of those around him is condemned to live as a slave of others. He showed through his own life that the radical independence of a saint consists not in his physical isolation from other men, but in his refusal to kowtow before the prevailing social idol, in his refusal to search outside his own deepest inspiration for an understanding of life's meaning and purpose.

The sage knew that we all come into the world alone, and we must leave it alone, in addition to facing all the intervening trials alone. Whether off on some distant mountain peak or in the company of men, we are alone, and not one bit less alone when we are in a crowd. Ramakrishna also knew that it is in the depths of solitude and aloneness that true spiritual values are found; they are never available in the marketplace of the world. Some would deny the necessity for this spiritual aloneness. Most of us fear it because we make the mistake of confusing aloneness with loneliness. We fail to understand that accepting the undeniable fact of aloneness allows for a far deeper sense of connectedness with the whole of life than would a merely superficial, clinging attachment to others.

As a result, instead of embracing our condition as something creative and sacred, we try to escape from it entirely. We tell ourselves: "Here is my father, my mother, my husband, my wife, my children, my kinsmen, my countrymen. My identity and my fortunes are inextricably linked with theirs." If we cling tightly enough to them, we believe we are safe. If we cling tenaciously enough, we needn't bother to find our own way, we needn't trouble ourselves to investigate this wondrous and terrible mystery of a universe on our own. We are safe. We are absolved of responsibility.

It is all very comforting. Repeated often enough, it may even become monotonously convincing. But it isn't true. Like a loosely woven garment that doesn't keep out the wind or the cold, the defects become distressingly clear. Sooner or later, we find that clinging to others is clinging to a hill of sand, clinging to something made to change, something changing and shifting before our eyes, unreliable—a child of the wind.

According to Hindu thought, each human life has a high purpose, a secret task. Hidden within every man, woman, and child is a vital spark of the Divine—the *Atman,* or Self. The *Atman,* as we have already seen, has no name, form, dimensions, or limitations of any kind. It is who we really are behind the compulsively busy surface of our lives. Beyond birth, beyond death, beyond pleasure and pain, the *Atman* shines as pure *Sat Chit Ananada* (Being, Consciousness, and Bliss). But the *Atman,* the perennial spring of life within, is hidden beneath the hardened layers of our social self, the layers of false personae that we have accumulated, mask upon mask, to protect ourselves from others, or to make ourselves more acceptable to them. It is precisely to uncover these masks and reveal "your original face before you were born," in the language of Zen, that each of us has come into incarnation.

In Ramakrishna's view, the life that does not fructify in the self-knowledge of God-consciousness is lived in vain. The Master believed that the world was made for that object alone; the experiences, the relationships, and the pleasures and pains that we undergo along the way are nothing but fuel for that inward journey of discovery. If, instead of using them as such, we regard them as sufficient in themselves; if we become attached to them and look upon them as ends in their own right, rather than means toward a greater goal, then we have sold our precious divine birthright for a mess of porridge. We develop possessive feelings toward our fellow pilgrims on the planet—individuals who, like ourselves, have incarnated to work out their own progress and not to serve as objects to fulfill the selfish ends of others. The final result is a tangled web of grief, jealousy, anger, envy, and pride, in which we become increasingly imprisoned, and which we use to imprison others in turn. The one overriding goal of life—to realize God, the true Self of all—fades completely from sight. We die in ignorance, compelled to be reborn again and to suffer and die once more. In this way, the cycle of birth, delusion, death, and rebirth spirals painfully on without an end in sight.

There is, however, a way to extricate ourselves from this cycle. Ramakrishna was quick to point out that those who cling to the Lord will easily come to recognize their transcendent kinship with Him. They will be able to detach themselves in mind, if not in body, from their dependence on others. The body, of necessity, has relations with many other bodies. These last for a limited time only and bring in their wake a mixed brood of pleasures and pains. But the inner man, the soul, has only one relation—God, the Divine Mother, the nearest and dearest of all. Remaining firm in that conviction, the waves on the surface of life are unlikely to sway the devotee very much. He becomes liberated while still alive.

The Master used to compare such a one to a duck that needs only to gently shake its body and any water clinging to the feathers will fall away. He also compared the devotee of God to a lotus flower with roots sunk deeply in the mud while its blossom floats unstained on the surface of the waves. In the same manner, the devotee might sink his roots very deeply in the world. He might be beaded all over with the water of the world. But the things of the world do not cling to him. They easily roll off his consciousness. Inwardly, he remains unstained.

"Do your duties, but keep your mind on God," the Master was to counsel, time and again. "Live with all—wife and children, father and mother—and serve them. Treat them as if they were very dear to you, but know in your heart of hearts that they do not belong to you." (T.S., p. 64)

At first this ideal might strike us as a bit harsh, even cold. It would seem to run against the grain of love, to subvert it and leave it wilted and lifeless. We can hardly imagine love without possessiveness; it strikes us very nearly as a contradiction in terms. In fact, as we shall see clearly demonstrated in Ramakrishna's relationship with his wife, Sarada Devi, spiritual detachment does not rule out a genuine warmth and sharing. It allows for a love which is not less real for being essentially impersonal and disinterested—a love which, on the contrary, is so much purer, less selfish, and more abundantly fruitful by virtue of its detachment.

We have seen that the young Gadadhar left for Calcutta shortly after his marriage. It was not until ten years later, during an extended stay which Ramakrishna made at Kamarpukur, that

Sarada Devi finally had the chance to make her husband's acquaintance. The teenaged Sarada was swiftly won over by the respect and gentle consideration that he showed for her. Ramakrishna, for his part, spared no pains in instructing his young wife meticulously in the arts of matter and spirit. While holding out the ideal of detachment from the world with one hand, the Master was careful to train Sarada in the duties of household management with the other. Hours of inspired outpourings on God and devotion alternated with earthy instructions on how to shop for vegetables, trim a lamp, receive guests, and sweep the floor. The sacred and the profane mixed and became as one.

In his training of Sarada, Ramakrishna left no stone unturned. And he reveals to us a surprising new face, something we hardly would have expected to find in the heedless madman of God—an admirable sense of proportion and a peasant's canny practicality. These qualities were increasingly in evidence as Ramakrishna the seeker of God became Ramakrishna the teacher of men. The one who traveled to the heavens astride the whirlwind set before others a graded and gradual ladder of ascent. He well understood that, for Sarada, the natural pathway of the spirit did not lead through a landscape of passionate ecstasies and restless strivings, but through a quiet and purposive dutifulness and attention to detail.

Ramakrishna watched calmly and patiently as Sarada's high destiny slowly unfolded. He knew that the Divine Mother was awakening within her. He only prayed that She not awaken too quickly or too violently. Once, when Sarada fell asleep exhausted during one of the Master's spiritual talks, a companion woke her saying, "You were asleep! You have missed such priceless words." But Ramakrishna admonished, "No don't wake her. Let her sleep. If she listens to everything I say, she will not stay on this earth; she will unfold her wings and fly away."[1]

Sarada didn't fly away, of course. She was far too filled with joy in her husband's presence to have considered it! She spent the happiest days of her life, buoyed by Ramakrishna's ever-cheerful nature and awed by the palpable aura of spirituality that radiated from him at all times. Soon, the Master returned to Dakshineswar and Sarada went to her parental home. Thereafter, the anguish of separation from her husband was constant. Sarada's personality underwent a silent metamorphosis. In the years that followed, she became more thoughtful, mature, and introspective. The last traces of a child's selfishness disappeared, and her compassion for others blossomed wonderfully.

At this time, without any direct word from her husband, Sarada was at the mercy of a host of vague rumors filtering back from Dakshineswar—Ramakrishna had become a Muslim, he walked around naked, he laughed and cried without cause, he had gone insane. As one distorted tale followed another, some of the villagers came openly to pity, or cruelly mock "the madman's wife." Sarada, extremely sensitive by nature, was tortured by these thoughtless remarks and increasingly shrank from all contact with her neighbors.

It hardly seemed credible, judging from what she had seen of her wise and gentle husband, that he had actually gone mad. Nevertheless, she couldn't lightly dismiss the taunting gossip from mind. She had to find out for herself if there was any truth in it. And above all, if Ramakrishna were in distress, her heart demanded that she be at his side to comfort and serve him. Accompanied by her father, in March of 1872, Sarada made the difficult journey to Dakshineswar on foot. She arrived ill and thoroughly exhausted. But an affectionate welcome from her husband, who seemed to have expected her, revived Sandra's spirits. It also dispelled immediately the questions about his sanity. For it was abundantly clear from his calm and cheerful manner that Ramakrishna had not changed at all.

The Master was pleased that Sarada had come, and he took it as a sign from the Mother that the time was finally ripe that they should remain together. Sarada was eighteen years old. The thread of her training, which had been broken off four years earlier, was taken up once more by Ramakrishna. And, as before, Sarada passed her days and nights ecstatically immersed in a rare marital bliss. Perhaps the most extraordinary thing about that bliss (and surely the most difficult for our jaded twentieth-century sensibilities to fathom) is that it was entirely sexless. While Ramakrishna and Sarada lived together in the same room, often sharing the same bed, their relationship remained chaste throughout. The Master reflected on it years later: "If she had not been so pure, if she had lost her self-control and made any demand on me—who knows? Perhaps my own self-control would have given way. Perhaps I would have become sex-conscious. After I got married, I implored the Divine Mother to keep Sarada's consciousness absolutely free from lust. And now, after living with Sarada all of that time, I know that the Mother granted my prayer" (R.D., p. 145).

We shouldn't think that Ramakrishna looked upon sex as something sinful. The thought would not have occurred to him, or to any Hindu uninfluenced by the moralistic dogmas of the Christian missionaries. Sexuality was a part of the natural order, of *maya*, no better and no worse than anything else in nature. From a certain standpoint, it could even be regarded as sacred. Indeed, in the philosophy of the Tantras, the coming together of the male and female is regarded as symbolic of the intercourse of Shiva and Shakti, Spirit and Matter, out of which the universe and its infinitude of sentient beings came to birth. On one occasion during the Tantric phase of his own *sadhana*, the Master observed an intimate rite between male and female practitioners that appeared to his purified vision emblamatic of this ongoing divine act of creation. The ritual union, far from appearing lewd or indecent, plunged Ramakrishna into spiritual ecstasy.

Nevertheless, Ramakrishna was well aware that sex-consciousness and God-consciousness are fundamentally incompatible. Sex thrives on duality and the sense of separateness and incompleteness, and that consciousness is diametrically opposed to the spiritual, which is a consciousness of unity and fullness. The Master would invariably counsel his young devotees that absolute purity in thought and act was a precondition for spiritual advancement. And he was very particular that they regard all women as mothers or sisters, or, even better, as manifestations of the blissful Mother of the universe.

The reasons for this will become even clearer if we look at their roots in Indian thought. According to Hinduism, man, in his fallen state of incompleteness, hungers for union with that which will make him whole. This yearning for fulfillment is the fuel for life itself, at every level of manifestation. In many, this

Married Life

primal urge expresses itself primarily on the physical level through union with the opposite sex. Just as a desert mirage holds out the promise of water, the mirage of sexuality holds out the promise of wholeness through cleaving to a twin of flesh. But the alluring promise turns out to be empty in the end. The fleeting pleasure that sexuality provides is only a distant echo of the joy of oneness that we obscurely seek through it. Inevitably, the energy of seeking for union is dissipated without attaining to its goal. And men and women remain frustrated, isolated, and incomplete as before.

Only now, disillusioned, we begin to search beyond the instinctual boundaries of physical life for a deeper meaning, a more profound union than that of the flesh. Science, philosophy, art, and civilization itself are the by-products of this groping search for the light. But the modern world is vivid testimony to the fact that even these pursuits, rewarding and productive as they are, lack the power to fill the yawning gap within.

As Ramakrishna was keenly aware, any attempt to gain fulfillment at the level of the body or of the mind alone is an exercise in futility. Mind and body are themselves only fragments, instruments, murky reflections of something awesomely vaster—something which can be sensed, but not seen, as it prowls at the shining fringes of consciousness. Man has called this entity God, Self, Mother, the Unnameable, and countless other names. And intuitively, in his most lucid moments, he has recognized that nothing short of union with It can satisfy his deep yearnings for fulfillment.

If the yogi, therefore, renounces sex and other worldly pursuits, it is not because they are sinful or unlawful, but, simply put, because they don't deliver the goods. He renounces them because they are illusions holding out a false promise they can never hope to fulfill, trapping one in the chronic delusion that the pot of gold lies at the end of the next rainbow of physical or mental conquest. By frittering away the vital energy in vain pursuits, they sap the inner being of the psychic fuel which alone can bring the seeker to God. It is for this reason that Ramakrishna held firmly that one must commit oneself either to the world or to the Spirit. One can't live under two flags at once.

In truth, one doesn't so much choose as get unavoidably drawn one way or the other. The aspirant who has tasted of the bliss of spiritual experience will necessarily find even the greatest physical pleasures insipid by comparison. The celibacy of these men and women will not appear, in their own eyes, as a great and heroic renunciation, but as a natural expression of a deeper yearning. Others—those who have given up the supreme joy of the divine in exchange for the transient pleasures of the world—will seem to them the true renunciates!

All of this is not to say that these aspirants will never be confronted by the natural stirrings of lust within themselves. Even Sri Ramakrishna was not altogether immune to temptation, although he was never seriously troubled by it. One evening, as he gazed at the youthful Sarada asleep by his side, the Master pondered over his options. "Oh, my Mind," he reflected, "this is the body of a woman. Men look on it as an object of great enjoyment; something to be highly prized. They devote their lives to enjoying it. But one who possesses this body must remain confined within the flesh; he can't realize God. Oh Mind, now don't be thinking one thing in private and outwardly pretending another! Be frank! Do you want this body of a woman, or do you want God?" (R.D., p. 145).

After he had reasoned in this way, Sri Ramakrishna stretched his hand out to the sleeping body of his wife, but it shrank back in horror. His mind also instinctively recoiled, into a deep state of *samadhi* from which the Master did not return until the following morning.

The choice that Ramakrishna gave to his own mind he also offered, in fairness, to his wife. "I have learned to look upon every woman as Mother," he told her. "That is the only idea I can have about you. But if you wish to draw me into the world, as I have been married to you, I am at your service." (T.L.R., p. 82) The prospect of renouncing their spiritual relationship and living together as an ordinary husband and wife, however, was just as unthinkable to Sarada as it had been to Ramakrishna. Nevertheless, she was occasionally troubled by the thought that she would never experience the joys of motherhood as did other women. She once revealed this to her husband. Tenderly, he reassured her that the day was not long off when her ears would be ringing from so many people addressing her as "mother," and that these spiritual children, some of them coming from foreign lands, would more than compensate for the offspring of the flesh that she would never have. We will see later how fully this prophecy would be realized.

In the India of old, a wife was expected to look upon her husband as God in human form, a living symbol of the Protector and Provider for all beings. By worshipful obedience and selfless service of her mate, the Hindu wife was believed capable of overcoming her own inborn egoism and rising to a divine level. In recent times, needless to say, this has degenerated largely into a matter of empty gestures and lip service, the old ideals having been replaced by the Western secular model of relations between husband and wife.

But Sarada Devi was inclined to take the ancient ideals quite literally. She viewed Ramakrishna, in her own words, as "God eternal and absolute." And, far from being merely a pious slogan, this was, for her, a heartfelt conviction based on what she had actually glimpsed in Ramakrishna. If Sarada was not the very last Hindu wife to regard her husband as a living God, she was certainly a member of a small and dying breed. Then again, Ramakrishna became part of an even smaller breed by taking the age-old tradition one step farther and treating his wife Sarada as God, the Mother.

Actually, some of the most ancient texts do speak of the husband's duty to look upon his wife as an embodiment of the Divine Mother and to worship her as such in thought, word, and deed. But over the centuries, Hindu males have conveniently chosen to forget about their side of the bargain. In recent times, the equation, superficial and formalistic as it has largely become, has run almost exclusively in the opposite direction.

In a historic act, the repercussions of which are still being felt in India today, the Master revived a largely forgotten tradition, and in the process elevated his wife and, symbolically, all of Indian womanhood to the pedestal of their former glory. In a rarely performed Tantric ritual, the *Shodashi Puja*, the adoration of the Divine Virgin, Ramakrishna worshiped Sarada in a formal ceremony with flowers, incense, and the chanting of mantras, in a manner similar to the rituals of the Kali temple. Remarkably, the shy and unassuming Sarada acquiesced without objection to being treated as a living Goddess. A startling change had come over her. She sat on the throne of the deity with a calm self-assurance, as if it were her rightful seat; her countenance radiated an unusual light. Gradually, she lost consciousness in ecstasy, as did her husband, and for several hours worshiper and worshiped remained united in an exalted state of oneness.

When the ritual was over, Sarada Devi was aware of a strange new power stirring within. Something which had been fitfully asleep had awakened briefly and then disappeared again, but not without leaving the curious telltale traces of its passage imprinted in her growing spirit.

It has been said quite accurately that Ramakrishna's first disciple was Sarada Devi. Others had come to Dakshineswar before her, lodged stonelike in their conventional niches of re-signed respectability. The spiritual life was at best an idle hobby for them, something to be toyed with as a palliative to boredom, but not to be taken up as a vocation, or as a serious challenge to their way of life. The fire had long since vanished from their breasts. Ramakrishna used to compare them to mature parrots, after the ring of colored throat feathers had formed, that could no longer be taught to speak. Still others, like Mathur and Hriday, were not so insensible to the Master's influence. Their feelings for Ramakrishna were genuine enough. They admired, even revered, him—but always at a distance, as one admires a beautiful work of art, without ever seriously thinking of becoming a work of art oneself.

The pure-hearted Sarada, on the other hand, did not rest content with revering Ramakrishna—she *followed* him, uncondi-tionally. Not that she was ambitious to become just like her husband or even considered that possible. But her life had no other object than to aspire to his lofty example. She came to Ramakrishna a perfectly clean slate, an uncarved block, pristine, as soft and pliable as warm wax, ready to be molded, anxious to be molded.

Out of that sensitive human material, Ramakrishna was to fashion a Goddess.

→>> *Chapter 8* <<←

Keshab Sen and the Brahmo Samaj

IF THERE WAS ANY ONE MAN WHO CAN BE SAID TO HAVE "DISCOV-
ered" Ramakrishna, that man was Keshab Chandra Sen, the in-
fluential leader of the Brahmo Samaj, a reform movement centered in Bengal. Not only did Keshab Sen introduce
Ramakrishna to the liberal intellectual elite of Calcutta and,
through them, to India and the world, but he also introduced
Ramakrishna to a world of life and thought previously alien to
him—a world foreign indeed to everything that Ramakrishna
knew and cherished—but not in the end impenetrable. It was
through this contact with the Brahmos and their brave new world
of enlightened reason that Ramakrishna's teachings were forged
into a form that could speak directly to the best minds of his own
day, and of our own.

For all their modern ideas, Keshab and his Brahmo followers were not ultimately unsympathetic. But neither were they
credulous devotees ready to accept anything and everything on
the authority of tradition or on the demands of faith. They did
not offer Ramakrishna unquestioning acquiescence. What they
did offer—bold challenges, the resistances of prejudice and a
skeptical, materialistic bent of mind—turned out to be even better, because it was more stimulating, drawing out of the priest
of Kali a spirited defense of divine reality which remains to this
day an unequaled clarion call to God. And, ultimately, after

99

they had tested the holy man and weighed his words, they offered themselves. For it was from out of the ranks of the younger and less dogmatically fixed of the Brahmos that the nucleus of Ramakrishna's own brotherhood of the heart was to be formed.

Keshab himself never became a devotee of Ramakrishna, at least not in any explicit or formal sense. He was too restlessly independent for that. But he did become Ramakrishna's lifelong friend—a friend indebted to Ramakrishna for some of the deepest and most abiding insights of the soul. But before we try to understand the curious friendship that developed between these two contrary geniuses of the spirit, it will be useful to look first at the movement which Keshab led so charismatically, so stormily, and at anguished moments so diffidently.

The Brahmo Samaj was founded during the first half of the nineteenth century by aristocrat and scholar Raja Rammohan Roy as a vehicle for disseminating his radical new social and spiritual thought. Born into an orthodox *brahmin* family, Rammohan Roy's eclectic studies of Islamic and Buddhist culture, as well as his social contact with Europeans at an early age, inspired him to challenge many of the archaic practices and inequities of Hindu society. In alliance with the British colonial authorities and native Indian freethinkers, he agitated for the abolition of child marriage, and, more successfully, for an end to *sati*, the ritual suicide of the widow on her husband's funeral pyre (*sati* was outlawed by the British House of Commons, largely at his instigation). He was also a bitter foe of the caste system and a supporter of the education of women well over a century before Mahatma Gandhi (who would call Roy "the father of advanced liberal thought in Hinduism") finally succeeded in arousing any significant public support for these reforms.

For being so far ahead of his times, Rammohan Roy was ostracized from his family and scorned as a social outcast. Nevertheless, he was able to garner a small following of like-minded iconoclasts out of which the Brahmo Samaj was formed in 1828.

The social ideals of the Samaj, however, were only one aspect of its program for the renewal of Indian life. Equally important, in Rammohan's view, was a reordering of the spiritual beliefs of the people. Out of the tangled jungle growth of popular Hinduism, the Raja felt it was necessary to prune those elements that could not stand up to the test of enlightened reason, so that India might return to the original purity of its ancient Vedic conception of the Godhead. In this endeavor, Rammohan opposed everything that smacked of idolatry and superstitious belief, rejecting the theory of Avatars, or Divine Incarnations, so central to Hindu devotional practice, and instead advocating a strict monotheistic worship of the Deity without name or form.

Raja Rammohan Roy envisioned his Brahmo Samaj as a universal religion embodying the core teaching of all the world's spiritual traditions, but discarding their nonessential and individualistic elements—a religion open to all castes, races, and nations without distinction, teaching the Fatherhood of God and the Brotherhood of Man. But this synthetic conception of religion, while unquestionably exalted, was far too colorless, far too tasteless, to have any real appeal to the vivid Hindu imagination on a popular scale. In the end, the Brahmo creed was less a living religion than an idealized wax dummy of a religion, lacking the native strength and authenticity of the real thing, and offering only its generalized outward appearance.

Nevertheless, Raja Rammohan Roy's ideas did fill a need for a sector of the new Western-educated class, which was poised uncomfortably between two worlds, groping for a way to integrate them and preserve what was best in each. The Brahmos were men who found themselves, by vocation and training, at the outer fringes of Hindu society, alienated from the ways of their own people but yearning for some lifeline to the spiritual values that had sustained that people over the centuries.

The scathing attacks of the missionaries and the haughty condescension of the British colonials toward all things Indian had unsettled these intellectuals. Seeing their world through foreign eyes, they felt embarrassed by the riotous exuberance of the Hindu tradition, and they wished to tidy it up to conform with the prim sensibilities of the conqueror's race. The incongruous result was that the worship of the Samaj came to be modeled on a Protestant church service, with hymns and silent prayer and grandiloquent preachers railing in solemn and finely turned ex-pressions against "sin" and for the industrious and sober moral virtues of an emerging middle class.

Still, for all its alien trappings, the Samaj remained essentially Indian at heart. Its views of the underlying oneness of religion and of the centrality of spirituality to life were entirely homegrown. Moreover, the readiness to accommodate the ways and thought of a conquering race within the broad framework of Hindu culture was how India had always dealt with incursions from the outside. Perhaps only the outer garb had changed. It was as if the loose-fitting and rough-spun cotton wearing cloths of Bengal had been replaced by shirt, trousers, coat, tie, and bowler hat. The result was a humorous, even a ridiculous, hybrid but not, as it turns out, a fatal one.

For all its pomposity, the Brahmo Samaj retained within itself a live spark of that genuine metaphysical searching which had animated India from its beginnings. And that live spark drew to it some of the best and most vigorous personalities of its time. After the death of Rammohan Roy, the leadership passed to the noble Devendranath Tagore (the father of the poet Rabindranath Tagore) and then to Keshab Chandra Sen. The doctrine of the Samaj underwent seismic shifts, as both Devendranath and Keshab left on it their own highly individual stamps. Through it all, however, the broad guiding principles of social reform and spiritual regeneration persisted.

Keshab Sen was an extremely complex man. He was far and away the most Westernized of the Brahmo leaders; educated in English schools, he never learned Sanskrit, as had his predecessors, and he grew up more familiar with the Christian Bible than with the Hindu scriptures. And yet, at the same time, he was arguably the most mystical of the Brahmo leaders. He was a zealous leader, but a changeable and painfully honest one, who suffered agonizing and frequent public reversals of opinion. He was a teacher of men, who remained at the same time an eager student of life. He once said, "I am a born disciple. . . . All objects are my Masters. I learn from everything." (T.L.R., p. 154)

Keshab's first love was for Christ; he had had a childhood vision of Jesus. But he came in later years to revere the Divine

Mother as well, though his attachment to Kali never molded his thought or influenced his public doctrine so profoundly as had his love for the Son of Man. On occasions, he seemed on the verge of embracing Christianity, and the missionaries were sorely tempted to call him one of their own. But Keshab's proclamations of the oneness of religion and his condemnation of the narrow exclusivity of Western Christendom gave the missionaries no solace. He said, "All truths are common to all, for all are of God. Truth is no more European than Asiatic, no more yours than mine" (T.L.R., p. 156).

In the end, Keshab Sen was too obstinately multifaceted to fit comfortably into any religion or ideology—even the one he struggled heroically, but unsuccessfully, to fashion himself.

Brilliant and with a restlessness to match, Keshab spoke with a spellbinding eloquence. He was an intense man, fair-skinned and handsome, with vivid, piercing eyes and the temper of a prophet, convinced that he had a "New Dispensation" to offer humanity that would heal its divisions and unite East with West. For all of his zeal for unity, however, Keshab remained painfully divided himself. He hungered mightily to crystallize the truths that he had discovered on his own personal Mount Sinai of vision into the form of universal laws and principles that he could proclaim for the salvation of the world. And yet, he remained a troubled, mercurial Moses, whose Ten Commandments were not set in stone, but scrawled in glowing letters on the air, letters which appeared to shift uncomfortably as he himself drew ever closer to the Divine Source of his inspiration.

Keshab was that rare leader who was not afraid to grow and admit his mistakes, that rare prophet willing to alter his revelation, even at the risk of appearing inconsistent or, worse, hypocritical. Perhaps most remarkable of all for a man of his standing and his abundant gifts, this revered leader of thousands had the humility to sit at the feet of a half-naked son of a peasant, and the wisdom to learn from him.

As with nearly all those who were to play a central role in his mission, Ramakrishna saw Keshab first in vision long before he met him in the flesh. The Brahmo leader appeared dreamlike with the body of a peacock, his tail proudly outspread, symbolizing the broad following he would attract, and sporting a brilliant ruby on his forehead as an emblem of the driving energy and ambition that would fuel his single-minded crusade. In the vision, Keshab exhorted his followers to listen carefully to what Ramakrishna had to say to them.

The Master was taken by surprise by Kali's words. He objected incredulously: "Mother, these people hold the views of 'Englishmen.' Why should I talk to them?" (G.S., p. 831) But the Divine Mother calmed him. In the dark age of irreligion that was dawning, men would be like that, She explained. The Brahmos were just the advance guard. Many would follow in their footsteps. On this note of mild foreboding, the vision ended.

A more favorable glimpse of Keshab came during a meeting of the Brahmo Samaj, to which Ramakrishna had been taken by Mather Babu. The Master saw there on an upraised dais fronting the large congregation of worshipers a row of grave figures engaged in silent prayer. Surveying the group with uncanny penetration, he singled out one among them for Mathur's attention. "Of all who are meditating," Ramakrishna revealed, "only this young man's float has bobbed under the water. The Fish is biting on his hook alone." (N.p., n.d.) The "Fish," of course, was God, and the promising young devotee, Keshab Chandra Sen. Keshab had not yet assumed the leadership of the Samaj at that time, and it was not until many years later that he and Ramakrishna would finally meet.

That first meeting took place in March of 1875. Inspired during a spiritual mood to pay the Brahmo leader a visit, Ramakrishna approached Keshab who had gathered with a few of his devotees at a garden villa near Dakshineswar. In all simplicity and joy of spirit, he said to the Brahmo leader, "People tell me you've had a vision of God. I want so much to hear about it!" But no sooner had he spoken than, buoyed by the thought of the vision, the priest of Kali broke into song. He sang touchingly a traditional *bhajan*, a tender song of love for the Divine Mother, but he was unable to finish it. As so often happened when Ramakrishna was moved to song, his emotions soon overwhelmed him, and he slipped silently into unconscious reverie.

If this show of emotions left Keshab and his disciples unconvinced, or even somewhat suspicious, the luminous tidal wave of inspired words that followed the Master's ecstasy left no doubt as to the sincerity and spiritual depth of their strange visitor. Ramakrishna spoke in vivid parables of God and of the impossibility of ever grasping Him fully with the limited tools of the intellect. He spoke simply and forcefully and gestured expansively. All the while, his eyes glowed with an otherworldly fire and flashed with compelling authority. It was a pure joy to watch him. The Brahmos were dazzled. They forgot to take lunch, abandoned their carefully planned program of prayer and ritual and listened spellbound well into the afternoon. In the midst of this, Keshab turned to his followers as he had in Ramakrishna's prophetic vision of him many years earlier and urged them to mark carefully the priceless words of truth.

If it is true that it takes a prophet to fully appreciate a prophet, then Keshab was in a unique position to savor the richness of vision of the humble priest of Kali. To be sure, the two men were separated by formidable gulfs of culture and education. The texture of their gifts—homespun, earthy, and direct on the one hand, subtle, refined, and aggressively zealous on the other—were poles apart. Keshab lived in a world of abstractions; Ramakrishna, in a concrete world of spiritual experience. Keshab was sharp and discriminating; Ramakrishna, broad and tolerant. Keshab was the very picture of sophistication; Ramakrishna, frank and uncalculating.

And, if they differed in style, the content of their visions was hardly less divergent. On the surface, Keshab's immaculate and rationalistic conception of religion would seem to have little in common with Ramakrishna's rainbow profusion of Gods and *sadhanas.*

But underneath the surface, beneath the duality of style and even substance—powerfully, invisibly—a shared tide of yearning for the Ineffable ran in both men. It was a tide that marked them out as true brothers of the spirit. The abundant differences that appeared to divide them were less barriers than the mutually attracting poles of a magnet. In Ramakrishna's simplicity, calm self-assurance, and gentle good humor, Keshab found a soothing complement to his own tortured oversophistication. He came to visit Dakshineswar often and reverently, delighting in the words, the songs, the frequent ecstasies, as a breath of fresh air for the soul. The Master evoked such a powerful sense of God's moment-to-moment living presence in Keshab that just to be with him fortified the Brahmo leader in his own vision of God. At Dakshineswar, the spiritual realm shone out brightly as intensely real, and the fractured world of organizational politics, of ambition and the clash of egos, receded to the vanishing point. It was a place to recharge the battery. If even a few days passed without having seen Ramakrishna, Keshab would grow restless for his company.

Keshab Sen learned many things at Ramakrishna's feet. But the greatest thing he learned was also the simplest—to love God intimately as the nearest and dearest companion of the soul. It was a lesson that would be repeated in various forms over the years of their acquaintance. One day, during a meeting of the Brahmo Samaj, the Master listened to one of Keshab's elaborate prayers, in which he praised God for His various attributes and virtues. For Sri Ramakrishna, accustomed as he was to addressing God in the most familiar and heartfelt whispers, the high-flown invocation sounded stilted and artificial. He confronted Keshab afterward:

> Why all of these statistics? Does a son say to his father: "Oh my father, you own so many houses, so many gardens, so many grottos, so many horses"? Does that do justice to any father? It is natural for a father to have these things and to put them at the disposal of his son. Is it also natural that he should be kind, beneficent, merciful, forgiving and so on. There is no surprise in that. God is our Father. If you think of Him and His gifts as something extraordinary, you can never be intimate with Him, you can never draw near to Him. Do not think of Him as if He were far away. Think of Him as your nearest! Then He will reveal Himself to you. . . . Don't you see that if you go into ecstasy over His attributes you become an idolater? (T.L.R., p. 160)

This last suggestion hit painfully close to home. Keshab objected strenuously that idolatry is the worship of stones and icons, whereas he worshiped the formless God.

"God is with form, and He is also without form," Ramakrishna responded softly. "Images and other symbols of Him are just as valid, just as evocative as your strings of divine attributes. In fact these attributes are not different from idolatry, but merely hard and petrified forms of it." (T.L.R., p. 161)

We can almost see the mischievous glint in Ramakrishna's eyes as he placed the Brahmos' own favorite whipping boy of idolatry firmly on their own doorstep. His doing so was not without its justice; even Keshab must have recognized that. The fact is that like all who have felt divinely called upon to knock down other people's idols, the Brahmos had left their own idols standing—and unavoidably so, because their own idols were invisible to them. Their reforming vision had been directed outward for so long that it had never occurred to them that the dreaded bugbear might be thriving so close to home!

Like all theorists, the Brahmos had ultimately failed to contort themselves into the mold of their own theories. The only alternative that is left in such cases, of course, is to impose those theories on others.

Ramakrishna was very little of a theorist himself. He was a spiritual realist who had scant patience for those to whom religion was often little more than an intellectual exercise conceived within a vacuum, something legalistic and devoid of the rich odor of life. For Ramakrishna, God was not an idea—He was a lived Reality. And that living God was not to be known by the mind alone, but by all of man's faculties, as well as by something mysterious beyond all of those faculties.

How facile to sit on a pious high horse of the intellect and proclaim that God is without form, to proclaim that worship of an image is a sacrilege and an abomination. But Ramakrishna knew that such talk came from those who had never actually struggled to know God, those who were content to speculate in a detached way about a curiosity that didn't touch them where they lived. Anyone who had grasped and wrestled, sweated and cried in agony to the Lord, would have known better. Anyone who had truly yearned for God would have called out to Him with every possible name, beseeched Him in every idol, sensed Him lurking in every man, woman, child, and beast, recognized

Him in every form and in every formless void, whether dreamt or remembered, perceived or imagined.

It was self-evident to Ramakrishna that a person who sought to know the Divine had to get off the high horse of abstraction to approach Him—as he had, as all the saints had—through concrete images and symbols. All fancy theories aside, the basic facts of our humanity—the mind, the body, the human heart, the limbs—drive us to take up images and symbols. Those images might be of wood or stone, or they might be mental categories and theological formulae. But what difference does it make whether we burn incense before a painted Madonna or a basalt Kali, or whether we envision in our minds a "compassionate" God? Both the word and the statue, if taken as ends in themselves, fall equally short of the Ineffable Reality which they attempt to represent. One is a visual image, the other a mental image; one appeals to the heart, the other to the mind. If one is false, then the other can hardly be true.

Actually, Ramakrishna would have said that neither one is false. Both are potentially true. From his standpoint, only the God that we picture as distant from ourselves is a false God. If a word or an image fosters an attitude of separation from God, then it is false. If it helps us come closer to Him, then it must be regarded as true. As Sri Ramakrishna insisted, "So long as God seems to be outside and far away, there is ignorance. But when God is realized within, there is true knowledge. He who sees Him in the temple of his own soul, sees Him also in the temple of the universe. As long as a man feels that God is 'there,' he is ignorant. But he attains knowledge when he feels that God is 'here.'" (T.S., p. 37)

Idolatry, from this practical point of view, is anything that makes the Divine seem out "there"—anything that acts as a barrier between ourselves and God, by being interpreted too externally, too literally, too dogmatically, too unyieldingly. Idolatry is when the image becomes opaque to the imaged as it exists in our own being. According to this perspective, idolatry is not a function of particular images but of the attitudes we bring to them. The man who sees the God that is everywhere palpably focused in a carved stone is not an idolater. The man who sees God *as* a stone most certainly is an idolater. And so is the man who sees God as a lifeless theory, an airy abstraction, an intellectual bludgeon to silence all opposing views.

The telling difference between these two idolatries is that, while the devotee's simple-minded idolatry is regarded as absurd, the scholar's is often confused for transcendental wisdom. The peasant who claimed that the God of the universe resided in his household shrine and nowhere else is rightly treated as a lunatic. The preacher who argues intricately to prove that his sect alone derives from God, on the other hand, is often honored as a great theologian and attracts a large following; but for precisely that reason, he is the more destructive of the two.

Ramakrishna held firmly that learned men who tried to teach the world religion before experiencing a dynamic contact with God themselves succeed only in sowing the seeds of confusion. He insisted that the Brahmos should reform themselves first, and only then tackle the world. To the young Brahmo, Mahendra Nath Gupta (the chronicler "M" of *The Gospel of Sri Ramakrishna*), who asserted during his first meeting with Ramakrishna that people should be made to understand that the images they worshiped are not God, the Master responded sharply:

> Making others understand—giving them lectures—that's all you Calcutta people think about! You never ask yourself how *you* can find the truth. Who are *you* to teach others? . . . Supposing it *is* a mistake to worship God in the image—doesn't He know that He alone is being worshiped? He will certainly be pleased by that worship. Why should *you* get a headache over that? It would be better if you struggled to get knowledge and devotion yourself.
>
> You talk of worshipping a clay image. Even if it is made of clay, there is a need for that sort of worship. God Himself has arranged for many ways of worship to suit the varied temperaments of His worshippers in their different stages of growth. A mother has five children. There is fish to be cooked. She prepares different kinds of fish dishes to agree with every kind of stomach. For one child, she cooks fish pilau, for another pickled fish, for another baked fish, fried fish and so forth. She has cooked all kinds

of dishes to appeal to their different tastes and digestions. (R.D., p. 264)

Ramakrishna had no quarrel with the Brahmo mode of worship. It was only when they claimed that their way alone was right that he was forced to smile. How well he knew that it is not God who is limited, but rather the human intellect that perpetually labors to cut Him down to its own lilliputian dimensions! He took every opportunity to urge the Brahmos to be more accepting and tolerant. With Keshab especially, he could be very frank. The Master once said to him: "You wish to be strict and partial. . . . For myself, I have a burning desire to worship the Lord in as many ways as I can; nevertheless my heart's desire has never been satisfied. I long to worship with offerings of flowers and fruits, to repeat His Holy Name in solitude, to sing His hymns, to dance in the joy of the Lord! . . . Those who believe that God is without form attain Him just as those who believe He has form. The only two essentials are faith and surrender." (T.L.R., p. 161)

In time, Ramakrishna's critiques of the Brahmos and, more to the point, the living example of his intense devotion and broad tolerance began to have their effects. The organization that had mocked the Hindu Gods came at Keshab's instance to accept them, in theory at least, as symbolic crystallizations of divine attributes. The practices of Hindu devotionalism also played an increasingly prominent part in Brahmo rituals, and the Divine Mother was frequently invoked in song and prayer.

For all these changes, though, a certain un-Indian grimness remained. On one occasion, the Master objected to Keshab: "Once someone gave me a book of the Christians. I asked him to read it to me. It talked about nothing but sin. Sin is the only thing one hears at your Brahmo Samaj, too. The wretch who says day and night . . . 'I am a sinner, I am a sinner,' ends up becoming one. A person should have such a burning faith in God as to say: 'What? I have repeated the Name of God, can sin still cling to me?' . . . If a man repeats the Divine Name, his body, mind, everything becomes pure. Why should one dwell on sin and hell and such things?" (T.L.R., p. 33)

But if the Brahmos too often approached religion with a stark and loveless seriousness that was ultimately self-defeating, it was also true in another, more profound, sense that they did not take their religion seriously enough. For many of its members, the spiritual ideals of the league were more a matter of idle Sunday sentiment than of passionate conviction. Ramakrishna saw this clearly reflected in the hollow theatricality of some the Brahmo rituals themselves. He spoke humorously of what he had observed at a meeting of the Samaj:

> The leader said: "Let us commune with Him." I thought: "They will now go into the inner world and stay a long time." Hardly had a few minutes passed when they all opened their eyes. I was astonished. Can anyone find Him after so slight a meditation? After it was all over, I spoke to Keshab about it: "I watched all your congregation commuting with their eyes shut. Do you know what it reminded me of? Sometimes at Dakshineswar I have seen under the trees a flock of monkeys sitting, stiff and looking the very picture of innocence. . . . They were thinking and planning their campaign of robbing certain gardens of fruits, roots, and other edibles . . . in a few moments. The communing that your followers did with God today is no more serious." (T.L.R., p. 159)

We should make no mistake, however, about the tone of Ramakrishna's remarks. The words may be pointed, ironic, but they were delivered with a smiling and kindly indulgence. And it was certainly true that Ramakrishna had no intention of re-forming the reformers. He recognized that they, too, were grop-ing for God in their own way. If their views were sometimes overly narrow and restricting, if their God was a bit too somber and one-dimensional, this was, in any case, nothing that a little love couldn't cure. So, more than arguments, Ramakrishna gave his love, he gave of himself. He shared everything, his visions, his laughter, his boyish enthusiasm and his artless words—those magical words which resonated with such a pure ring of truth that the highest eloquence seemed empty by comparison. This openness proved irresistible. You might disagree with Ramak-rishna, but you could hardly help but love him. Once you had loved him, how could you fail to understand him better?

To understand Ramakrishna was to understand his love for

the Divine Mother. And more than a few of the Brahmos were deeply stirred by that wonderful love. It would surely have surprised Raja Rammohan Roy to know that, forty years after his founding of the Samaj, a goodly number of its leading figures would be weeping tears of joy at the mention of Kali's Name. But that is precisely what came to pass. It is a measure of Ramakrishna's deep influence on the Brahmos that the organization formed, among other things, to combat image worship and the Gods came within a single generation to embrace the conventions of Hindu devotionalism.

Not that Ramakrishna would have bothered himself about changing organizations. If he was concerned with change at all, it was with changing men, enkindling men with his unique savor of ecstatic love for God. In that task, he succeeded wonderfully with Keshab Chandra Sen.

Ironically, as Keshab's views widened and his spirituality blossomed, his hold on the Brahmo Samaj weakened, to such an extent that in 1878 a schism split the group into two rival organizations. The occasion for the split was a scandal attending the marriage of Keshab's thirteen-year-old daughter in contradiction to the Samaj's own campaign against child marriage. Ramakrishna remained friendly with both sides in the dispute. It did not seem to him that Keshab had done anything wrong. He had only discharged his duty as a householder in arranging the best possible match for his young daughter. If there was any error, it had come much earlier, in the attempt to impose a uniform standard of morality for all to follow. The Master would reflect: "Birth, death, and marriage are all subject to the will of God. They can't be made to obey hard and fast rules. Why does Keshab try to make such rules?" (R.D., p. 162).

Sri Ramakrishna viewed many of the Brahmo social ideals in a similar light. He compared their agitation against caste to an attempt to rip out the green boughs of a palm tree, rather than wait for them to turn brown in the natural course and fall off of their own. To those who felt that the purpose of life was a philanthropic "doing good to others," he counseled that it was best to do good to oneself spiritually before anything else; mere "social work" without a deep grounding in the wisdom and compassion of the soul invariably produced as much harm as good.

Nevertheless, the Master took pains not to impose his views on the Brahmos. He knew that a true understanding must be allowed to ripen in its own time. Impatience accomplishes nothing of value and argument still less—least of all when it appears to convince. To change a man's mind is easy, a cheap trick; to change a man is more difficult. But that is what Ramakrishna aimed for. He didn't want people to *believe* what he told them, he wanted them to experience it for themselves. He would pray to Kali: "Mother, do not let me become famous by leading those who believe in beliefs to me! Do not expound beliefs through my voice" (T.L.R., p. 183). In all humility, he urged the Brahmos: "I have said whatever came into my head. Take as much of it as you want. You can leave out the head and the tail."

He said these things out of his keen awareness that Truth is not something external to man; it is not an ideology, a flag to wrap around oneself, a garland of slogans. Truth bubbles up from within as the purest spring water and flows out in silence, almost imperceptibly. And if a man has so occupied himself with the bustle of opinion as to ignore the gentle upwelling of spiritual Truth, then there is no help for it. Each person hears what he or she is ready to hear at the moment and accepts only that which resonates within, rejecting the rest.

This knowledge made Ramakrishna accepting. Each of us dances to a tune no other hears; each dances as the Mother makes him dance. And in a sense, each dancer is perfect, as each one who has awakened from the dance is also perfect. The Master would address the Brahmos with a gentle smile: "You are in the world. Stay there! It is not for you to abandon it. You are very well as you are, pure gold and alloy, sugar and treacle. . . . We sometimes play a game in which one must gain seventeen points to win. I have passed that limit and I have lost. But you clever people, who have not won enough points can continue to play" (T.L.R., pp. 164–65).

Toward the end of 1883, Keshab Sen took seriously ill. Ramakrishna visited him in his Calcutta home. The appearance of the Brahmo leader was shocking. He was a mere skeleton, gaunt and weak, barely able to walk. When he made his way painfully and with difficulty to bow before Ramakrishna, the Master, to everyone's surprise, didn't make the usual polite inquiries about his health. He launched straightway into talk about God and devotion, seeming barely conscious of his surroundings.

After some time, Ramakrishna turned to Keshab and smiled. "Why is it that you are ill?" he asked.

> There is a reason for it. Many spiritual feelings have passed through your body; therefore it has fallen ill. At the time an emotion is aroused, one understands very little about it. The blow that it delivers to the body is felt only after a long while. I have seen big steamers going by on the Ganges, at the time hardly noticing their passing. But oh, my! What a terrific racket is heard after a while, when the waves splash against the shore! Perhaps a piece of the bank breaks loose and falls into the water.
>
> An elephant entering a hut creates havoc within and ultimately shakes it down. The elephant of divine emotion enters the hut of the body and shatters it to pieces. (G.S., p. 322)

Ramakrishna went on to cite his own bout with dysentery as evidence for this: "Hriday used to say, 'Never before have I seen such ecstasy for God, and never before have I seen such illness.' I was seriously ill with stubborn diarrhea. It was as if millions of ants were gnawing at my brain. But all the same, spiritual talk went on night and day. Doctor Rama of Natagore was called in to see me. He found me discussing spiritual truth. 'What a madman!' he said. 'Nothing is left of him but a few bones, and still he is reasoning like that!' " (G.S., p. 323).

The Master urged Keshab to leave off all worldly concerns and speak only of God. The Brahmo leader listened to Ramakrishna's words tranquilly and was evidently deeply consoled by them. But Keshab's mother, unable to look upon her son's illness so philosophically, pleaded with Ramakrishna to bless her son and cure him. "What can I do? God alone blesses," the Master replied, and then he added thoughtfully:

God laughs on two occasions. He laughs when two brothers divide land between them. They put a string across the land and say to each other, "This side is mine, and this side is yours." God laughs and says to Himself, "Why, this whole universe is Mine; and about that little clod they say, 'This side is mine and that side is yours!'"

God laughs again when the physician says to the mother weeping bitterly because of her child's desperate illness: "Don't be afraid, mother. I shall cure your child." The physician doesn't realize that no one can save the child if God wills that he should die. (G.S., pp. 323–24)

The sorrowful implications of these words were not lost on the gathering, and all became silent. Just then, Keshab was seized with a fit of coughing and had to retire into his inner chamber.

The two holy men were not to meet again. In a little over a month, Keshab was dead, at the age of forty-six. In the end, it is said, he became radiant. As his body grew weaker, his spirit flared up; he laughed and wept in ecstasy, and talked aloud to the Divine Mother. He spoke only of God, and his last words, as he sunk into the release and rapture of death, were, "Mother! Mother!"

→>> *Chapter 9* <<←

The Devotees Come

M<small>OST OF THE BRAHMOS, AS WE HAVE SEEN, WERE TOO SMUGLY</small> well established in life, too self-satisfied, and too respectably sober to stake all on God. They liked to talk about religion, but generally stopped there. Few were prepared to make sacrifices, and fewer still had the fire in them that drives a man to God.

Nevertheless, there were notable exceptions—idealistic young men whose lives still seemed rich with infinite possibilities, lives that were about to be revolutionized in ways they would not have understood, still less anticipated. Generally, they came to Dakshineswar for the first time out of curiosity. If there were deeper motives, they were hardly aware of them. But underneath the surface, something seethed in these young Brahmos as it had seethed in the young Gadadhar decades earlier. Something drove them onward to seek—for what exactly they would not have been able to say. They would not have believed (as Gadadhar had believed) that they were seeking God. For the most part, they were not religious men at all. Some led bohemian lives that were the very antithesis of conventional piety.

The first recruits of Ramakrishna's future inner circle to be drawn to Dakshineswar were Ramachandra Datta, a young doctor, and his cousin, Manmohan Mithra. Intrigued by a reference to the saintly devotee of Dakshineswar temple in the journal of the Brahmo Samaj, of which they were members, the cousins decided to find out for themselves what sort of holy man he was. Western educated, they looked upon themselves as atheists, or perhaps agnostics—open-minded enough not to close all the accounts on the God of their fathers, but too much the products of their rational age to have had much commerce with Him. Still, inwardly, they were not at peace. Like many of their Calcutta peers, they had turned to the Brahmo Samaj in the restless search for deep values in a world seemingly cut loose from the moorings of tradition. It was not long, however, before the platitudes and empty rituals of the brotherhood came to appear depressingly sterile and unsatisfying.

When the cousins first ventured to Dakshineswar, they came well armed with a healthy skepticism and some less-than-flattering stereotypes of holy men; from the start, however, it was clear that that the unassuming priest of Kali could not be made to fit into any of their stereotypes. Warm, affable, and palpably down-to-earth, Ramakrishna had nothing in common with the cold and ascetic yogi, the wild-eyed religious fanatic of their imaginings. His artless familiarity put them immediately at ease, and they were charmed by the genuineness of the man, his country humor, and his boyish directness. Moreover, there was a quality to his presence, something intangible but nonetheless vital and intensely real, that stirred them profoundly. In Ramakrishna's small room by the Ganges, the world with all its endless cares and calculations seemed to recede almost to the vanishing point. One felt revived there, refreshed by an invisible spring of purity. It was a new experience for the young men from Calcutta, and one they could neither account for nor resist.

Soon Manmohan and Ramachandra were making the joyous pilgrimage to Dakshineswar every Sunday without fail. Nevertheless, if the artless child of the Divine Mother had won their hearts without so much as a fight, their minds were not so easily conquered. Even after the cousins had become intuitively convinced of the existence of a living spiritual truth beyond the range of the senses (and the overwhelming presence of Ramakrishna himself was evidence enough of that), their materialistically trained intellects continued to throw up doubts for some time to come.

"Does God really exist?" Ramachandra demanded bluntly

on one occasion. This point-blank directness delighted the Master, and he replied with obvious relish, "Of course He exists. You don't see the stars during the daytime, but that doesn't mean that stars don't exist. There is butter in milk, but how could anyone guess that simply by looking at milk? To get the butter you have to churn the milk in a cool place. To get the vision of God you have to practice mental disciplines—you can't see Him just by wishing" (R.D., p. 169).

This straightforward and practical approach toward spirituality impressed the cousins greatly. At long last, here was a holy man who didn't attempt to prop up religion by references to hoary Sanskrit *slokas*, or biblical chapter and verse. Here was someone who spoke directly from out of his own living experience of God, who didn't insist on blind faith, but asked only for a sincere willingness to put his propositions fairly to the test. And Ramakrishna himself was the most compelling argument to do just that—Ramakrishna, ever cheerful, with a buoyant enthusiasm for life and a smile that melted away resistance as the morning sun melts fog. This Ramakrishna, transfigured by a tremendous inner joy and driven to share it freely with all, seemed incapable of holding anything back; he spoke plainly, without mystification or the priestly double-talk that the religious use to veil their own uncertainties; he poured out his knowledge, his enthusiasm, and his unselfish love as a fountain of light to guide them on their way. Little wonder the cousins were drawn irresistibly to Dakshineswar and inspired to apply the Master's spiritual teachings to their own lives.

Still, not all among their relatives and Brahmo friends sympathized with this growing attachment to the eccentric priest of Kali. Once when Manmohan was preparing to leave for Dakshineswar, his aunt argued forcibly to restrain him from going. He was somewhat shaken by her arguments at first, but, after considering the matter carefully, his own best instincts won out and he determined to go. When Manmohan entered the Master's room, however, he was surprised to see the ever-bright Ramakrishna seated on his cot looking wan and depressed. "Why are you sad?" he asked. "You see, there is a devotee of mine who likes coming here," Ramakrishna told him. "But his aunt doesn't approve; she tries to prevent him. It makes me sad to think that some day he may listen to her and stop coming" (R.D., pp. 168–69).

Such thrilling demonstrations of the Master's omniscience and tender love were almost more than Manmohan could bear. His devotion became inflamed beyond all bounds, so much so that it rapidly became unbalanced. For all of its strength and adolescent intensity, Manmohan's attachment to Sri Ramakrishna was becoming narrowly jealous, and it was mixed with an uncomfortably large quotient of self-regarding spiritual pride—an explosive combination that promised trouble. The inevitable crisis was not long in coming.

Manmohan was seated in a group of Ramakrishna's admirers one Sunday when he heard the Master praise the "unequaled devotion" of one Surendra Nath Mithra, a wealthy businessman. Having secretly harbored the conceit that his own devotion was without peer, Manmohan was deeply wounded by this casual remark. He stormed from the room with the bitter resolve never to return again. "Enjoy yourself with your devotees; you don't need me—to you I'm a nobody," (R.D., p. 171) he addressed himself mentally to Ramakrishna. And as the weeks passed, his anger, instead of abating, was nurtured beyond all reason to the point of obsession. When Ramakrishna sent emissaries to his home, Manmohan refused to talk with them. He shunned everybody and everything that could possibly remind him of the Master. Eventually, at the cost of great personal inconvenience, he moved several miles outside of Calcutta to try to exorcise Ramakrishna and his messengers from his life altogether.

Inevitably, however, the self-imposed exile was powerless to banish the ghost of Ramakrishna from Manmohan's mind. In his more lucid moments, he was forced to concede that, just underneath the self-destructive frenzy of hatred, his love for the Master had hardly changed at all. But Manmohan was like a crazed marionette flailing about in the violent turmoil of his emotions, no longer able to control himself. And his career and private life were in ruins.

One day as Manmohan went down to the Ganges to bathe, the sacred river vividly reminded him of Ramakrishna. He recalled with what gentle affection and reverence the Master would speak of the river as "Ganga Ma," treating it as a conscious and tender Mother for all beings. Closing his eyes a moment in wistful reflection, Ramakrishna appeared with shocking realism before his inner sight; but when he opened them again, Manmohan's shock was multiplied many times over. It was as if the vision had taken tangible shape before him, for there in a rowboat gliding swiftly toward shore was Ramakrishna himself! Bursting violently into tears, Manmohan was about to collapse into the water when the Master's disciple Niranjan (the future Swami Niranjanananda) caught hold of him and dragged him on board. Slowly recovering consciousness from his spontaneous ecstasy at the sight of the long-awaited Manmohan, Sri Ramakrishna gazed at him tenderly. "I was so worried about you that I had to come," he whispered. Manmohan fell sobbing at the Master's feet. "It was all because of my wounded vanity!" (R.D., p. 172) he cried out. And Niranjan rowed toward Dakshineswar.

Ramakrishna loved his young disciples with a mother's love, patient, forgiving, and tenaciously loyal. He recognized in their youthful dedication and energy, their earnestness, and their bright sincerity the very qualities which had fueled his own journey to God, and he wished to nurture and bring to fruition these divine qualities within them. The purity of his vision allowed Ramakrishna to see through the thin veneer of personality and to perceive directly the divine spark yearning for expression deep within a true spiritual aspirant; once he had seen that spark, nothing that happened could convince him that it wasn't there. Once he had welcomed someone, as he had welcomed Manmohan, into his brood, he could never let him go, whatever came to pass. The contradictions, the shortcomings, the stumbling along the way, the thousand weaknesses that flesh is heir to, didn't matter. Only God mattered—God struggling fitfully within, yearning to be free of the bonds of the flesh.

All of this is not to suggest that the Master was blind to the faults in his devotees, or so dazzled by the indwelling divine spark as to ignore the human failings which often threatened to smother it. In reality, he was one of the canniest judges of men. He could read more from the carriage of a body, the shape of a forehead, the glow in a man's eye, than most can discover from years of intimate acquaintance. Each soul was an open book for him, and he knew all of its dark secrets and all of its bright possibilities.

But, while he undoubtedly saw a man starkly and without illusions, it is also true that Ramakrishna didn't measure him by the same yardstick that the world uses. His vision had penetrated too deeply for that. He had seen how the best of men are rifled through with hidden failings, and how even the worst have the bright seed of redemption within them. Moreover, he had penetrated beyond the cherished myth of freedom to a vision of man spinning in a vortex of forces beyond his control. It would not be an exaggeration to say that Ramakrishna had peered behind the curtain of the puppet theater and observed the Mother at work pulling all the strings that man, in his ignorance, imagines he holds himself. It was a vision that burnt to ashes any temptation to lay blame, to judge, or to condemn. The very act of seeing all was, for Ramakrishna, the act of forgiving all. Even to speak of forgiveness is too harsh; for in a world where God alone acts, what is there to forgive, and who is there to be forgiven?

But this cosmic vision did not make Ramakrishna indiscriminate in his dealings. The heady transcendence of good and evil, which the seer experiences when he perceives that God Himself has manifested as both, did not in any way blunt the Master's ability to distinguish between the two when he returned again to the realm of duality in which his devotees functioned. Indeed, he always insisted that, of all men, the spiritual aspirant has to be the most discriminating in his choice of environment and companions. The good inspire one to pure deeds and exalted thoughts, while the bad drag one into the depths of illusion and have to be avoided at all costs. God is in the tiger, no doubt. But the man who embraces the tiger, on that account, will surely come to regret doing so, the Master would tell his young devotees.

And what is true of tigers is true, too, of human tigers. The Master taught that those who live without spiritual light, completely enslaved to the beast within, are to be avoided at all costs by the person who aspires for a higher life. Ramakrishna himself was physically repulsed by such people, and suffered an unbearable burning sensation in his body, crying out in pain, if they sat next to him. If a worldly soul touched an item of food, even inadvertently, Ramakrishna would sense the impure vibration without being told and refuse to eat it. Yes, God is in all beings, but some had turned their backs so totally on that Inner Divinity and lived in such a suffocating and loveless darkness of spirit that they were, at least for the moment, effectively beyond all hope or healing. Ramakrishna would have nothing to do with them.

But if you showed the smallest glimmer of compassion or truthfulness, gentleness or reverence, sincerity, or remorse, then a cartload of sins would be forgiven, and you were welcomed with open arms. Any sin could be forgiven. Only the stony coldness of indifference could not be forgiven.

In this, Sri Ramakrishna differed radically from the conventionally pious religious men of all nations, who look only to the external "sins" of others and not to their inward states of openness to reform. What they fail to realize is that the "sinner" may be closer to redemption than many a solid citizen who, while he may have avoided committing public offense, yet lives perversely cut off from the wellsprings of joy, love, and truth within himself. It is for this reason that the great sages have always looked more to the motivations of their fellow men than to their outward actions. Far be it from a Christ of the whores and publicans and a Ramakrishna to hold themselves aloof from the foibles of flesh and blood.

But if these holy men mixed with sinners, scrubbed the wounds of lepers, and mopped the mud huts of untouchables with their long matted hair, they did these things not to uplift or to purify or to set a good example for others. They did it because they felt every festering uncleanliness of the body or spirit of every man, woman, and child to be their own. They bore the sins of the world in their own being—and not just metaphorically, not in some magical or supernatural sense, not in a single transcendental moment of sacrifice nailed to the bloody lumber of cruelty and ignorance, but every moment, in the living awareness of their unity with humankind. They bore our sins not in their dying, but in every moment of their living among us, in every tender moment of reaching out to suffering humanity. And because they understood us perfectly, because they felt every wrong turn of our body, mind, and spirit viscerally in their own being, they did not condemn—they were far too practical for that. They alleviated.

The reader will remember Surendra Nath Mithra, whom Ramakrishna had praised, causing Manmohan such terrible anguish of spirit. If Manmohan's great demon was jealousy, then Surendra's was drink. And this habit, aside from the havoc it wreaked in Surendra's life, was a source of acute embarrassment to the other devotees, who feared it would reflect badly on Ramakrishna himself. It was this concern with scandal that caused Ramachandra Datta to approach Surendra one day and earnestly press him to give up the bottle. But Surendra would have none of it. "The Master would certainly warn me if it was really bad for me. He knows all about it," Surendra insisted. "Very well then," Ramachandra agreed. "Let's go and visit him now. I'm sure he'll tell you to stop drinking" (R.D., pp. 173–74). Surendra consented to the test, and vowed that he would do whatever Ramakrishna asked. His only stipulation was that Ramachandra not bring up the subject.

Arriving at the temple a short time later, the devotees found the Master seated under a tree appearing radiant and detached, as if he were only partially conscious of his surroundings. Immediately after prostrating themselves before him, Ramakrishna turned to Surendra and spoke as if he were picking up the thread of something just said: "But Surendra, why when you are drinking wine, do you have to think of it as just ordinary wine? You should offer it to the Mother Kali first and then drink it as Her *prasad.* Only you must be careful not to get drunk. Don't let your footsteps stumble or your mind wander. At first you'll feel only the sort of excitement that you usually feel; but that will soon lead to spiritual joy" (R.D., p. 174).

It was Ramakrishna's way to guide each of his devotees gently along the path most natural to him. He was careful not to impose his will on another. He knew that to do so, even with the best of motives, risks doing violence to nature. Above all, he was convinced that nothing good could come from the mere suppression of an impulse: "A river has no need of barriers. If it dams itself up, it stagnates and becomes foul." (T.L.R., p. 183) Better, as in Surendra's case, to divert the stream than to block its flow.

The moralist, of course, wouldn't understand this. And he wouldn't be likely to appreciate the subtlety of Ramakrishna's advice to Surendra. From his perspective, a thing is either right or wrong, black or white. If drinking is an evil, then it must be stopped at all costs, he would insist.

But for a man of spiritual vision like Sri Ramakrishna, nothing can be said to be evil, in and of itself. An act becomes evil only when we make it so. And what man has made evil, through his slackness and indulgence, he can just as easily make good by respect and reverence and vigilant care. Moreover, by looking at Surendra without passing judgment, Ramakrishna was able to make a wonderfully astute psychological observation—something the moralist, with his built-in blinders and one-dimensional worldview, would have missed entirely. He saw, paradoxically, that Surendra's drinking expressed a healthy impulse to a greater freedom and a fuller joy. However imperfectly, however wrongheadedly that impulse had been channeled, the fact remained that the very urge that drove Surendra to drink was the same one that was driving him to God. And that impulse had to be respected at all costs.

So Ramakrishna didn't insist that Surendra give up drink. On the contrary, he urged him to take his habit to its logical conclusion and use it, consciously and with full control, for the same aims toward which it had heretofore been blindly striving— a wider freedom and more spiritual joy in life. In doing so, Ramakrishna was skillfully applying an ancient Tantric principle: Leave the impulse in place, but transform it by changing its context. Let Surendra drink, but let his drinking become, by a simple shift of attention, a sacrament, a tool for the expansion of consciousness. And Ramakrishna's advice turned out to be precisely on target. The simple ritual act of offering wine to the Divine Mother worked, almost miraculously, to redeem a shameful and private indulgence and transform it into something life-giving. Like the high priest before the altar, Surendra now lifted his glass with a sharp thrill of devotion.

Wine and its effects have, for centuries, been emblematic in the East of the divine inebriation of God-realization. Rama-krishna himself often employed the metaphor in conversation, and at times, during his own ecstasies, he would actually reel like a drunkard, his voice slurring and his eyes swimming in disarray. Seeing drunken men stagger down the road from his hackney carriage, as he rode at night through Calcutta, the Master would jump out of the cab and dance in tipsy rapture with the unsus-pecting inebriate!

Needless to say, Ramakrishna's spiritual state was a far cry from the ordinary drunkenness that it so superficially resembled, just as Rumi's wine of ecstasy has little in common with the article sold under the counter in the bazaars of Asia. Surendra's wine, on the other hand, was literal enough, and yet, by some incomprehensible alchemy, the erstwhile poison was transmuted into something as beneficent as the wine of poetry. Under its influence, the dammed-up waters of his love for the Divine Mother burst forth gloriously, and Surendra contracted Rama-krishna's own disease, weeping freely like a child, singing the Mother's praises. At times, the cup of Surendra's newly awakened devotion would overflow, and he would rise spontaneously to states of ecstatic absorption. He had attained all of this by living up to his part of the bargain perfectly, by using wine for one purpose alone—to open himself consciously to the Mother, and never for the sake of mere indulgence. As a result, his mind did not waver and his steps did not falter in drunkenness ever again.

While Ramakrishna could show a maternal tolerance for the human weaknesses of his devotees, he was never in the least bit slack with himself. By our present day standards, his life-style certainly appears harsh and austere. For a man never to touch alcohol, women, or even money will barely seem credible to many. Even some of Ramakrishna's contemporaries wondered about his dispassion at times, and tested it in a variety of ways. Ramakrishna was not offended when they did this. Indeed, he always insisted that a disciple has a responsibility to test his teacher as thoroughly as a money changer tests his coins. One devotee followed through on this advice by concealing a single coin under the Master's mattress, in order to probe the depths his well-known aversion to money. Incredibly, the moment Sri Ramakrishna lay down on his bed he cried out in pain, so sensitive had he become to even the unseen presence of money, which he had always considered as one of the two great corrupting influences (the other was lust) that drag a seeker away from the spiritual ideal. In keeping with Ramakrishna's ideal of spiritual poverty and absolute dependence on the Divine Mother for everything, his physical surroundings were utterly simple, and he refused all of the comforts which his wealthy devotees would have happily provided.

And yet, as we have seen, there was nothing of the puritan in Sri Ramakrishna. He loved life with a passion that no mere pleasure seeker can hope to equal, and throughout his life he maintained the breathless wonder of a child at the opulence of creation. If his way was lean and shorn of nonessentials, it was not the bitter leanness of the reformer, but the leanness of the superb spiritual athlete who knows exactly what he has to do to win the race and then goes ahead and does it; it was the leanness of a lover.

Even after he had won love's gold, Ramakrishna saw no reason to change his ways. Perhaps he imposed the most exacting standards on himself as an example for his devotees to follow. But if that was the case, then it was also true that he never held unrealistic expectations for others. He never demanded that others be more like him; he revered the God in each man too much for that. It was enough if a person became more like himself by fulfilling his own unique destiny along the path that the Mother had carved out for him alone. Ramakrishna knew that the Mother's paths are as infinite and varied as the Mother Herself. And he had learned to look upon Her creation with a reverent but dispassionate eye, recognizing that all things without exception proclaim Her greater glory. As a result, he felt no anxiety to fit others into some preconceived mold, but instead guided the devotees with an acute sensitivity to their individual needs.

In determining the spiritual needs of those who came to Dakshineswar, Ramakrishna always took into consideration the person's station in life. What was appropriate for a student was not appropriate for a renunciate, what was appropriate for the renunciate was not valid for the householder, and so on. While he could never for a moment question the fact that spirituality was the finest fruit on the tree of life, Sri Ramakrishna had come to understand that it was not the only fruit. He therefore counseled moderation, especially for his married devotees. He was keenly aware that life in the world consists in a series of unavoidable compromises, and that it is not possible for someone with a family to support to give the mind totally to thoughts of God. The Master reflected with a smile on the delicate balancing act that was required of a devotee in the world:

> I tell people that they must fulfill their duties in the world as well as think about God. I don't ask them to renounce all. One day in the course of a lecture Keshab [Chandra Sen] said, "Oh God, grant that we may be plunged into the river of devotion and attain the ocean of *Sat Chit Ananda* [Being, Consciousness, Bliss]!" The women were present sitting behind the screen. I pointed them out to Keshab and said, "If you are all plunged in at once, what will become of them? So you must come out of the water from time to time, immerse yourself and come out alternately." Keshab and the others began to laugh. (T.L.R., pp. 187–88)

The point was made with characteristic good humor, but it was not any the less serious for Ramakrishna's playful tone. He always insisted on his married devotees fulfilling their duties faithfully. To do anything less in the name of religion was both morally indefensible and spiritually counterproductive. If, as sometimes happened, a disillusioned householder approached him with the idea of "renouncing the world," the Master would sternly bring the straying family man back to reality. He knew that, in the vast majority of cases, the impulsive desire to renounce didn't come from genuine dispassion, but from mental weakness in the face of worldly troubles. He was far too keen-eyed an observer of men to imagine that most were inspired to flee from hearth and home out of the purity of their love for God!

He counseled his devotees in the world to aspire to the ideal of the legendary King Janaka, who succeeded in ruling his realm and attaining the knowledge of God at the same time. This required a delicate balancing act—giving both God and Caesar their due but siding inwardly with God: "When you are at your work use only one hand and let the other touch the feet of the Lord.

When there is a break in your chores, take His feet in both your hands and place them over your heart." (T.S., p. 70)

In the final analysis, Ramakrishna taught, as all great souls do, that it is not the external circumstances of life that bind us to the earth, but our attitude toward these circumstances: "It is only the lunatic who says, 'I am enchained' who ends up being so. The mind is all in all. If it is free, then you are free. Whether in the forest or the world, I am not in bondage. I am the son of God, the King of Kings. Who then dare put me in chains?" (T.L.R., p. 189).

While setting forth this ideal, Ramakrishna was well aware how difficult it could prove for men to realize in actual practice. One of the many names of the Divine Mother in India is "Bewitcher of Worlds." And it is certainly true that the Master, who had wrestled with Her for so long, was in a better position than most to appreciate the subtlety of Her magic. He would compare the Mother's *maya* to a fisherman's net, snaring one and all in its tightly woven web of delusion. Some struggle awhile and became hopelessly entangled. Others, with net in mouth, bury their heads deeply into the mud, hoping vainly that what they don't see won't harm them. But now and again, a vigorous and determined soul manages to slip through with a big splash. When that happens, the Divine Fisherwoman applauds wildly and exclaims in unbounded admiration: "Whoops, there goes a big one!"

And so it happens that a person caught up in the net of lust and greed, which are the very warp and woof of the Mother's net of *maya*, do occasionally slip through to freedom. Yet it happens only rarely, and only the strongest and most heroic of souls are capable of it. Surely it is because he understood how formidable were the odds against his householder devotees that Ramakrishna was, as a rule, not very rigorous with them.

His real hopes lay with the young men who had not yet become entangled in the net of the world, young men without ties who were prepared to renounce all for the spiritual life. The core of this group—the future monastic disciples—started coming from the year 1879 onward. We will meet some of the more remarkable of them in the next chapter.

→≫ *Chapter 10* ≪←

The Coming of Rakhal and Naren

Among Ramakrishna's oft-repeated parables, there is a lovely one about the mythic homa bird of the Vedas; it describes the state of the *nityasiddha*, the born-adept, whose intense nostalgia for the spirit forces him to recoil from the world almost from birth itself:

> The bird dwells high in the sky and never descends to earth. It lays its egg in the air and the egg begins to fall. But the bird lives at such a dizzy height that the egg hatches while falling. The fledgling comes out and continues to plummet. But it is still so high that its wings unfold and its eyes open. Then the young bird finds that it is dashing down toward the earth and will be killed instantly. When it sees the ground rushing to meet it, it soars up toward its mother in the sky. Then its one goal is to reach its mother.
>
> Boys like Rakhal are like that bird. From their earliest childhood they see the emptiness of the world, and their one thought is how to reach the Mother, how to realize God. (N.p., n.d.)

The Rakhal to whom Ramakrishna referred was Rakhal Chandra Ghosh, the future Swami Brahmananda, first abbot of the Ramakrishna Mission, and a revered saint in his own right.

129

As a youth of intense spirituality and unwavering devotion to the Master, Rakhal was the one Ramakrishna considered to be, in a special sense, his spiritual son. Born to a wealthy land-owning family in the village of Sikra, near Calcutta, Rakhal was naturally affectionate and mild mannered, boyish, and a bit of a dreamer—a bit too much of a dreamer, indeed, for his parents' comfort. Like the young Gadadhar, Rakhal showed little fondness for academia. A mediocre student, he preferred fishing, gardening, and singing devotional songs to the deadening routine of the classroom. And true to Ramakrishna's analogy of the homa bird, one imperative thought haunted Rakhal's formative years: "God is our Father, our very own. How shall I reach Him?"[1]

This budding otherworldliness was more than a little alarming to Rakhal's parents. Their solution (the usual one) to marry him off at the tender age of sixteen did nothing to stem the rising tide of his dispassion. Ironically, it had exactly the opposite effect, for, as fate would have it, Rakhal's new brother-in-law was Manmohan Mithra, in whose company he would visit Dakshineswar for the first time.

Rakhal's coming was, in the most literal sense, an answer to Sri Ramakrishna's prayers. The Master had implored Kali fervently: "Mother, I want someone for my constant companion. Bring me a boy, who is like myself, pure-hearted and intensely devoted to you." (E.C., p. 14) Some days later, he had a vision of an unknown youth standing alone under a sprawling banyan tree within the temple compound. In a subsequent revelation, Kali appeared and placed the same boy on his lap with the puzzling declaration, "This is your son." (E.C., p. 15) The Master was alarmed at first, thinking that he would produce a child by sex. But Kali smiled at his naive fears, and reassured him that the boy was not a son of the flesh, but a worthy progeny of the spirit who would live up to the highest ideal of renunciation. In yet another vision, Sri Ramakrishna watched this "spiritual son" dancing together with the youthful Sri Krishna atop a giant lotus blossom whose petals shimmered ethereally on the waves of the Ganges. Bewitched by the exquisitely graceful dance, the Master's consciousness soared. Some moments later, on returning to his senses, Ramakrishna was astonished to see the very youth of his visions walk through the open door of his room, accompanied by Manmohan. At first, he could do little more than gape in wonder. Then, recovering his balance, he turned smiling broadly to Manmohan. "There are wonderful possibilities in him," (E.C., p. 16) the Master affirmed as he gazed with unconcealed pleasure at Rakhal.

From the very beginning, there was an electricity between boy and man which was hard to account for. It must have puzzled Manmohan that they chatted together with the easy familiarity of dear old friends. Oddly enough, however, it didn't seem to surprise either Rakhal or Ramakrishna that their relationship should start out full-blown. Evidently, it was immediately clear to both of them that theirs was to be no ordinary relationship. Each instinctively recognized in the other the materialization of his own deepest and most secret prayer; Rakhal was thrilled beyond words to meet someone who actually knew God, and Ramakrishna was equally thrilled to find an unencumbered soul who yearned as deeply as he himself had yearned to know Him. In no time at all, they were inseparable companions.

Rakhal felt absolutely free with Ramakrishna. There was a joking, playful quality in this relationship between two of God's eternal children. The seventeen-year-old disciple would lean on his Master's lap, climb onto his shoulders, and play a variety of games with him. The guileless child in Rakhal—the child who society generally anesthetizes by the coming of adolescence—found a welcome haven at Dakshineswar; the childlike freedom and security which Sri Ramakrishna offered Rakhal quickly ripened into a spiritual joy for the young disciple. As the Master later recalled, "No words can describe Rakhal's mood during that period. He was in a state of ecstasy most of the time. He was like a little infant, helpless in its mother's arms and surrendering itself completely to her—always conscious of the divine relationship." (E.C., p. 17)

Ramakrishna responded with a love that was maternal in every sense. He fed Rakhal tenderly with specially prepared dishes, and fussed over him as anxiously as a doting mother. The Master, who perceived even his human loves as reflections of the divine loves of the mythic past, felt the way mother Yashoda felt with her child, Krishna. In truth, there was no longer any such thing as a "human love" for Ramakrishna. To love man as man alone was not possible for him. He could only love the God in man, which is to say he could only love the *true man* behind the veil of personality. And in the pure-souled Rakhal, that God, that *true man*, was hardly veiled at all. At times, just the sight, or even the thought, of Rakhal was sufficient to kindle the flame of Sri Ramakrishna's spiritual consciousness.

"Why is my spiritual feeling awakened at the sight of Rakhal?" he once reflected. "The more you advance toward God, the less you see of His glories and grandeur. The aspirant at first has a vision of the Goddess with ten arms; there is a great display of power in that image. The next vision is that of the Deity with two arms; there are no longer ten arms holding various weapons and missiles. Then the aspirant has a vision of Gopala [Krishna as a cowherd boy] in which there is no trace of power at all." (G.S., p. 177)

Ramakrishna had now come full circle from his worship of Kali in the temple to his worship of Kali within the temple of the human form. As his intimacy with the Mother increased, the Mother appeared to him in increasingly more intimate guises. While previously he had had to struggle to find Her, now the Master was unable to avoid Her. But it was in his devoted young followers, like Rakhal, that the Divine Mother shone most brilliantly. And it was through his loving and patient guidance of these pure souls that Sri Ramakrishna now worshiped the God in man.

Although Ramakrishna perceived the God in Rakhal and worshiped that indwelling Divinity with the love of an indulgent mother for her dearest child, he did not hesitate on that account to administer stronger medicine when called for. On one occasion, while massaging Ramakrishna with oil, Rakhal pleaded with the Master to grant him the boon of *samadhi*. At first, Ramakrishna ignored him, but, when the badgering persisted, he turned to Rakhal and scolded him for his presumptuousness. Deeply hurt, Rakhal smashed the bottle of oil on the earth and ran off through the temple grounds, crying bitterly. No sooner had he reached the gate, however, than his feet locked firmly beneath him. Paralyzed, unable to move another step, he collapsed in a quivering heap at the center of the path.

Ramakrishna sent his nephew Ramlal to fetch Rakhal. With gentle diplomacy, Ramlal finally succeeded in assuaging Rakhal's anger, and the two young men returned together to Ramakrishna's room. The Master turned to Rakhal and smiled knowingly: "You see! You could not go outside the circle I drew around you! . . . You were angry with me. Do you know why I made you angry? There was a purpose behind it. Medicine acts only after the sore has been opened." (E.C., pp. 20–21)

This incident introduces several intriguing questions. Was Ramakrishna really angry at Rakhal's desire for spiritual ecstasy (a desire hardly foreign to his own heart, after all)? Did Rakhal's own deeper instincts restrain him from leaving the temple compound, or is was it the Master's spiritual power which prevented him leaving the charmed circle of the Kali temple? And just what was the nature of the "sore" which the Master was opening up to the influence of his medicine? Was it Rakhal's impatience, his greed for spiritual experience, his childish temper, that was being mercifully exposed to Ramakrishna's stinging, but healing, balm?

We can ask these questions more easily than we can answer them. The full import of the incident is shrouded in the depths of two souls, guru and disciple, and we can never hope to know the whole of it. One thing is certain, though; the Master's medicine *did* have an effect. For a few days later, while massaging Ramakrishna's feet, Rakhal attained spontaneously, and for the first time, the transcendental state of *samadhi* for which he had pleaded.

In the months that followed, Rakhal progressed rapidly under Ramakrishna's watchful gaze. Those who knew him marveled at how serene and gentle he had become. Repeating the Name of God just under his breath at all times, he appeared to be continuously absorbed in a mellow bliss. In short order, as a result of his growing capacity for spiritual concentration, psychic powers developed in Rakhal of their own—among them, the ability to read a man's character at a glance and uncover his hidden motives. Thinking to protect the Master from disturbance by insincere and unworthy visitors, Rakhal used this penetrating gift to screen all who came to Dakshineswar, refusing to allow into Ramakrishna's presence any but those he perceived to be earnest seekers. When the Master came to know of this, however, he was not at all pleased: "It is mean-spirited to use your powers in this way," he told Rakhal. "A person who pays the least attention to occult powers can't live in God-knowledge. Don't take any notice of them when they come to you." (E.C., p. 28) Reflecting on this lesson with his own disciples many years later, Swami Brahmananda mused, "It is easy to acquire occult powers, but hard indeed to attain purity of heart." (E.C., p. 29)

It was precisely toward fostering this inward purity in his disciples that Ramakrishna worked tirelessly as a spiritual teacher. He used to say that only the pure can see God. And he felt that all spiritual disciplines have one aim alone—the purification of the turbid waters of the self. Ramakrishna had seen that only the mirrorlike clarity of a mind cleansed of prejudice, ill will, and sensual strivings could faithfully reflect the indwelling Divinity.

Ironically, it was with those who were closest to embodying this ideal of purity in their lives that Ramakrishna was the most severe in pointing out the least divergence. One day, he remarked to Rakhal: "I can't bear to look at you. I see a veil of ignorance over your face. Tell me, have you done anything wrong?" (E.C., p. 24) Greatly upset, Rakhal searched his conscience, but could find nothing. Finally the Master prompted him, saying, "Try to recall if you have told any untruth." (E.C., p. 24) Instantly, Rakhal recalled a lie that he had told in a jesting way to a friend. It was a very small affair, what society tolerantly calls a "white lie." But for Sri Ramakrishna there was no such thing as a "white lie." He understood that every untruth has its price in deception, and the greatest deception, oddly enough, is for the deceiver and not for the deceived. A man tells a lie, and then to cover that lie tells another lie, and so on down the line, until he is so busy fabricating a reality that he can no longer distinguish himself what is true from what is false. By being habitually false with others, he inevitably loses the capacity for being true with himself. And the worst thing about it, from Ramakrishna's perspective, was that a mind rendered twisted and cunning by its own falsehoods was no longer capable of knowing God, who is straightforwardness and simplicity itself.

He told his disciples:

> The virtue of truthfulness is most important. If a man always speaks the truth, and holds to the truth tenaciously, he will realize God; for God is truth. I prayed once to the Divine Mother, saying: "Mother, here is Your knowledge, here is Your ignorance—take them both and give me pure love for You. Here is Your purity, here is Your impurity—take them both and give me pure love for You. Here is Your good, here is Your evil—take them both and give me pure love for You." . . . I mentioned all these things in turn, but I could not bring myself to say "Here is Your truth, here is Your untruth—take them both." I gave up everything at Her feet, but I could not bring myself to give up truth. (E.C., pp. 23–24)

With the consent of his parents, Rakhal came to spend almost all of his time now at Dakshineswar serving the Master and looking after him during his states of absorption. It was not long, however, before it was Ramakrishna who was looking after Rakhal, and not the other way around. Rakhal's ecstasy while massaging the Master's feet turned out to be only the first of many that followed. And just as with Sri Ramakrishna during the stormy days of his own youthful *sadhana*, Rakhal's frequent spiritual moods effectively incapacitated him from doing any work, and rendered him in almost permanent need of assistance himself.

By now, though, several others had come to take Rakhal's place. Foremost among them was Latu, the poor servant boy of Ramachandra Datta. Latu was so taken with the personality of the Master during his visits to Dakshineswar that he obtained Ramachandra's permission to remain there full-time as Ramakrishna's personal attendant. He was a country boy, orphaned during childhood, and brought up by relatives amid the crushing poverty of rural Bihar. Coming to Sri Ramakrishna in his midteens, Latu was illiterate, frank, and unsophisticated, speaking a crude Bengali picturesquely overlayed with a thick Hindi accent that would launch Ramakrishna into peals of good-natured laughter. And Latu, for all his contact with Calcutta's intellectual elite, remained essentially rough and uncultured his whole life. The Master's comically ill-fated attempts to tutor him were doomed from the start, and he soon abandoned them.

But if Latu evinced little interest in book learning or the fine points of elocution, he showed a far greater aptitude for spiritual matters. On one occasion, Sri Ramakrishna mildly reproached him for resting during the evening: "If you sleep, then when will you meditate?" (R.D., p. 177) Latu took the rebuke to heart and all but renounced sleep; he meditated the entire night, serving Ramakrishna faithfully during the day with only the briefest pause now and again for a nap. This strict regimen soon bore fruit. Latu had wonderful visions. He learned how to dive deeply into the inner world—too deeply at times! So profound was his meditation, that once, while he prayed alone on the bank of the Ganges, the flood tide came swirling in around him without his even becoming aware of it. If Ramakrishna hadn't arrived at the crucial moment to rouse him from trance, Latu would have been carried away by the rising current.

On another occasion, Ramakrishna found Latu sitting within one of the small shrines of Shiva adjacent to the temple of Kali absorbed in profound meditation. As the day was sweltering and Latu sweating profusely, the Master started fanning him with one of the large plaited hand fans reserved for the Deity. After some time, when the young devotee returned to external awareness and saw what Sri Ramakrishna was doing, he was stunned. He had always regarded himself as a servant and was unaccustomed to being served himself. But with infinite sweetness and tenderness, Ramakrishna began chatting familiarly so as to relieve Latu of his embarrassment. It was a poignant and revealing moment. Latu lost all self-consciousness, and his heart swelled mightily with love for this Christlike saint who was a humble servant of his servants.

One day, Ramakrishna inquired enigmatically of Latu if he knew what God was doing at that very moment. Latu had to admit that he didn't. So the Master told him: "God is passing a camel through the eye of a needle." Latu understood immediately that Ramakrishna was referring to him—unwieldy, crude, unformed, God was, nevertheless, molding him into a worthy recipient of His grace. Years later, Swami Vivekananda would say of

Latu, the rough-hewn son of a peasant, who had by then become the revered Swami Abhutananda: "Latu is Ramakrishna's greatest miracle. Without any education at all, he acquired the deepest wisdom, just by virtue of Ramakrishna's touch" (R.D., p. 178).

This brings us to Vivekananda. Many would say that Vivekananda himself was Ramakrishna's great miracle. And he certainly was, though in quite a different sense from Latu. While Latu had approached Sri Ramakrishna rough and unformed, Vivekananda (at that time called by his given name, Naren) had come, if anything, overformed. Latu came ignorant, an empty vessel. Naren came as a huge ocean liner teeming with knowledge. Latu came to learn. In a sense, Naren came to unlearn what he already thought he knew too well, to empty himself of preconceptions, and to open himself to a simplicity and quiet power that made all his vaunted knowledge and opinions seem petty and insubstantial by comparison.

This revolution would not take place overnight. Naren came to Dakshineswar as a raging bull, and it was not enough for Ramakrishna to grab him by the horns. He had to hold on to those horns manfully, and hold on and on during the entire heady dance of resistance, until the bull, exhausted, dropped to his knees in grateful defeat. That, too, would come to pass. And after the bull had sunk to his knees and owned defeat, he became magically transfigured, like Saul in the desert, into a dancing ball of flame to enlighten the world. Naren became Vivekananda. And Vivekananda became Ramakrishna's Saint Paul, broadcasting the good news of his Master's advent to the world.

Naren was born Narendranath Datta to a well-to-do family of *kshatriyas*, the caste of warriors and kings, and he was a true scion of the ancient line gifted with a crusading temperament to rival those of his noble ancestors. He had less in common with his own father, Viswanath, who was a lawyer of the Calcutta High Court, a cosmopolitan man of the world, a linguist, and a highly cultivated lover of the arts and literature, of fine food and stimulating conversation. Viswanath was a skeptic—but a skeptic possessed of deep compassion and an almost reckless generosity. He had a high opinion of himself (not without cause) and an aristocrat's confident air of superiority. As a father, Viswanath was faultlessly mild with his children. It is said that he never lost his temper, though at times he was sorely provoked by Naren, as we shall soon see. When Naren asked his father for advice on how to conduct himself in life, the seasoned old veteran of the world answered in a way that was typical of him: "Never show surprise at anything." (R.D., p. 187) It was a prescription that he had followed himself. A gentleman, in the original sense of the term, he never failed to view the world with a wry and indulgent smile.

If Viswanath was mild mannered and urbane, Naren's grandfather, Durgcharan, was more passionate. He had abandoned home and fortune and the promise of a brilliant career at the age of twenty-five to become a wandering monk. Durgcharan simply disappeared one day. And he never again returned to the worldly life that he so precipitously abandoned.

There was more than a little of Durgcharan in young Naren—enough, indeed to make everyone palpably uneasy; the memory of Durgcharan's renunciation remained a painful one for the Datta family. They were understandably anxious that the talented Naren, who bore Durgcharan such an uncanny physical resemblance, might follow in his grandfather's ascetic footsteps. And their worries were not baseless. Naren had responded passionately to the ideal of renunciation from earliest childhood. He loved to watch *sadhus* pass through his neighborhood calling out for alms, and gathering in the temples to smoke chillums and trade their wanderers' tales.

While his contemporaries dreamt of wealth and power, Naren filled himself with visions of the pilgrim life, free as a billowing cloud of summer. The romance and fearless independence of that life evoked images of faraway places and prodigious feats of self-mastery. To Naren, these lean monks seemed the very embodiments of a heroic freedom. They were giants forging their own way through the world, heedless of the the views of society, slaves to no man—conscious, liquid sparks of the very boundlessness through which they wandered. Just to see an ochre-robed ascetic transported Naren to a purer, truer world.

Naren took a special pleasure in offering alms to *sadhus*. He didn't limit himself to a few pennies or a handful of rice as others did, but gave indiscriminately, compulsively—once going so far as to strip down in the street and pass on his fine-spun and costly wearing cloth to a ragged hermit. Not surprisingly, such extremes of generosity alarmed his parents. But to attempt to reason with the boy once he'd set his mind on something was futile. Even locking Naren in his room whenever a begging *sadhu* approached on his daily rounds didn't help. Naren would simply pick up anything at hand in his room and toss it out the window to the passing holy man.

On matters of principle, Naren was willful in the extreme and harder to control than a untamed colt. And, like a colt, his awesome energy could lash out in sudden and unpredictable gusts of random vitality. At times, when thwarted, that excess vitality would boil over, turn destructive, and he would take up a piece of furniture and smash it to bits in an explosive fit of rage. Naren's mother, Bhuvaneshwari, found that if she repeated the Name of Shiva at such times the storm would pass, the boy would become calm again. Bhuvaneshwari reflected, only half in jest, that she had prayed to Shiva for a son, and he had sent one of his demons instead!

But if there was a demon in Naren, it was God's own demon, for Naren was obsessed with God. While his friends busied themselves with the games of childhood, Naren would play at meditation, sitting naked except for a thin cotton loincloth before painted and gaily festooned clay models of the deities that he had purchased for a few pennies in the local bazaar. And there was more than just a child's earnest mimicry involved in these spontaneous rituals. When Naren would close his eyes in meditation, he invariably saw an inner light that gradually spread and imparted a wonderful sense of joy. On one occasion, a cobra slithered right by Naren as he prayed before his clay idols. His young companions called out to him in alarm, but Naren didn't stir. It was not courage or youthful bravado that rendered him unresponsive to their warnings. In a world apart, he simply hadn't heard their cries.

This same awesome capacity for concentration crowned everything that Naren took up with success. And Naren took up everything that caught his fancy. He was an expert gymnast, he

SRI RAMAKRISHNA

swam, he rowed, he rode horses. He was skilled at debate, and a master of language. "When he spoke," a friend recalled many years later, "there was a strange power in his eyes that would hold his listeners in thrall." (N.p., n.d.) A born leader with great charismatic powers, Naren nevertheless bore his leadership role lightly. He didn't abuse his strength, but remained evenhanded—a youthful Solomon in his keen sense of justice, and a faultlessly loyal friend. Little wonder that his fellow students flocked around Naren and idolized him as they did.

Not least of Naren's abundant talents was his mastery of Indian dance and of music, both the popular devotional songs, the *kirtanas,* and the exacting classical traditions of ancient Bengal. Naren's encyclopedic musical knowledge combined with his voice of ethereal sweetness inspired the great maestros of the day to proclaim that the boy would soon be recognized as the finest vocalist in the land. Conveying far more than mere technical polish and artistic brilliance, his voice had a haunting, plaintive quality that deeply moved all who heard it. When Naren sang, he lost himself in an interior world. It was clear to those who watched these stirring performances why Naren regarded music as the "highest form of worship." In the future, Ramakrishna himself would marvel at the depth of the pathos and the joy and the naked yearning that Naren could evoke, and he wouldn't let a single gathering pass without somehow inducing him to sing.

Added to these artistic gifts was Naren's astounding photographic memory. He could recite verbatim practically everything he had ever read. And he read everything he could get his hands on—hungrily devouring a diversity of works from Shakespeare, Wordsworth, and Western science and philosophy to the Ramayana and the Hindu epics. There were no bounds to his curiosity and seemingly no limits to what he was capable of mastering once he'd set his mind to it. The future looked very bright indeed. Nothing was realistically beyond his grasp. But when Naren considered what exactly it was that he wanted to grasp with the prodigious talons of his genius, what fruit of life was the most worthy of him, the same image invariably recurred. Let us turn to his own description of many years later:

Every night, as I went to bed two visions floated before my mind's eye. One of them pictured me as a successful man of the world, occupying the foremost place in society, with great wealth and immense power, and I felt that it was well within my ability to carve out such a place for myself. A moment later would come the other vision in which I found myself a wandering monk, dressed in a loincloth, living on a chance morsel of food and spending the night under the trees, depending solely on God. I felt that it was in me to live that sort of life too. Of the two visions, the latter appealed to me more, and I thought that the life of the monk was the noblest thing on earth, and that I would one day embrace it. (L.R., p. 328)

Nevertheless, as Naren grew older the simple faith in the God of his childhood wavered under the successive blows of Western rationalism, to which his study exposed him. During his college years, the conflict between belief and the endless questioning of a keenly honed, critical intelligence reached a crisis of intensity. Naren was very much influenced by Western thought at this time. He corresponded with the English philosopher Herbert Spencer, who was astonished at the "precociousness of his philosophic intellect." (T.L.R., p. 225) For Naren, however, philosophy was never a sterile intellectual exercise, but a matter of the utmost personal importance. It would not be an exaggeration to say that he recognized no aim in life other than the discovery of Truth. He struggled manfully with all of the great questions— the nature of creation and death, the existence of evil. He even dared to reason about the existence of God, and before too long he found himself in the only place that pure reason, untempered by intuition, could ever take him—at the dead end of an uncomfortable agnosticism.

Naren could not believe in a thing without becoming passionate about that belief. So Naren become a passionate agnostic, a passionate social and religious critic. He joined the Brahmo Samaj. But the very passion with which he took up these new beliefs was, paradoxically, working silently to undermine them. You can become a passionate agnostic, perhaps, but you can't really succeed in making agnosticism passionate—and therein lay

Naren's difficulty. It just was not possible for him to dedicate himself enthusiastically to negation and doubt. There was too much of the idealist in him for that. The concepts that satisfied Naren's intellect left his heart essentially cold and indifferent. And any belief that Naren couldn't *feel* as intensely and as palpably as he could *think* it was ultimately unsatisfying to him.

Naren yearned for a faith that he could embrace with his whole being, an integral faith, stretching far beyond the narrow circle of universal reason, a faith wide enough to encompass the universe, and deep enough to hallow it. But at the same time, he hesitated to leave reason's bright and sharply ordered arena. He longed—perhaps more than anything else—to believe in the God of his childhood. By middle adolescence, however, that naive faith was no longer possible; Naren's childhood God had already come to appear to him a child's God, and he was forced to wonder if Divinity was not merely the imaginative creation of mankind's long childhood, as many Western philosophers so persuasively argued.

If God actually exists, Naren reasoned, then there must be solid, irrefutable evidence of it. Somewhere there must be men and women who had put Him to the test and proved Him in the laboratories of their own experience as plainly and as unsentimentally as the Western scientists had proved out the laws of nature in their laboratories. Legend spoke of the existence of such holy seers, but did they exist in anything more than legend? And, if they did exist, then where were they to be found?

It wasn't that Naren hadn't searched. When Devendranath Tagore spoke eloquently of God, Naren had the temerity to wonder out loud: "But sir, have you seen Him?"[2] The revered spiritual teacher was forced to admit that he hadn't. And not only Devendranath Tagore, but all the other preachers appeared to be in the same boat. What were their sermons but collections of old bones, inert things, quotations from scriptures, holy sayings, curiosities that had little or nothing to do with life, as they themselves lived it? Preachers cited earlier preachers, and those preachers had cited still earlier preachers, and so on endlessly throughout history. Perhaps God was nothing more than a creation of the preachers, a musty old rumor passed down the centuries by men afraid to face up to the emptiness of their own lives, men afraid of death.

Throughout these years of painful questioning, however, Naren maintained an exemplary purity and self-dedication that are hard to account for in a young man, who had, to all outward appearances, lost his faith. He remained celibate, refusing numerous offers of marriage, maintained strict vegetarianism, and generally lived in the taut asceticism of someone whose vision is firmly fixed to higher ends than the usual. Naren may indeed have lost sight temporarily of just what exactly those ends were supposed to be, but he had not forgotten that they were there. He had not forgotten that his life was an offering and a flame, consecrated to a great purpose, and possessed of a deep, if hidden, meaning. He felt that much unshakably in his bones, and instinctually he shrank from the usual adolescent rounds of pleasure seeking and self-centered concern.

So it is clear that, while Naren may have discarded God, God had not discarded Naren, or allowed him to abandon the ideal of a spiritual life that had ennobled his childhood. That ideal had survived barely tarnished by the heavy weather of skepticism. But it was no longer clearly visible. It had become obscured in a feverish haze of thought and theory, and now it was not so much a conscious choice as an unconscious and proudly stubborn clinging. Naren was lost in this mental fog, wandering, now this way and now that, as impelled by the conflicting demands of head and heart. Noticing his unsettled condition, Naren's cousin, the devotee Ramachandra Datta, counseled him earnestly: "If you seriously want to live a spiritual life, you ought to talk with Ramakrishna. You won't find anything at the Brahmo Samaj." (R.D., p. 193) Naren took Ramachandra's advice to heart, and a few days later he visited Dakshineswar for the first time.

As we have seen, Ramakrishna was granted intimations from the Mother before the coming of his closest disciples. More than simple visions, these were symbolic revelations of the devotee's character, and of the nature of his future relationship to Ramakrishna. Nowhere is this clearer than in the richly meaningful vision in which Ramakrishna suddenly found himself soaring on a luminous pathway through progressively more subtle worlds. From the everyday plane of matter, he ascended to the realm of pure thought, and from there to the divine heaven of the Gods and Goddesses. Finally, he pierced the luminous barrier between the world of relativity and the sphere of the Absolute. In this world beyond the worlds, which even the Gods could not hope to penetrate, seven venerable sages were seated rapt in the silent contemplation of the Eternal.

Ramakrishna gazed in awe at the radiant sages whose bodies were composed of the light of pure consciousness. As he looked on, a portion of the surrounding luminosity became detached and resolved itself into the figure of a divine child. The child ambled over to one of the seers and clasped him affectionately in his soft arms, rousing him from superconsciousness. As the sage returned to outward awareness, the expression of pure delight in his eyes showed that the child was the beloved of his heart and infinitely dear to him. "I am going down. You must come too," (R.D., p. 199) the child insisted. And the sage expressed his mute agreement with a tender look of assent. Finally, the yogi returned to *samadhi* and, as he did so, a fragment of his body and mind broke loose descending to earth in a ball of radiance.

In recounting this experience, Sri Ramakrishna concluded with the words, "No sooner had I seen Naren than I recognized him to be that sage." (R.D., p. 199) The reader may have already guessed the identity of the child. As the Master himself later confirmed, and as his relationship with Naren would bear ample witness, the divine child was none other than Sri Ramakrishna himself.

Let us turn to Naren's own account of his first meeting with the Master:

> After I had sung a Brahmo song for him, he took me in hand to the northern veranda. . . . To my great surprise, he began to weep with joy. He held me by the hand and addressed me very tenderly, as if I was long familiar to him. He said, "You've come so late! Was that right? Couldn't you have guessed how I've been waiting for you? My ears are nearly burned off listening to the talk of these worldly peo-

ple. I thought I would burst, not having anyone to tell how I really felt!" He went on like that—raving and weeping. And then suddenly he folded his palms together and began addressing me as if I was some divine being, "I know who you are my Lord. You are Nara, the ancient sage, the incarnation of Narayana. You have come back to earth to take away the sufferings and sorrows of mankind." I was absolutely dumbfounded. I said to myself, "What kind of man is this? He must be raving mad! How can he talk like this to me, who am nobody—the son of Viswanath Datta?" But I didn't answer him, and I let this wonderful madman go on talking as he chose. . . . Then he took my hand and said, "Promise me you'll come back here soon, alone." I couldn't refuse his request; it was made so earnestly. So I had to say, "I will." (R.D., pp. 194–95)

After this perplexing encounter, Naren returned with Ramakrishna to the room where several other devotees were gathered, and immediately the Master launched into one of his inspired monologues: "God can be seen and spoken to just as surely as I am seeing you and speaking to you. . . . If anyone really wants to see God, and if he calls upon Him—God will reveal Himself, that's for certain" (R.D., p. 195). Simple words spoken in the unsophisticated idiom of peasant Bengal, but how wonderfully sincere and affecting. Ramakrishna was speaking from the heart. Nothing could have been clearer than that. And Naren felt intuitively that here, at long last, was a man who had actually practiced what he preached. Even physically, the half-naked country priest seemed the very picture of spiritual renunciation—wiry and alert, with the bright intensity of one who has attained the heights of ecstasy, yet serene, with the suffused glow of a contemplative who has plumbed the very depths of the ocean of peace.

Seemingly against his own better judgment, Naren was powerfully moved by Ramakrishna. But how was it possible to reconcile this lucid and saintly figure now before his eyes with the bizarre scene on the veranda just minutes before? Naren was frankly puzzled. "Well, he may be mad," he thought to himself. "Yes, he *is* mad. But how pure! And what renunciation!" (R.D.,

p. 196). With these observations, Naren took his leave and returned to Calcutta.

Given the quirkiness of this experience, it would hardly be surprising if Naren had broken his word to Ramakrishna and never returned again. Certainly, he must have felt tempted to forget the whole episode. But Naren could neither forget the strange priest nor comprehend him. Indeed, it was precisely because he could not comprehend the Master that he could not forget him. Naren prided himself on the ability to judge a man and gauge his worth on sight. Ramakrishna, however, eluded judgment. He did not fit into any of the familiar categories; the ordinary weights and measures just didn't seem adequate. Ramakrishna, in short, was a riddle and a challenge in every possible sense; his devotion challenged Naren's intellectual assumptions, his ecstasies and his eccentricities challenged Naren's sense of propriety, his serenity challenged Naren's restlessness. Challenged, Naren had no choice but to return to Dakshineswar. Little could he have guessed how much more unsettling, how much more deeply challenging to everything he thought himself to be, this second visit would prove!

Let us return again to Naren's own vivid account:

> "He [Ramakrishna] was in a strange mood. He muttered something to himself which I couldn't understand, looked hard at me, then rose and approached me. I thought we were about to have another crazy scene. Scarcely had that thought passed through my mind than he placed his right foot on my body. Immediately, I had a wonderful experience. My eyes were wide open, and I saw that everything in the room, including the walls themselves, was whirling rapidly around and receding, and at the same time, it seemed to me that my consciousness of self, together with the entire universe, was about to vanish into a vast, all-devouring void. This destruction of my consciousness of self seemed to me to be the same thing as death. I felt that death was right before me, very close. Unable to control myself, I cried out loudly, "Ah, what are you doing to me? Don't you know I have parents at home?" When the Master heard this, he gave out a loud laugh. Then, touching my chest with his hand,

he said, "All right—let it stop now. It needn't be done all at once. It will happen in its own good time." To my amazement, this extraordinary vision of mine vanished as suddenly as it had come." (R.D., p. 197)

Naren struggled, as he had after his first bizarre meeting with Ramakrishna, to wrest some sense out of this latest episode—but with no greater success. He wondered at first if Ramakrishna hadn't somehow managed to hypnotize him. On reflection, however, this seemed highly unlikely. A weak mind may perhaps be hypnotized against its will by a stronger mind. But Naren prided himself on his mental strength, and, in any event, the tremendous experience that the Master had communicated with a touch hardly qualified as a hypnotic stupor!

Nevertheless, Naren was on his guard during his next visit to Dakshineswar, convinced that, if he remained vigilant, such a thing could not happen to him again. But it did happen again—this time, however, with a very different outcome. When Ramakrishna touched him lightly, Naren immediately lost consciousness. Even afterward, he had no recollection of what had taken place during the trance. Speaking about this incident later with his devotees, Ramakrishna revealed that Naren had become temporarily unconscious of his present identity, but cognizant of the larger context of his spiritual destiny. In that state, the Master questioned him minutely about his past lives and the nature of his present mission and future fate.

What Naren told him at that time accorded with Ramakrishna's intuitions and confirmed what had already been revealed to him in his own vision—that Naren had attained perfection in meditation during a previous incarnation, and that the realizations of that lifetime, while temporarily eclipsed from his consciousness so that he might be free to accomplish a very great task for the good of the world, would be revealed to him as soon as his work was accomplished. Ramakrishna discovered that on the very day Naren learned his true identity, he would give up his body by an act of will.

The Master did not reveal any of this to Naren when he recovered his outward consciousness; Naren probably wouldn't have believed it, in any event. The special regard with which the Master treated him—a regard which deepened still further as a result of this latest revelation of the boy's true nature—remained bewildering and embarrassing to Naren. While he could not help but be touched by the Master's affection, he didn't for a moment understand it or feel worthy of it.

Naren was hardly the only one mystified on that account. More than a few questioned what the Master saw in him. The boy's charm had a rough edge, and not all were instantly won over to it. He was too negligent of ordinary social conventions, too willful and supremely self-confident for the tastes of some. Naren appeared argumentative. He didn't show any of the usual deference to the views of elders, and went so far as to dispute openly with the Master. He condemned Ramakrishna's views on image worship, and casually dismissed his visions, from the standpoint of Western psychology, as hallucinations of an over-stimulated religious imagination. He didn't even stop short of abusing Kali, whose worship he did not support. No wonder there were those who felt deeply offended at Naren's outspokenness and regarded him as an arrogant schoolboy with a badly inflated opinion of his own worth and of the value of his opinions.

These views did not appear to bother Naren. Still less did they trouble Ramakrishna. "Let no man judge Naren, for none is in a position to fully understand him," he cautioned. And far from being offended by the boy's combativeness, the Master delighted in it. No fisherman was ever more thrilled by a strong tug on his line than Ramakrishna was by the bold resistance of this scrappy teenager. For the Master knew from experience what every fisher of men knows from the gut—that the stiffer the struggle the greater the prize in the end. Sri Ramakrishna could see that Naren's resistance, far from being brute obstinacy, or "argument for argument's sake," was, in actuality, a sign of his obsessive quest for Truth. And Ramakrishna knew that that head-strong passion could not fail to tunnel its own way through to the treasure house in the end.

He told Naren: "If you can't accept God with form or any of the commonly held ideas about Him, because they are the product of human thought—it doesn't matter. So long as you have faith in a God, in a Controller of the Universe, and you pray to Him with all sincerity, 'Oh, Lord! I am ignorant of Your true nature. Do reveal Yourself to me as You really are.' " (N.p., n.d.)

Ramakrishna recognized in Naren's furious and obstinate strength a divine power. He could see clearly that, once it had exercised itself in questioning and doubt and thoroughly exhausted them, that same power would one day lead a multitude of weaker souls to God.

So Ramakrishna was supremely patient with Naren. The more Naren thrashed about the better, as far as he was concerned. This feisty "big one" was not about to get away, in any event. Naren was hooked. His struggles could only drive the hook still deeper. In the meantime, the sport of it was a wonder to behold, and a strong tonic for Sri Ramakrishna. One aspect of the Master's yearning had been fulfilled by Rakhal—his gentle, contemplative side—and Rakhal's coming had been a literal fulfillment of Ramakrishna's prayer to the Mother for a mild and affectionate spiritual son. But Ramakrishna had made a prayer of a sterner sort as well. Sensing, perhaps, that the very best that was inside of him would come out only under the fire of battle, the Master had prayed, "Mother, send me someone who will dispute my realizations!" (T.L.R., p. 234)

It was a prayer that Naren's coming was to answer in excess.

→≫ *Chapter 11* ≪←

Taming the Bull

AT THE SAME TIME THAT NAREN FOUND HIMSELF DISAGREEING strongly with much of what Sri Ramakrishna stood for, he was utterly incapable of resisting the man himself. While Naren had grown up accustomed to the doting warmth of a close-knit family, as well as the admiring, almost idolizing attention of his classmates and friends, neither the fickle adulation of his peers nor the grasping attachment of family members had prepared him for anything so sublimely nurturing as the divine love of Sri Ramakrishna. In later years, he would declare, "Ever since our first meeting, it was the Master alone who always had faith in me—no one else, not even my own mother and brothers had that kind of faith. That faith and that love have bound me to him forever. The Master was the only one who knew how to love and who really loved. Worldly people only feign love to gratify their own self-interest" (R.D., p. 216).

More than anything else, it was this love that mellowed Naren and softened his philosophy and brought him gently back to God. If Ramakrishna—a mere mortal—could love so purely and so selflessly, then was it likely that the Creator's love for his creation could be anything less? Somehow, just to see Ramakrishna in the flesh was enough to make the unseen God seem less improbable, more concretely conceivable—not that Naren subscribed for a moment to the idea current among some of the other devotees that the Master actually was an Avatar, an incarnation of God. If God does exist, then logic (not to mention plain common sense) told Naren that He must be very far transcendent of that groping, stumbling biped known as man.

This belief in the "otherness" of the Creator stood in stark contrast to Ramakrishna's profound vision of the unity of the Mother with Her creation. It was inevitable that sooner or later these incompatible positions would clash. Just as inevitably, it was Ramakrishna's truth of experience which prevailed in the end over Naren's mental constructs. The telling confrontation was sparked when, at the Master's urging, Naren read some works on *Advaita* Vedanta. Far from being edified by the cosmic breadth of the Vedantic vision, the young man found himself dizzied by it. The sweeping nondualism appeared indiscriminately to erase the fundamental distinctions on which the philosophical assumptions of the West and of the Brahmo Samaj are based.

Naren was not wrong in sensing a deep challenge to his way of thinking. The philosophical dialectic of the West, which he had adopted as his own, is basically analytical. The analytic intellect struggles hard to make sharp distinctions between things, to untangle the knotted threads of events and trace out the pathways of order in the seeming chaos of the world. It works by dividing and conquering, by breaking the universe into logically manageable chunks and then manipulating them according to the dictates of the intellect. The price paid for the convenience of fragmenting the world (as we are only now discovering to our cost) is that we forget that it was ever whole to begin with. We pay in the coin of illusion—the illusion that the artificial entities of our own creation exist in actual fact and that the universe is a collection of loosely bound, independent "things," whose fundamental truth consists in their separateness and not in their unity with the rest of the cosmos.

When he first came to Ramakrishna, Naren did not yet perceive the shortcomings of such a one-sided view of things, or its dangers. He had deeply imbibed the spirit of Western thought. By comparison, the wisdom traditions of India were still virgin territory for him. So it is not hard to imagine Naren's sense of vertigo when suddenly confronted for the first time with a philosophy based on synthesis rather than analysis—a teaching that asserts that all is One, and that the distinctions don't matter, that the dividing lines are nothing but arbitrary boundaries etched in thought on a purely mental world—a world which, for all of its consensual reality, doesn't ultimately exist. These ideas struck him not just as sloppy thinking, but as fundamentally blasphemous. Were God and man, stones and trees, morality and immorality, and everything else besides, mere fancy, illusions of a fragmenting intellect? Was individuality to be dissolved with a casual wave of the Vedantic wand, and everything sloshed together as equal and indistinguishable elements of some mixed up, formless, and tasteless cosmic soup? Naren thought it absurd. And he ridiculed the sages who wrote such patent nonsense. The whole lot of them must have been out of their minds, he told Ramakrishna. But the Master only smiled indulgently, telling him, "You may not be able to accept these truths at present. But is that any reason to condemn the great *rishis* who taught them? Why do you try to limit God's nature? Keep calling on Him. He is truth itself. Whatever He reveals to you, believe that to be His true nature" (R.D., p. 205).

Ramakrishna had faith that, given time, Truth would unfold itself within the questing spirit of Naren by a natural process like the blossoming of a flower; it would be best not to interfere with this process. Ramakrishna certainly never felt that he needed to convince Naren of anything through argument, a sport which the young devotee was all too adept at in any event. As a result, the Master sagely refused to do battle on Naren's home territory. He knew only too well that the truth of nondualism is not a matter of words, but of the towering experience behind them. Naren, on the other hand, like most who use words well, was rather overawed by their power. Words were Naren's native element. He swam in conceptualization as a shark in water. He employed language sharply, bluntly, and caustically at times to cut through the shams of society and reveal the hypocrisy beneath the surface.

Naren's critical intellect was central to his spiritual quest as well. He employed it as a sharp blade of discrimination to cleave the real from the false, and to clear the strait and narrow path to Truth. But, while intellect had helped Naren reach the threshold of Truth's temple, it could not lead him into the sanctum. Beyond its limited and proper sphere, conceptualization cannot pass.

As Sri Ramakrishna himself reflected with graphic emphasis: "Knowledge has entry only up to the drawing-room of God, but love can enter into His inner apartment." (T.S., p. 48)

Just as many years earlier Ramakrishna had needed to put to sword the vision of Kali at the dramatic climax of his own path, so had Naren now reached that stage where he would have to transcend verbal and intellectual symbols if he were to penetrate intuitively the magic circle of nondualistic Truth. Ramakrishna, however, did not tell Naren to take a leap beyond the mind. He did something far more sensible than *telling* him—he *showed* him.

It was an unforgettable lesson and one that Naren couldn't argue with because it came without words. Naren had been speaking mockingly to a companion about the teachings of Vedanta. "Can it be that this waterpot is God," he asked sarcastically, "and this jug is God, and everything we see is all God, and all of us are God too? What could be more absurd!" (R.D., p. 206). Attracted by their merry peals of laughter, the Master came over and asked Naren what they were talking about. But before Naren had a chance to respond, Ramakrishna touched him lightly and Naren fell into a trance.

With that liberating touch, the blinders fell away from Naren's eyes, and suddenly the reality, which he had been ridiculing just moments before, was shining clear as daylight. In a flash it was revealed to him that everything actually *is* God, that nothing whatsoever exists but the Divine, that the entire universe is His body, and all things His forms.

In framing this experience with words, the impression is unavoidably created of some sort of brainstorm, a whirlwind of insight during which Naren's thoughts fortuitously clicked into place. Actually, it was nothing of the sort. Naren didn't reason any of this out; there was no mental process involved at all. He didn't think it—he *saw* it. In an instant it dawned on him with the blinding intensity of vision that the objects in front of his eyes, the thoughts passing through his mind, and the people around him, that everything, everywhere was radiating the light of God as unmistakably as the sun the light of day.

This powerful realization did not fade when Naren left Dakshineswar. While dining at home, the food before him, the plate on which it sat, the mother who served it, and he who consumed it, were all revealed to be radiant forms detached from God for the purpose of His play of the One as the many. When he crossed the street, the carriage that was speeding toward him and his own body appeared as extensions of the same mighty Being. When Naren sat, God was sitting; when Naren walked, God was walking; when Naren talked, God was talking.

And so it continued for several days as the young man drifted about the workaday world like a specter through a dream—curiously subdued, indifferent to everything. His parents feared that he was ill. Naren hardly ate or spoke, and his glazed eyes bore the faraway look of the saints and the dying. As the days passed and the intensity of this experience slowly faded, his focus shifted from the perception of God in everything to a complementary sense of the unreality of the world as it presents itself to the senses. In the shadow now of his radiant experience of Divinity, nothing seemed substantial to Naren; he knocked his head against the iron railing in Cornwallis Square just to convince himself that it was indeed real, that he was real.

Only gradually did this strange intoxication begin to ebb and his usual reactions set in once more. Even after the episode had become little more than a memory, however, the sure conviction born of experience that what the scriptures reveal about nondualism is a verifiable fact became firmly established in his consciousness. Naren didn't dare to speak lightly of Vedanta again. Indeed, within a little over a decade, as the world-renowned Swami Vivekananda, he would be proselytizing vigorously for these very teachings from lecture platforms throughout India, Europe, and America. Ironically, the one who had mocked the doctrine of Oneness as meaningless nonsense was fated to become its most passionate exponent in modern times.

But the faith growing daily in the young devotee's heart was about to be tested severely. In 1884, Naren's father died suddenly, leaving behind a prodigious and unexpected pile of debts and seven hungry mouths to feed. As the eldest son, the crux of the burden fell on Naren's inexperienced shoulders. Quite against his kingly instincts, Naren was forced to tramp exhaustedly the streets of Calcutta begging for employment. And for the first time in his life, he tasted the bitterness of rejection. Down on his luck, Naren was shocked to witness many of his erstwhile "friends" shunning him. Those who would once have cannily regarded it as very much in their own best interests to do Naren a favor now turned a deaf ear to his plight. It was a painful object lesson for the idealistic young man on the fickleness of human ties. As if to further underscore the point, Naren's own relatives brought suit in court, squabbling like a flock of greedy vultures over a carcass for what little remained of the Datta estate. Meanwhile, Naren's immediate family members were skipping meals and growing thin. When his mother would inquire if he had eaten, Naren, loath to partake of their meager supplies, usually claimed to have taken food at a friend's house. But the truth was that none of his friends had so much as asked if he were hungry. It was a novel experience. The world that had seemed so nurturing and secure to Naren was collapsing around him. What was worse, no one cared. No one even appeared to notice.

In the thick of these troubles, a well-meaning acquaintance tried to console Naren with a song about God's grace. In his present bitter state of mind, however, the pious lyrics grated like salt rubbed in an open wound and Naren exploded in fury: "Be quiet! That fanciful nonsense is all right for people who live in the lap of luxury—people who have no idea what hunger is—people whose nearest and dearest aren't going about in rags and starving. No doubt it sounds true and beautiful to them—as it did to me in the old days. But now I've seen what life is really like. That song is just a pack of lies" (R.D., p. 210).

This outburst exposes the painful depths of soul-searching that Naren was undergoing. But in truth, the harsh words blurted out in the heat of emotion and of raw pain were exaggerated. Naren had not really abandoned his faith. To be sure, it would have been difficult to guess that from what he was saying to his young companions—that God either didn't exist or was positively heartless if He did, and that, in either case, it was just so much wasted breath to pray to Him or expect any sympathy or help. Naren proclaimed all of this with the perverse pride of the rebel. But, troubled as he surely was, he could never fully bring himself to believe his own words. He had seen too much since coming to Ramakrishna not to suspect a divine purpose behind the outward drama of the world, a purpose and a necessity behind even the most incomprehensible suffering, a purpose that was not any less real for being hidden from the intellect and opaque to all merely human standards of judgment.

This truth was startlingly confirmed for Naren one night after an exhausting and famished day of searching vainly for work. As he lay down weary, preoccupied with the anxious buzzing of innumerable concerns, suddenly it was as if screen after screen was lifted from his mind's eye. All of the tortuous polarities that had been haunting him—good and evil, justice and mercy, poverty and wealth, joy and sorrow—were wordlessly and instantly reconciled. And Naren saw clearly that things were perfect just as they were. Once again, it would be wrong to suppose that Naren had reasoned all of this out. It was not so much that his problems were *solved* intellectually as it was that they *dis-solved*. Nothing had changed; only the perceiver had changed. Looking upon the world with vision transformed, even the shadows of his troubles no longer appeared. Naren's fatigue was gone. He was filled with light and peace, and at the same time the powerful determination arose within him to follow in his grandfather's footsteps and cast off the shackles of the world once and for all.

Naren was careful not to reveal his intention of renouncing the world to anyone at the time, not even to Sri Ramakrishna. But when the day arrived on which he had secretly vowed to take up the robes of the renunciate, the Master himself showed up unexpectedly at his home and asked Naren to accompany him to Dakshineswar. They left together by carriage, soon arriving at the temple where Ramakrishna passed into an ecstatic mood. Suddenly, he gripped Naren's hand. With tears pouring freely down his cheeks, he sang a familiar *bhajan*. Ostensibly it represented Krishna's words of love for Radha. But Naren knew that the plaintive lyrics referred to him alone: "I am afraid to speak, I am afraid not to speak, for the fear rises in my mind that I shall lose you" (R.D., p. 213).

Naren struggled in vain to stem the rising tide of his own tears. When they burst forth in a torrent, some devotees who were present asked what the matter was. Ramakrishna smiled knowingly. "It's just something between the two of us," he replied (R.D., p. 213). Later on that evening, after the others had left, the Master confided to Naren in private: "I know you have come to the world for the Mother's work; you can never lead a worldly life. But, for my sake, stay with your family as long as I'm alive" (R.D., p. 213).

Naren gave Sri Ramakrishna his pledge to stay. Soon thereafter, he did succeed in finding temporary work as a translator in various law offices. This provided a measure of relief to his hard-pressed family. But the employment was sporadic. At best, it allowed for a hand-to-mouth existence that was hardly much more secure or comfortable than before. The oppressive burden of poverty, the sheer uncertainty of not knowing where the next meal was coming from, weighed heavily on Naren and he finally appealed in desperation for Sri Ramakrishna to pray to Kali for his family's welfare. But the Master countered with the suggestion that Naren pray himself. "You don't accept the Mother. That is why you suffer so much,"[1] he revealed, and then he added pointedly that the Mother was sure to grant whatever Naren asked of Her directly.

Naren had faith in the Master's words, and went to the temple fully intending to pray for his family. However, as he stood before the imposing figure within the inner sanctum, it was as if he were struck dumb. Kali appeared vividly before him as a living presence. And in that exalted presence, he forgot all about his Brahmo prejudices against idol worship. Incredibly, he also forgot why he had come. Instead of imploring the Mother to grant him financial security, as he had intended, Naren prayed fervently for the spiritual wealth of detachment, love, and wisdom. When he returned to Ramakrishna and revealed what had happened, the Master sent him back to try again. But just as before, Naren's intention to pray for the welfare of his family melted tracelessly from his mind in the dazzling presence of the Universal Mother. Only on the third attempt did he finally manage to recollect his purpose in coming. But this time as he stood before Kali, the thought of asking for material benefits seemed so mean and small-minded ("Like being graciously received by a king and then asking for gourds and pumpkins," (R.D., p. 214)

Naren later recalled) that his shame prevented him from uttering a single word of the prayer.

When he returned again to Ramakrishna, however, the strangeness of his own reactions in the Kali temple struck Naren forcibly. It occurred to him that he must have been been tricked by Ramakrishna, and he argued with the Master that, since he had intoxicated him and made him incapable of praying as he had intended, it was his responsibility to do the praying for him. At first Ramakrishna resisted, saying that he was no more capable than Naren had been of begging Kali for worldly favors. But Naren pursued him and Ramakrishna finally relented. "All right," he agreed, "they will never lack plain food and clothing" (R.D., p. 215). This promise proved accurate. For all their financial problems, Naren's family never again went hungry.

Perhaps the most significant thing about this incident is that it marks the beginning of Naren's acceptance of Kali after ridiculing Her for so long. And it is interesting to note that, just as with Totapuri, it was the experience of suffering and the resulting realization of the impotence of the personal will to achieve its ends that finally drove Naren into the Mother's waiting arms. It was a chastening experience for Naren to discover that his own best efforts were not enough to insure the well-being of his family. Fate had gifted Naren with an iron will and abundant personal power. But fate had also been gracious enough in the end to show him that there was a still greater will and more potent power against which even his own daunting energy could not prevail. In his extremity, Naren had no other recourse than to cry out to that great Shakti for help and deliverance.

If Naren came to Kali in distress, though, he stayed on in love. He soon discovered, as Ramakrishna had before him, the ineffable sweetness of addressing God intimately as Mother.

Naren spent the rest of the night singing a hymn that Ramakrishna had taught him, "Mother, You are the Savior." The following morning, the Master was overjoyed, just like a little child. To a visitor who happened upon the scene, he pointed to the sleeping Naren and said, "Narendra has accepted Kali. That's very good, isn't it?" And then gaily he repeated again to no one in particular, "Narendra has accepted the Mother. It's very good. What do you say?" (R.D., p. 215).

Chapter 12

The Market of Joy

From a lone figure calling plaintively from the rooftop for sincere devotees of God to gather around him, Ramakrishna had been transformed in a few short years into the busy focus of a rapidly expanding brood of kindred souls. "When the Lotus blooms, the bees come of their own accord," (T.S., p. xiii) the Master was fond of saying. And the maxim certainly proved true of Ramakrishna. They surged hungrily to him from all walks of life, and they represented every conceivable spiritual point of view—believers in the formless God, devotees of Vishnu and of Shakti, Christians and Brahmos, dogmatic religionists and radical freethinkers. If you had asked them why they were there, you would have gotten as many different answers as there were visitors. But in a sense all the reasons boiled down to one reason alone—the bees had come for the nectar. And in that quest none went away disappointed.

There were pious young boys like Hari Nath Chaterjee (the future Swami Turiyananda), who at age fourteen, during an encounter on the streets of Calcutta, was struck dumb by the indescribable radiance of the Master's face. There were distinguished pundits, men of massive dignity like Vidyasagar, who found his long years of scholarship confounded and enlightened by a living wisdom infinitely beyond the dry logic of books. And there were simple day laborers and lawyers, mendicants and poets. There were inspired lovers of God like Gopala Ma, an orthodox widow who was blessed for a time with the almost continual vision of the child Krishna, her chosen deity. There were also celebrated men of the world like Girish Chandra Ghosh, the founding genius of modern Bengali theater and a notorious bohemian whose dissolute ways gradually evaporated in the gentle sunshine of Ramakrishna's patient and all-forgiving love.

Frequently on weekends and holidays, the Master's simple dwelling would overflow with eager refugees from the stressful rounds of Calcutta. These spirited gatherings had none of the gravity or self-conscious holiness of religious groups like the Brahmo Samaj. Instead, the atmosphere was relaxed, the mood warm and festive. Joy was the hallmark—pure, cleansing, and uplifting—a joy as refreshingly different from the ordinary pleasures of the world as nectar is from brackish sea water, to use one of the Master's own graphic analogies. The divine nectar of true spiritual joy satiates even the thirsts one didn't know one had whereas, Sri Ramakrishna always insisted, the salt water of ordinary sensual pleasures, though appearing to offer refreshment, actually exacerbates the thirst that it is taken to quench. It does not, of course, follow that all will choose the nectar!

To be sure, the rare and subtle nectar of God-communion that Ramakrishna served up often proved tasteless to those of grosser appetites. Others came to savor it only gradually over time, while still others found it offensively cloying from the start. And so, paradoxically, while many devout souls enjoyed a veritable "market of joy," a foretaste of heaven on earth, others were unmoved or even made uncomfortable by the ardent atmosphere at Dakshineswar. It is a mystery of the diversity called man—one pilgrim might be agape with the vision of a radiant saint pulsing with God-consciousness, while the fellow sitting next to him might be seeing only a gaunt scarecrow prattling on like a moonstruck child about his Divine Mother. To the worldly devotee of "woman and gold," this unassuming devotee of Kali could only have seemed a comic figure, a country bumpkin, not without a certain charm—but laughably naive, if not deluded or worse.

The contemporary sage Neem Karoli Baba used to say that when a pickpocket sees a saint he sees only his pockets. It follows that when a man whose heart has been completely given over to the pursuit of worldly pleasures sees a man of God he notices only those things to which his desire system has sensitized him— power, status, outward polish, and sophistication. Well, no one could have accused Ramakrishna of sophistication. And it was certainly the case that the fat and satisfied Calcutta babus, worshipers of mammon and everything English, would find nothing to detain them at Dakshineswar. If they came once, they would certainly not make the same mistake twice!

But many others did return for a second look—or perhaps it would be more to the point to say that they were powerless to keep away. Just what exactly it was that lured them back they themselves might have been unable to explain. But whether comprehended or not, the pervasive magic could not fail to work on them. For Ramakrishna's destined spiritual children, Dakshineswar quite simply felt like home. And Sri Ramakrishna seemed strangely familiar, an intimate companion of the distant past whom one cannot quite place. This curious spiritual déjà vu—the feeling not merely of "having been there before," but in some primal way of belonging there "from the beginning of time," as it were—was shared by many of those who ventured to the Dakshineswar temple for the first time.

A revered miracle-working contemporary of Sri Ramakrishna, the enigmatic fakir Sai Baba of Shirdi in central India, once likened his devotees to birds with strings tied to their legs. When the moment became ripe for one of them to come to Shirdi for the first time, the great Baba asserted that he would simply reel in the string which he had held in his hands all along. Sai Baba's analogy, apart from describing the occult relationship between guru and disciple, which is said to span many lifetimes and to have transcended the ordinary constraints of space and time, captures the subjective experience of the aspirant who meets his Master for the first time. What the devotee realizes at that moment—not rationally, not even consciously, but viscerally—is that he has been tied to this remarkable being in whose presence he suddenly finds himself all of his life, if not longer, by an invisible cord of the spirit. It is as though he were Plato's caveman existing in a dim and mysterious twilight world. All along, he has dwelled in the very shadow of the Master's radiance without ever having looked upon it directly. And now, in a moment's turning, he gazes for the first time at the sun.

This brilliant access of revelation, instead of seeming strange or fantastic, has the savor of inevitability about it, like waking from a dream into a greater reality which immediately strikes one as obvious, self-evident. The aspirant who one day discovered himself in the Master's presence at Dakshineswar was not surprised at it. He sensed that he was in that place toward which his steps had been leading, unknowingly, all along. It was not so much that he had awakened as that he had arrived at long last at the place he was meant to be.

This sense of long-awaited fulfillment was most clearly experienced by the future monastic disciples of Sri Ramakrishna. Like Rakhal and Naren, these young men were all, to one degree or another, psychic exiles from a higher and purer realm who felt themselves to be in the world but not of it. Each in his own way had been groping for the spiritual direction that would lift him from out of the twilight realm of shadows, in which he knew himself at heart a stranger, and back into the light of his True Self. Each had been knocking on the Mother's door, knocking so long and monotonously that he might well have forgotten why he was knocking, or even—like one entranced—that he was knocking at all. In most cases, he would have all but given up hope of ever getting a response. But, no matter. At midnight of the dark night of the soul, the door is suddenly flung open. In a flash, a being with beautiful, smiling eyes is beckoning graciously for him to enter. Sri Ramakrishna is greeting him with a joyous gaze, as a mother greets her long lost son, and he knows intuitively that he has returned home. Such is the timeless poetry of meeting the guru. But it is a poetry which was real enough for those who have lived it. The wide-eyed thrill of this initial contact is nicely captured in the account of Hari Prassana Chaterjee, the future Swami Vijnananda:

> I felt in Ramakrishna's room a tangible atmosphere of peace. The devotees present seemed to be listening in blissful absorption to the words which poured from the Master's lips. I don't recall what he said, but I still remember the

transport of delight I experienced then as if it were yester-
day. For a long while I sat there, besides myself with joy, and
my whole attention was concentrated on Sri Ramakrishna.
He did not say anything to me, nor did I ask him anything.
One by one the devotees took their leave, and suddenly I
found myself alone with him. Sri Ramakrishna was looking
at me intently. I thought it was time to depart, so I prostrated
before him. As I stood up to go, he asked, "Can you wrestle?
Come, let me see how well you wrestle!" With these words
he stood up ready to grapple with me. I was very much
surprised at this kind of challenge. I thought to myself,
"What kind of holy man is this?" Anyhow, I replied, "Yes,
of course I can wrestle."

Sri Ramakrishna came closer, with a smile on his lips.
He caught hold of my arm and began to shove me. But I was
a muscular young man, and pushed him back to the wall. He
was still smiling and holding me with a strong grip. Gradually I felt a sort of electric current coming out of his hands
and entering into me. That touch made me completely helpless; I lost all my physical strength. I went into ecstasy, and
the hair on my body stood on end. Then Ramakrishna let
me go. He said, smiling, "Well, you are the winner." (R.D.,
pp. 236–37)

Typically, the Master sat cross-legged on a small wooden
cot placed just in front of the larger bed on which he slept; these
were the only items of furniture in the austere but spacious room.
The devotees approached his quarters through the temple court-
yard, often pausing briefly on the way to pay their respects to the
Mother Kali. Entering Sri Ramakrishna's room, they would prostrate before him in the Hindu fashion, perhaps offering some fruit
or a handful of sacred betel leaves or milk-sweets as the prescribed
ritual gift to a holy man, before sitting down on grass mats placed
upon the floor to listen to the conversation.

The whitewashed walls of the room were bare except for the
colorful pictures of various incarnations and Gods—among them,
Sri Chaitanya and Nityananda (the medieval Bengali prophets of
bhakti yoga), the Divine Mother Kali, and a small print of Christ
rescuing Peter from the sea. Incense was burned daily before

these images, and crimson *kumkum* powder, emblematic of the Divine Mother, was smeared on the glass frames as a token of worship. The room had high ceilings and was bright and airy, with grated windows and large wooden doors opening out onto a colonnaded veranda.

From the veranda, one could look toward the luxuriant temple garden, or out over the vast liquid expanse of the Ganges, whose concrete embankment lay just a few yards below. It was a restful, timeless landscape, but full of life, movement, and color. In season there were fantastic dream castles of cloud, turning brilliantly in the tropical sun, metamorphizing as they scudded in off the Bay of Bengal. The heavy scents of jasmine, gardenia, and rose mixed with the river breezes. And the bright air echoed with the calls of fishermen, the solemn chanting of the priests, the cries of noisy flocks of parrot and doves, the high-pitched call of egrets, and the endless chatter of innumerable small birds. Sparrows, seemingly oblivious to human presence, flitted freely about on the floor of Ramakrishna's room in search of a single grain of rice or sugar. Chameleons lay in motionless vigil on the plastered walls, waiting interminably for a stray insect to wander their way. Now and again, a toad could be seen huddling pensively in a corner. The doors generally stayed open all day long. And all day—and often well into the night—man and beast entered freely and left freely, forming a swirling slow-motion tide of life and yearning around the serenely seated figure of Ramakrishna.

Ramakrishna sat on his simple cot as a king on his throne. He was a true king of the devotees, a child-king presiding over a daily court of love. But no monarch could have been less affected by the fealty and honors showered upon him. Visitors were impressed immediately with how utterly without egotism, or the least hint of self-consciousness, was this little poor man of God. You couldn't have guessed from his manner or appearance that he was the revered guru of so many. Except during the cool months of winter, he remained half-naked, with only a plain cotton cloth wound loosely around his waist. He was thin, at times almost to the point of looking emaciated, and brown-skinned, with a short, scraggly beard of mixed black and silver. Most remarkable were his eyes, piercing and yet kindly, bright

and laughing. Often those eyes remained half-shut, as if Ramakrishna were at one and the same time gazing inward toward the
depths of the Self and outward at the devotees assembled before
him.

Both in physical appearance and manner, Ramakrishna was
simplicity itself. No one could have been more unassuming or less
bothered with making an impression on others. He seemed all but
unconscious of the great power that flowed through him to those
gathered at the foot of his cot. In a boyish zeal, inspired insights
would bubble out as pure water from a spring—lightly, joyously,
and without effort or strain. His musical speech lacked preten-
sion, or any attempt to convert or even to persuade his listeners.
In a fundamental sense, he was not even aware of having listeners.
He spoke to the other who was not an "other" at all, but an
extension of his own Self. And he never felt he was telling you
anything that you didn't already know, deep inside. This conviction lent an extraordinary intimacy to his talk.

Ramakrishna was, by nature, incapable of holding himself
aloof. From the moment a newcomer arrived, the Master would
be chatting with a transparent sincerity. Invariably, after the
briefest civilities, the conversation would turn to God and devotion; everything else seemed insipid to him. It was not unusual
that within minutes Ramakrishna would be taking a perfect
stranger into his confidence, speaking of his most intimate visions
and other spiritual experiences in the same easy manner that
others talk about the weather or the price of a loaf of bread—but
always without a hint of pride or boasting. Like the child of God
he was, the Master would say, "Mother showed me this. . . .
Mother told me. . . . Mother revealed. . . ."

At times during such talk, the Master would fall spontaneously into a peculiar absentminded state. The chronicler "M"
(Mahendra Nath Gupta) compared these moods to the condition
of a fisherman who has just felt a tug on the line. The angler is
"alert . . . he grips the rod . . . he will not speak to anyone." (G.S.,
p. 78) This deep transport of spiritual feeling is referred to as
bhava samadhi in the language of yoga. Again there were times
when Ramakrishna would suddenly enter an unseen world of
vision and start talking to Kali as if She were standing right by

his cot: "Hello, Mother! I see that You too have come. How You are showing off Your Benares sari! Don't bother me now, please. Sit down and be quiet." (G.S., p. 319) It happened so naturally and without ceremony that one would hardly have imagined that anything out of the ordinary were occurring. But in a sense, that made it all the more startling.

Some reacted, as Naren had at first, with a vague sense of pity for the deluded, if cheerful, son of a peasant. Others were touched with awe. But however one regarded Ramakrishna's visions and ecstasies, it was plain to see that they were intensely real to him. Here was a man for whom the Divine Mother of the universe existed so tangibly, so personally, as to actually take visible form before him. Here was someone who chatted and joked with God, someone whose earthy faith in spirit had compelled spirit to clothe itself in sensible earth. It was a faith that clearly formed a seamless garment with his life, a faith that had shattered forever the barrier between "this world" and the "other world," and had bridged the gulf between the human and the Divine. All of the usual dualities, between which men spend their lives uncomfortably suspended, had become reconciled in Sri Ramakrishna's case, and what remained, at the level of his personality, was a unity—an absolute correspondence of thought with word, word with deed, aspiration with realization.

Even the skeptics couldn't help but admire the integrity of the man. It was a marvel how patently different this *brahmin* priest was from the "great men" of the world. In a society where posturing and facade often took precedence over genuine feeling, here was someone whose every emotion was reflected sensitively in his fluid features, whose every thought found instantaneous expression in speech. "The Mother has put me in such a state that I can't hide anything from anyone," (G.S., p. 390) Ramakrishna once stated. And at every moment he was giving fresh evidence of that central law of his being.

Recognizing Ramakrishna's transcendent artlessness, the devotees bestowed upon him the title of *paramahamsa* (literally, "great swan"), which refers to the holy man who swims freely and joyously upon the waves of the world without being in any way stained by them. The *paramahamsa* often flaunts the conventions of society; sometimes he is flamboyantly eccentric, acting like a ghoul or a madman, or even remaining insensible as a clod of earth; Ramakrishna claimed that this behavior was sometimes on account of the intensity of divine emotions, and at other times merely a ruse to discourage the unwelcome attention of curiosity seekers. Often the *paramahamsa*, in his undefended openness to the reality around him, resembles most of all a young child. The Master recounted how certain spiritually advanced souls, in aspiring to the station of the *paramahamsa*, would associate with children in order to absorb directly something of their natural spontaneity, much as the Hasidic masters of eastern Europe would stop and question youngsters in the streets in order to cull untainted wisdom from their lips. Ramakrishna described the childlike sublimity of the true *paramahamsa* from his own experience:

> The *paramahamsa* is like a five-year-old child. He sees everything as filled with Consciousness. At one time I was staying at Kamarpukur when Shivaram [Ramakrishna's nephew] was four or five years old. One day he was trying to catch grasshoppers near the pond. The leaves were moving. To stop their rustling he said to the leaves: "Hush! Hush! I want to catch a grasshopper." Another day it was stormy and rained hard. . . . When Shivaram saw the lightning, he exclaimed, "There uncle! They are striking matches again!"
>
> The *paramahamsa* is like a child. He can't distinguish between a stranger and a relative. He isn't particular about worldly relationships. . . . He doesn't keep track of his whereabouts. He wanders here and there without concern. . . . He sees everything as Brahman." (G.S., pp. 490–91)

Certainly, Ramakrishna fit his own description better than anyone. A boyhood friend from Kamarpukur, who visited Dakshineswar toward the end of the Master's life, was amazed to find his old companion exactly as he had remembered him. It was as if time had frozen in its tracks for Ramakrishna alone. Despite the invading gray hair and lined skin, all the mannerisms, all the playfulness, all the irrepressible and mischievous energy of the ten-year-old Gadadhar were still there virtually unchanged. Now he laughed, now he wept, now he sang, now he danced, now he spoke rapturously of God.

But if a visitor praised him for his childlike devotion, he only laughed. Far be it from Ramakrishna to try to impress anyone; the opinions of men counted for little. Only the Mother's approval mattered—which is not to say that he tried to impress the Mother either! You didn't try to impress the Mother—how absurd! How could a Mother fail to be impressed by her own child? There was nothing one had to *prove* to Her; there was nothing that one had to merit by virtue of good deeds and devotion, so far as Ramakrishna was concerned. Intimacy with the Mother wasn't something one earned; it came with birth as a sacred trust. We have only to lay our claim to it by calling out to Her for the affection which is rightfully ours.

The Master offered the analogy of an infant who is given colorful toys to play with. So long as it is occupied with these baubles, the Mother leaves the child to play to its heart's content. But the moment it tires of them and cries out for the Mother Herself to come, then She abandons everything and rushes over to take the infant into Her arms, embracing and kissing it. In the same way, the Divine Mother has given us the beguiling toys of Her material creation to play with. But the moment they lose their fascination and we cry out for God, our Divine Mother, She rushes to take us up firmly in the embrace of undying Oneness. Sri Ramakrishna's point is that, whether we are aware of it or not, the Divine Mother is with us even now. She waits patiently to give us everything we sincerely desire. And, more than anything, She longs to give Herself. But She refuses to impose on our freedom. She gives us only what we ourselves demand of Her.

Ramakrishna knew better than anyone that there are infinite ways to approach God, the Divine Mother. It all depends on what you are seeking from Her. Those craving mercy approach Her as a defendant approaches an all-powerful judge pleading for forgiveness. Those craving material benefits approach Her as a customer approaches a merchant, bargaining for a more advantageous deal. Those seeking heaven present themselves like a job candidate armed with a resume of good deeds and worthy virtues. But for those who desire none of the things She offers, but who crave only the Mother Herself, groveling in the dust and begging and whining to be given what is ours by divine birthright seems not only demeaning, but self-defeating.

"God is our Father and Mother, isn't He?" the Master insisted. "Therefore, we should force our demands on God. If the son calls for his patrimony and gives up food and drink as a means to enforce his demand, then the parents hand his share over to him three years before his legal time" (G.S., pp. 96–97). Man fancies himself a slave, but in reality he is a prince; each of us is heir to the highest throne of all, according to Ramakrishna. However, through the veiling power of delusion we have forgotten our high ancestry and have come to accept our degraded condition as natural, ceasing to aspire for the one great consummation that life has to offer us.

Ramakrishna likened our situation to that of a tiger cub brought up by lambs. Before long the young tiger is bleating, eating grass, and even thinking of itself as a meek and helpless lamb. But when a grown tiger arrives on the scene and drags the frightened young beast to a pond, it sees for the very first time its true reflection in the still waters and awakens instantly to its true nature.

Ramakrishna was like that mature tiger awakening us to our tiger nature. His teachings in *The Gospel of Sri Ramakrishna* fill over a thousand pages. But the more we read these words, the greater becomes the conviction that they amount to many different ways of saying the same thing. "Wake up!" Ramakrishna seems to be insisting over and over again. "You are not what you think you are. The kingdom of God's joy is within you. Realize it. Throw off the shackles of narrow selfhood and know yourself to be a blissful child of God!" The stirring echoes of this credo reach us powerfully in the exhaustive transcripts "M" compiled. Nevertheless, we can't fail to sense, as we pore through them, how much of the impact of Ramakrishna's words lies between the lines, how much of it is untranslatable—a matter of a gesture, a sigh, a look of liquid fire. From the many descriptive hints that "M" gives us, however, we can reconstruct something of what it must have been like to sit in the Master's presence and listen to his incandescent words of love.

When Ramakrishna spoke, his tongue appeared to trip over itself in an innocent eagerness to express himself; at times there was the hint of a stammer. He spoke ungrammatically, confusing the formal and familiar "you," as if the distinction meant nothing to one who perceived God equally present in all beings. To sensitive ears, Ramakrishna's conversation could seem crude or at times vulgar; he didn't shrink from speaking frankly of acts and parts of the body not generally referred to in polite conversation. Legend has it that the worldly-wise Girish Chandra Ghosh once unknowingly uttered a profanity within Ramakrishna's hearing range, only to apologize profusely when he realized that his guru was there beside him. Undaunted, and with the amused purity of a small child, Sri Ramakrishna proceeded to run through a formidable recitation of, it seemed, every vulgar expression in the Bengali language. Girish was visibly overwhelmed. Bowing reverently before the Master, the renowned playwright exclaimed in awe: "Well, it seems that you are my guru and my better in this department as well!"

In all things, Ramakrishna was accustomed to speaking his mind without inhibition. He didn't stop to weigh his words. They flowed out in pure ecstatic excess. They flooded over his listeners, enveloped them, awakened them. When he uttered even the most familiar truths of religion, they sounded fresh and vital, as if one were hearing them for the very first time. He gave freely of his knowledge with the artless generosity of a child sharing a handful of berries with his best friend; he never preached. Even when dealing with the most profound verities, the Master wasn't in the least bit sanctimonious or solemn.

The sheer impact that his words could have is beautifully conveyed by Sri Ramakrishna's account of his meeting with one of the most celebrated pundits of Bengal:

> When I first heard that the pundit was coming, I got frightened. After all, I'm not even conscious of the cloth that I'm wearing. I had no idea how I was going to reply to his questions. I said to the Mother, "Apart from You I don't know anything, I am completely ignorant of these scriptures and other matters." So I told the people here, "You just stay where you are. I'll feel encouraged by your presence."

When the pundit finally arrived, I was still a bit nervous. I sat quietly gazing at him and listening to him. Just then I saw the entire contents of the pundit's mind revealed to me by the Mother. What is the use of reading the scriptures if one has no discrimination or dispassion? There [Ramakrishna pointed at his own body] I felt something creeping up to the head. All my fear was gone and my self-consciousness vanished. I raised my head and words began to flow from my mouth. I felt as if someone were replenishing my thoughts as I spoke them. At Kamarpukur when people measured out grain, one person would be pushing the grain forward as another measured it out. It was like that. I myself didn't know what I was saying. When I recovered external consciousness a little, I saw the pundit weeping and his body soaked with tears. (S.R., pp. 320–321)

We shall never know what Ramakrishna told the pundit on that day. But in a sense, what he said doesn't matter. The significance would not have been anything that a pale transcript could have captured. A great holy woman of twentieth-century India, the Jillellamudi Mother, once said that even profound words of wisdom, when they are uttered by the ignorant, become just more words of ignorance. The corollary is that wise words, spoken by one who has fully assimilated their essence, have a potency all their own, which goes far beyond the mere verbal formula. So it was with Sri Ramakrishna's words to the pundit—their efficacy would not have come from the uniqueness of the thought, or the artifice of the expression. It is unlikely that the Master told him anything that he had not heard or read in scripture countless times before. Rather, the patent authority and ring of impersonal truth, the overwhelming power that the words conveyed, was vital. And as evidence of that power, the pundit's tears are more eloquent than any words.

The Master looked upon himself as a mouthpiece; he never felt personally responsible for the expressions of Truth that coursed through him. If the learned men who came to Dakshineswar were amazed at the profundities uttered by an unschooled village *brahmin*, then Ramakrishna himself was not any less amazed. He once asserted: "You know I am a fool. I know nothing. Then who is it that says all of these things? I say to the

Mother, 'Oh Mother, I am the machine and You are the operator. I am the chariot and You are the charioteer. . . . I do as You make me do. I speak as You make me speak. . . . It is not I! It is not I! It is Thou! It is Thou!' " (G.S., p. 891).

Or as he affirmed: "Rain-water falling on the roof of a house flows down to the ground through the spouts shaped grotesquely like tigers' heads. One gets the impression that the water comes from out of the tiger's mouth, but in reality it comes from the sky. In the same way the holy teachings that come from the mouths of Godly men seem to be uttered by those men themselves, while in reality they proceed from God." (S.R., p. 75)

Of course, those who conceive a God locked in an eternal, chilly silence, light years away from any concern for the infinitely petty affairs of earth (which He presumably abandoned as soon as He created it), will find this idea hard to credit. Some assert that God is silent, and that He speaks to man, if at all, only through His silence. But Ramakrishna surely wouldn't have agreed. Ramakrishna's whole life was a dialogue, and God spoke to him continuously—through the beauty of the world, through the aspirations of his heart, through friends and events, through dreams and visions. And not least of all, God spoke to him through the words of holy men. For he was firmly convinced that God, not only speaks *to* man but also *through* man, indeed that God speaks through the voice of every man who renounces his small self in order to live in the boundlessness of the life divine.

However, the question can be asked, if it is a fact that Truth is utterly beyond the range of verbal expression, as the sages unanimously testify, then why do these same sages speak about sacred things at all? Why don't all who have experienced the Ineffable maintain a wise silence, as Trailanga Swami of Benares and countless other silent sages in the many spiritual traditions of the world have done?

Ramakrishna once hinted, with characteristic wit, at an answer: "After the vision of Brahman, a man becomes silent. He reasons about *It* only so long as he has not realized *It*. The bee buzzes so long as it is not sitting on the flower. It becomes silent when it begins to sip the honey. But then again, sometimes intoxicated by the honey it buzzes again." (G.S., p. 103)

Presumably, Ramakrishna's intoxicated bee doesn't buzz so

as to describe the nectar, but rather to rejoice in it and to attract his bee comrades to the sweet feast. Similarly the holy man who speaks after the attainment of his goal doesn't do so with the intention of snaring that ever-elusive bird of Truth in the net of words. He speaks in order to urge his fellows on. It is as if he were saying, "Look, there is something wonderful here. Now you come and experience it for yourself!"

Ramakrishna explained what impels certain great souls to teach, in the following way:

> There are two classes of *paramahamsas,* one affirming the formless Reality and the other affirming God with form. . . . *Paramahamsas* [who believe in the formless reality] are only concerned with their own attainment of the goal. They are not interested in guiding others. But those *paramahamsas* who believe in God with form keep the love of God even after attaining the Knowledge of Brahman, so that they may teach spiritual truth to others. They are like a pitcher brimful of water. A portion of the water can be poured into another pitcher. These perfected souls describe to others the various spiritual disciplines by which they have realized God. They do this only to teach others and to help them in spiritual life. With great effort men dig a well for drinking water, using spades and baskets for the purpose. After the work is complete, some throw the spades and other implements into the well, not needing them anymore. But some place them near the well so that others may use them. (G.S., p. 500)

From this we can understand that the saint speaks in order to offer up practical tools for living a spiritual life, rather than with the intention of communicating the Truth beyond words. Even if he tries to communicate that Truth, there is simply no way for him to satisfactorily translate his highest experiences into words.

The Master learned this lesson the hard way. Once, noticing the upward surge of the *kundalini* force through his body, Sri Ramakrishna resolved to share the wonderful experience with his devotees by giving a running account as it took place. He succeeded well enough in describing his changing mental and physical sensations until the rising energy reached the throat center (the *visudha chakra,* the fifth of the seven psychic centers arrayed along the spinal column). At that moment, Ramakrishna's running commentary broke off suddenly in midsentence, and his body became stiff in wordless rapture. The experiment was over—or was it?

When after a time he returned to an awareness of his surroundings, the Master felt dejected by this failure. Ramakrishna, as we have seen, had no taste for secrets. The experience of *samadhi,* moreover, was something so marvelous that it seemed unconscionable to keep it selfishly to oneself. Burning to communicate the rapture to his devotees, he stubbornly determined to try again. But when the inevitable happened, and the second and even a third attempt to utter the unutterable ended as abruptly as the first, it finally dawned on him that nature was not about to be cheated. Sri Ramakrishna burst into anguished tears. "Well I sincerely want to tell you everything," he confessed. "But Mother won't let me. She gags me and I am unable to say a single word!" (L.R., p. 141)

Perhaps the Master was thinking of this ill-fated experiment when he remarked, "Once a salt doll went to measure the depth of the sea. It wanted to tell others how deep the water was. But it could never do so, because no sooner did it get into the water than it melted away. Now who was there to report the ocean's depth?" (N.p., n.d.)

Still, this crowning experience literally demands some sort of expression. If one can't speak of it, one stammers it, if one can't stammer, one grunts, if one can't grunt, one gestures wildly. The sheer impossibility of it hardly deters the pilgrim on fire with God from struggling to convey a taste of his own higher spiritual experiences to his companions. And since words—stiff, ungainly, one-dimensional artifacts that they are—prove peculiarly ill-suited as a medium for communicating the fluid bliss of the spirit, Sri Ramakrishna often turned to song.

Hardly an hour would pass but the atmosphere of the room by the Ganges would thicken with the hypnotic strains of Bengali devotional music—songs at once seductive and electrifying, with heady, spiraling melodies so distinct in tone from the solemn religious hymns of the West. On occasion, troupes of professional musicians were on hand to pay their respects to Sri Ramakrishna.

But more often it was the devotees themselves who sang in chorus the rhythmic praises of Shiva and Krishna and Kali, beating small kettle drums, clanging cymbals, and playing a variety of Indian stringed instruments—the livelier and more passionately the better, so far as Ramakrishna was concerned. These soaring *kirtanas* never failed to kindle in the devotees a high state of spiritual fervor.

If any hesitated to join in, the Master would protest: "One can't be spiritual as long as one has shame. . . . Great will be the joy today. But the fools who won't sing and dance, mad with God's name, will never attain Him. How can one feel any shame or fear when the names of God are sung? Now sing, all of you!" (G.S., p. 186).

Frequently, Ramakrishna himself would break into one of his favorite *bhajans*. The Master was endowed with a voice of unearthly sweetness and force, which seemed at times the very garment of his ecstasy. One couldn't help but be struck by it. It was as if a door had swung open momentarily through which one could glimpse the glowing furnace of the Master's love for God.

Sometimes, Ramakrishna sang in order to drive home a point. When the wealthy householder devotee Mani Mallick came to the Master shattered by the loss of his beloved son, Ramakrishna responded with a rousing goad to faith:

> To arms! To arms! Oh man, death invades your home in
>   battle array
> Get up into the chariot of faith, and arm yourself with the
>   quiver of wisdom
> Draw the mighty bow of love, and hurl, hurl the divine
>   arrow, the holy name of the Mother!
> (T.L.R., p. 217)

This martial chant had a wonderfully stimulating effect on the bereaved father, restoring his courage in a way that pious words alone would have been unable to accomplish.

Not that Ramakrishna needed any such excuse to sing. Does a bird need an excuse to sing? Still less a saint! Generally, there was no calculation; Ramakrishna didn't *choose* to sing—he was chosen by song. Song gushed out of him without warning like molten rock from a fissure. The lyrics were rapturous:

Is Kali, my Mother, really black?
The Naked One of darkest hue
Lights the Lotus of my heart.
(G.S., p. 486)

Swept up in the mood, everything else vanished—message and motive, rhyme and reason. Song became a raw force of nature, a whirlwind, a sudden beating flurry of inspiration on the wings of the heart. And on the wings of song Ramakrishna would soar to ever-fresh heights of intoxication. Inevitably, he brought many along with him; those who were present at such moments were surprised to find themselves powerfully caught up in the updraft of inspiration which Ramakrishna had unloosed upon the gathering.

On occasion, the Master would improvise words on the spot. But more often, he sang the well-known *bhajans*, adaptations of poems by revered Hindu saints of the past. Conversational and direct in tone, these lyrics are veritable catalogs of *bhakti* yoga. Most were composed during the great medieval flowering of devotionalism in the vernacular Hindi and Bengali, rather than in the Sanskrit of the pundits; they are even today an enormously popular heritage of that most democratic of all creeds, the people's religion of love, in which fervor is more important than scholarship, and yearning greater than ritual:

How are you trying, O my mind, to know the nature of
    God?
You are groping like a madman in a dark room
He is grasped through ecstatic love; how can you fathom
    Him without it?
(G.S., p. 107)

The songs Ramakrishna rendered again and again offer us a revealing window into his own spiritual ideals. They portray a God who, like Krishna, the sweetheart of the *gopis*, is simulta-

neously the eternal lover of each and every soul—a God who, to
appearances, can be every bit as elusive, jealous, even mischievous
as a human lover, but a God whose heart is tender at the core,
soft like wax, melting utterly from the least heat of genuine
devotion, a God who cares little about external actions and much
about the inward disposition of the heart. Above all, they represent a God who can be approached freely and without fear almost
as an equal—a God, moreover, who doesn't wait to be approached, but who Himself approaches man begging for his love:

> Oh, no one has found out who He is
> Like a madman He roams from door to door
> Like a beggar He roams from door to door.
> (G.S., p. 826)

Among Ramakrishna's favorite *bhajans* were those of the
Bengali poet devotee of the Divine Mother, Ram Prasad, whose
lyrical and insistent invocations of Kali had made such a deep
impression on the young Gadadhar at Kamarpukur:

> This bitterly contested suit between the Mother and Her
>   son—
> What sport it is! says Ram Prasad. I shall not cease torment-
>   ing You
> Till You Yourself shall yield the fight and take me in your
>   arms at last.
> (G.S., p. 613)

But Ramakrishna didn't restrict himself to Kali. He often
sang of Radha's incomparable love for Krishna, which he regarded as an ideal of the unwavering vision that sees in all the
world nothing but the divine Beloved. As one of the *bhajans* has
Radha telling her companions:

> To you my Krishna is nothing but a name
> But to me He is the anguish of my heart
> You hear His flute's song only with your ears
> But, oh, how it resounds within my deepest soul!
> (G.S., p. 613)

The Master was also fond of the enraptured lyrics of the great Vaishnava revival:

> Oh when will dawn that blessed day
> When tears of joy will flow from my eyes
> As I repeat Lord Hari's name?
> Oh when will dawn that blessed day
> when all my craving for the world
> Will vanish straightway from my heart
> And with the thrill of His holy name
> All my hair will stand on end?
> Oh, when will come that blessed day?
> (G.S., pp. 315–16)

The bald lyrics can be conveyed, but not the pathos and the fire, still less the contagious effect that singing them in the Master's presence could have—a blessed contagion for which Ramakrishna invariably strove. His ideal in music was active, never passive. The success of a *kirtana* was not in its technical rendering but in its fervor. The *kirtana* needed to be moving, even in the most physical sense: "Music should be so alive as to make everyone get up and dance!" (N.p., n.d.) the Master insisted. But, if the ultimate end of devotional music was dance, then the end of dance was stillness. For the final stage of rapturous movement overtaking itself is the transcendent stillness of *bhava samadhi*.

Frequently, as he danced with the devotees forming a circle around him, the Master would suddenly freeze in place, his eyes becoming fixed and glazed over, his lips parted and slightly upturned into a beatific smile which suffused his countenance with a palpable glow of joy. At such times, if Sri Ramakrishna were not immediately supported, there was every danger of him crumpling on the spot like a spent marionette. To prevent Ramakrishna from injuring himself in this way, a devotee always followed at his side, ready to catch hold of him should he suddenly fall into trance. By all accounts, these spontaneous flights of the spirit were thrilling beyond words. All eyes would be riveted to the silently eloquent form of the Master in ecstasy.

The festive atmosphere, the intensity of singing and dancing in the joy of the spirit, however, was just one note in the *raga* of Dakshineswar—a high note to be sure, but there were others. As the mood changed, song might give way to conversation, or conversation to silence. Time ruled all. Each phase of the Dakshineswar day had its own logic, its own special activities and character. Morning was shrouded in a deep meditative stillness, broken just before dawn by the loud cawing of crows and the first tentative stirring of the breezes. It was a time when Ramakrishna, and any of the devotees who had stayed overnight, would venture out into the chill air to bathe in the Ganges. As the orange glow of dawn swelled over the temple compound, it was greeted by an urgent cacophony of bells, horns, conches, and the sweet, flowing cadences of the *suprabhatam* hymn awakening the Divine Mother in the temple, and the divine indweller in the heart of man, to a new day rich in spiritual possibilities.

Though the Master no longer had any formal priestly duties to perform, he would sometimes go to the Kali temple to worship, after a fashion, or to converse with the Mother. In his own room, he used to bless the new day by waving camphor lamps and incense, and chanting the Divine Names of God. Afterward, he might stroll through the garden or sit out on the porch for some light talk with companions.

With the precipitous ascent of the tropical sun, the first visitors from Calcutta would start arriving by carriage or boat, and Ramakrishna's room would take on an animated air. At noon, all would lunch, and then spread out mats to rest comfortably through the hottest part of the day. After the siesta, the atmosphere was free and informal. Ramakrishna might perhaps enjoy a leisurely smoke from a small clay hookah prepared by one of the devotees. Here and there, off to the side, a heated discussion might be in progress on some spiritual or philosophical question, while visitors entered and left the room freely.

In late afternoon, tea and light refreshments were often served, or the Master would smilingly distribute the fruits and sweets which had been offered to him; sometimes with special affection he would feed a particular devotee by hand as a mother feeds her child. Casual visitors, come to worship at the Kali temple and attracted by the happy sounds, often thronged the verandas around the Master's room to catch a glimpse of the busy "market of joy." And boatmen floating down the Ganges paused on their way to savor the mingled strains of song and animated talk and laughter that drifted over the languid waters.

With the approach of dusk, the purposeful busyness of the daytime gave way to a deepening peace. Ramakrishna used to say that the twilight hour just naturally awakens in us an awareness of God's power. The bright day, which had seemed all but eternal while it lasted, is suddenly and unaccountably fading, giving way to the womb of mystery. Over the darkening waters of the river at Dakshineswar, the plumes of distant funeral pyres briefly catch fire in a final incendiary gesture of the dying light. Great flocks of egrets wheel and plunge through the scarlet air, and once again the sounds of musical instruments and chanting drifts in from the temple sanctum to mark the sacred transition between light and darkness. Inside Ramakrishna's room, an oil lamp is lit on its niche, and the Master chants the sacred names of God, then sits silent, engrossed in thought. Perhaps one of the devotees is slowly fanning him with a large plaited hand fan.

By now most of the visitors have left for their homes in Calcutta, and the atmosphere has returned to its natural intimacy. The evening is a time for quiet talk and contemplation. Frequently, Ramakrishna directs one of his young devotees to the meditation hut by the Ganges, within which he himself had spent so many sleepless nights in divine communion as a youthful priest of Kali. Others who are staying the night at Dakshineswar spread their mats inside Ramakrishna's room or go out onto one of the verandas to enjoy the cool evening air. There is no set routine concerning when the Master will retire for the night. Frequently he sleeps little, or not at all.

On one occasion, a young disciple, Yogen (the future Swami Yogananda), who was staying inside the Master's room, awoke in the middle of the night to find Ramakrishna missing from his bed. The young man's faith was not yet completely firm, and an awful doubt troubled him. Could the Master have gone to his wife, who was living in the nearby music tower? Was it possible that his appearance of purity was nothing but a sham? Tortured by his own faithlessness, Yogen nevertheless felt driven to investigate. Concealing himself from view near the entrance to Sarada's quarters, he watched and waited. It wasn't long, however, before Ramakrishna surprised him in his vigil, approaching from the direction of the sacred grove where he had been engaged in meditation. Yogen blushed with shame. But far from being offended, Ramakrishna praised the young man's vigilance. "You are quite right—before you accept anyone as your guru, you should watch him day and night," (R.D., p. 233) he gently reassured him.

Many of Ramakrishna's young devotees were fortunate in having an opportunity to do just that. The Master lived very much in a fishbowl with scarcely any privacy, or any time to himself. The conditions at Dakshineswar resembled those in the legendary *gurukulus* of the past, where the teacher actually lived with his pupils and taught as much out of the daily circumstances of life as from formal verbal instruction. At all times, several of Ramakrishna's future monastic disciples would be living with and serving their guru. It was a priceless opportunity, a spiritual hothouse of intensive striving and often spectacular growth in consciousness for those able to live away from their homes for days at a stretch. Some like Rakhal, Latu, and later Baburam (the future Swami Premananda) had freed themselves of family ties and were able to stay full time at Dakshineswar.

Ramakrishna's influence on those who lived within his orbit was manifested at every level, from the most mundane to the most metaphysical. His was a flame that burned and enlightened and that melted down the fixed metal of the whole person, only to remold it again in a simpler, truer form.

This transformation of character was Ramakrishna's greatest miracle and his most enduring legacy. Just how it was accomplished is the subject of the next chapter.

→≫ *Chapter 13* ≪←

The Spiritual Guide

In the course of the last chapter, we saw how a song, a word, or a touch from Ramakrishna could awaken the dormant spiritual consciousness of his devotees. In those who were poised to receive it, even a casual glance from the Master during one of his ecstasies might release a veritable flood tide of bliss. Nevertheless, dramatic transmissions of this sort were just the highly visible tip of the iceberg. The greater part of the Master's influence manifested far more quietly, far more subtly. It was less through enlightening mystical flashes than by the steady sunlight of his own being that Ramakrishna stimulated the aspiring souls that had gathered around him to growth.

Essentially, Ramakrishna taught by example. Not that he regarded himself as a "teacher," or consciously set himself up as a role model for all to follow. No one could have been simpler, less authoritarian, or more self-effacing than Ramakrishna. Nevertheless, without intending it—without for the most part even being aware of it—Ramakrishna exerted a tremendous sway on those who came within his orbit. Like his divine namesakes, the Avatars Rama and Krishna, there was something transcendently bewitching about Sri Ramakrishna. To see him was to feel drawn irresistibly to him; to be drawn to him was naturally to try to emulate him in every way. The Master didn't say to anyone, "You must do as I do." He didn't have to. Just to be in his presence was to find one's whole being turning toward the ideal of God-dedication which Ramakrishna so radiantly personified, as a blossom turns toward the sun. It is some measure of the impact of that example that sixteen of the young men who were eagerly spending their every leisure hour at Dakshineswar would, a few years hence, wander the length and breadth of India as the first renunciates of the Ramakrishna Order of monks.

For most of us, the ideal of renouncing all in the quest for God will appear heroic, almost superhuman. We may wonder what could possibly motivate a band of Western-educated students at the height of their physical and intellectual powers to sacrifice everything that men generally cherish in the pursuit of a goal which seems, at best, quixotic and elusive. We would do well to remember, however, that in Ramakrishna's immediate presence the spiritual goal seemed neither quixotic nor elusive, but eminently practical. If Ramakrishna had merely lectured about God-realization, as other religious teachers contented themselves with doing, then it would have been surprising if anyone had responded by staking his all on the pursuit of it. But Ramakrishna exuded God-realization. He didn't teach it; he was himself the teaching; he was himself concrete proof that higher states of consciousness are real and attainable.

The power of such a living example is beyond reckoning. In our Western spiritual tradition, we need only look to Saint Francis of Assisi. The ideals of Francis, while revolutionary in the deepest sense, were hardly new. For centuries, no doubt, preachers had been preaching the virtues of holy poverty and holy joy comfortably from their pulpits. But then, in a flurry of divine inspiration, a rich man's son in central Italy threw down his fine silk cloak and wandered off into the countryside garbed in sackcloth, radiating the ecstasy of owning nothing, and possessing everything in God. Alone among his contemporaries, this rich man's son had resolved to put Christ's words in the Gospels to the acid test of experience. And alone he had proven them both practical and true. The sublime spiritual contagion that Francis unleashed continues to reverberate to this day. The small band of divine madmen which he inspired swelled into a veritable army of Franciscan renunciates. In time, however, the purity of the original ideal of renunciation became watered down as succeeding generations grew increasingly distant in spirit and time from the wellspring of inspiration.

But those who followed directly in the footsteps of Saint Francis, the barefoot friars minor who kept strictly to their mentor's rule of absolute renunciation, would, paradoxically, never have considered that they were renouncing anything at all; could one who had gazed deeply into the divinely beaming eyes of Francis imagine for a moment that, by following his joyous lead, he was *renouncing?* Quite the reverse, he would realize that he was *embracing* a way of life and of truth infinitely more valuable than any trifles he might have given up in the process.

With the upsurge of holy power that accompanies the advent of a great soul, such as Francis, the normal human tendency toward a narrow self-seeking gets overriden by the ecstatic awareness that one's true well-being is better served by giving than by getting, by surrendering than by grasping. In that supercharged atmosphere, renunciation happens naturally, without either strain or lingering regret; nothing could be simpler, or less self-conscious. Just as Saint Francis had before him, Sri Ramakrishna, by his sheer authenticity and enthusiasm, galvanized a band of dedicated followers to set their sights higher and broader and finer than they would ever have imagined possible.

But the revolution took place quietly and without fanfare. And the revolutionized would hardly have been aware of the vast changes occurring within them until the work was done. To be present week after week at the foot of Ramakrishna's small cot was to find oneself gradually weaned from the coarse pleasures of the senses—pleasures which came, in the Master's joyous presence, to appear puny, even pathetic, in comparison to the boundless rewards of the Spirit which he embodied. To watch the little poor man of Kali in the barest surroundings radiate a holy good cheer like a monarch of happiness was to grasp what the scriptures of all the world's sacred traditions mean when they proclaim with a single voice that the fountainhead of joy exists within oneself, and that it is futile to seek it anywhere else. No wonder so many of Sri Ramakrishna's faithful were turning away from the harsh glitter of externals to seek the hidden treasure of the heart.

The Master rejoiced in this spirit of renunciation which was quietly spreading among his young disciples and recognized it as a sign of the Mother's special grace on them. He did everything within his power to fan the flame of dispassion which the Mother had lit. But he regarded the urge toward outward renunciation as only the first step on the path; he couldn't rest content with it. He prayed continually to Kali to grant his spiritual children ecstatic love for God. He knew that man's best efforts count for very little in attaining it. Renunciation and ascetic resolve certainly help to purify the being, to simplify and rid life of nonessentials, and thereby clear the way for Love's descent. But when Divine Love comes, it comes as a pure gift. When it comes, it comes as a bolt of lightning, a flame out of the night. It comes as a miracle.

Ramakrishna, of course, had full faith in the Mother's miracles. And he knew that of all of Kali's miracles, of all of Kali's gifts, the gift of *Prema*—boundless and unconditional Love—is the greatest. He also knew that Kali would heed his call. She had never failed him in the past when he had cried out for his own sake. He knew that She would not fail him now that he cried out to Her for the sake of his devotees, on whom She had already poured out so much of Her grace.

Ramakrishna was not to be disappointed.

The Sanskrit word *guru* literally means "destroyer of darkness." The guru is the light-giver who ignites the sacred flame of love and wisdom in those with whom he comes into contact. It is commonly held that without the live contact with a man of spiritual realization none can attain Truth. While Sri Ramakrishna never questioned the central importance of this person-to-person transmission from guru to disciple, he saw the guru as essentially a middleman, a torch in the hands of God and a conduit for His grace. In fact, whenever he spoke from the highest standpoint, the Master invariably taught that God is the sole guru; the human teacher is only His instrument. He once declared:

> If someone addresses me as "guru," I say to him, "Go away you fool! How can I be a teacher? There is no teacher except for *Sat Chit Ananda* [the Divine bedrock of Being,

Consciousness and Bliss within all beings]. There is no refuge except for Him." . . . Learn from me as much as I have
told you. But if you want to know more, you must pray to
God in solitude. . . . The son of the house can give a beggar
only a small measure of rice. But if the beggar asks for his
train fare, then the Master of the house must be called. (G.S.,
p. 853)

These are chastening words, especially so in our own day
when self-proclaimed gurus who promise a quick and easy enlightenment abound. Sri Ramakrishna's question, which he posed
on occasion to the gurus of his own time, was: How, when the
all-mighty Lord of the universe exists within each one of us and
guides our every step, can a mere mortal propose to enlighten
another? Ramakrishna naturally rejected all such claims as sheer
egotism. Ironically, it is those who are the purest channels for
God's healing and guiding energy who feel least responsible for
the works that get accomplished through their agency. Great
saints like Ramakrishna have always understood that it is exactly
proportional to their divestiture of the very "I" which could lay
a claim to guruship that the true guru—the divine *Sat* Guru—is
able to work through them for His own ends.

Only if God were really separate and at a distance from man
would it be possible to speak of one person guiding another
person to Him. But as the sages never tire of insisting, God is
nowhere if He is not here, now, within each of us not as some
abstract or latent potential, but as the very Being, Consciousness,
and will to Bliss which constitute our primal nature. These divine
qualities should not be regarded as static entities floating isolated
in the inaccessible depths of awareness, but as ceaselessly active
forces drawing us to themselves. Sri Ramakrishna used to liken
God to a magnet, and man to a piece of iron. The iron of human
nature is at every moment being powerfully attracted by the will
towards perfect joy and completeness, which is the dynamic
expression of the God within us. But we have badly dulled our
own sensitivity. In many cases, we have covered our mental
faculties so thickly in successive layers of worldly desire that we
are effectively unaware of this pull toward the Source.

Yet the magnetism is there, whether we perceive it or not. The human guru may be instrumental in reawakening us to it, but he is no more responsible for its existence than the sun's reflection in a pool of water is responsible for the heat of the day. The guru is just a mirror. He reflects the God-force at work within the disciple in an outward and visible form. But he can only reflect what is already there. He is the tool God may choose to use in revealing His presence to men. But the guru is just an agent, the Master was always quick to point out; he can do nothing of himself.

This is not to deny, of course, that the guru can offer tremendously potent assistance to the spiritual aspirant. Ramakrishna was in full accord with the age-old mystic wisdom which holds that the help of an inspired guide is essential for those who would attain the Divine. While it is true that God is the only guru, the Master affirmed the complementary truth that the one who has attained the consciousness of God is not in any way different from God Himself. The actions of the God-realized saint are so powerful precisely because they do not arise out of the small personal will, but from the realm of impersonal wisdom, the God within. Ramakrishna insisted, however, that only an individual with a genuine "commission from God" is a true spiritual teacher. Others can parrot the words of truth. But without the backing of a divine power, those words will amount to very little in the end.

The Master once compared the guru to a physician of the soul. There are three grades of physicians, he asserted. The lowest grade merely prescribes the therapy and leaves it for the patient to carry it through. The middle range of physician reasons with the patient and explains the necessity for keeping the diet and taking the medicine. But the most conscientious doctor doesn't just prescribe a cure or encourage the patient to pursue it on his own; he administers it directly, even forcing the sick man's mouth open and pouring the medicine in himself, if need be. Only that way will there be no question of his instructions being faithfully followed.

So, too, with spiritual teachers: The incompetent guru limits himself to setting forth the abstract principles and rules of spiritual life, and then leaves it up to the student to assimilate them or not depending on his own level of motivation and understanding; the mediocre guru, on the other hand, reasons with the pupil and tries to persuade him of the validity of his instructions. But the most exalted spiritual guide, the one with the true commission from God, can't rest content with a merely verbal teaching (though he doesn't ignore that either). He depends on more forceful, more direct and, therefore, less corruptible means for getting the message across.

In the Hindu scriptures, several forms of *diksha* (usually translated as initiation, but actually encompassing all forms of the direct transmission of spiritual power) by which the guru may communicate his inner realizations are enumerated. There is the *diksha* by verbal teachings, the *diksha* by touch, the *diksha* by glance, and the *diksha* by telepathy. But of all the *dikshas*, the highest, the most refined and delicate, and the most subtly potent is the *mouna diksha*, the initiation of silence.

All of the other forms of communion are dualistic, tied to the distinction between subject and object, between giver and receiver. But in the communion of silence, there is neither giving nor receiving. In that silence, the walls that separate guru and disciple have ceased to exist. In that silence, what is in the heart of the guru is also in the heart of the disciple. The indivisible Truth has wordlessly flashed between them, and for a timeless instant guru and disciple are One. Sri Ramakrishna used all of the tools at his disposal—speech, touch, thought, glance. But, as was the case with other Spiritual Masters, his most important work was accomplished in silence. In silence, he conveyed the subtlest and most profound essence of what he had to share. In silence, Ramakrishna's inner being contacted the disciple directly causing each one to resonate, if only distantly and faintly at first, with the Master's own fathomless capacity for ecstatic knowledge of God.

This gift for awakening spontaneously the latent spirituality in others is the special magic of the saint. Once the Master was taken to the Calcutta museum by Mathur. He thrilled to the myriad wonders of the Mother's creation on display there. But most of all, he marveled at the painstakingly reconstructed dinosaur skeletons—huge cages of bone turned to stone through age-

The Spiritual Guide

long contact with minerals in the soil. These fossils struck Ramakrishna as analogues for the transforming effect of *satsang* (the association with a holy man). Like the giant reptiles of old, the devotee, from no virtue of his own, simply by maintaining contact with a person of divine realization, finds himself gradually made over into something altogether new, the difference being that, in the case of the dinosaur, the tissue of life is transformed into stone, whereas, in the case of the devotee, a heart of stone is unaccountably rendered supple and alive.

The heart that does not thrill continually to God's miracle of creation is a heart of stone. But the heart that beats in rhythm with the passage of stars through space and with the nearer, but no less awesome, flow of limitless love within its own confines is alive in God. And the paramount miracle of the saint, and Ramakrishna's special miracle, was that in his presence that which is dead truly comes back to life. The saint is like the spring; at his magical touch a thousand withered, gray limbs of inner perception and feeling burst effusively to bud.

Others might preach God, but Ramakrishna made one feel the presence of the living God. For others (even the ostensibly religious), Divinity was hardly more than a vague dream to be dreamt in some undefined future or some saccharine afterlife state. But for Ramakrishna, that dream was anything but a vague and honey-coated imagining. For Ramakrishna, the dream was alive here and now. And in Ramakrishna's presence, the dream came alive in oneself.

But is that spiritual world, which stirred to joyous life in Ramakrishna's presence, really a dream? Or is the matter-of-fact world of consensus the real dream? There is no doubt how Ramakrishna would have answered that. The world has been drained of its Holy Mystery, the King of Kings has been deposed from His throne, he would have insisted. Man sees no further than the tip of his own nose, and he calls what he sees "Reality." Ramakrishna believed that we are living in *kali yuga*, the dark age of untruth—a fallen and topsy-turvy era, when black has turned white and white, black, and in which foreground and background, dream and reality, have exchanged places. In that mad world, only the madman of God is truly sane.

189

So Ramakrishna offered a radically different way of looking at things. At Dakshineswar, the usual perceptual order was dramatically reversed; the spiritual realm—for most of us hazy and indistinct—became concrete and sharply defined, while the mundane world of the senses—the painfully literal, solid, and coarsely substantial world of everyday experience—was revealed to be the thinnest of veils overlaying the radiance of the Infinite. In his attempts to reinforce the devotees in the spiritual reality, Ramakrishna would return again and again to the central axiom of his teachings. "God alone is real; all else is false," (G.S., p. 125) he would insist. And to be with him at Dakshineswar was to see what he meant, to come face to face with the bliss at the core of life so tremendous that all else is dwarfed by comparison. No wonder those with an aching nostalgia for the spiritual realm (fellow "hemp smokers," (G.S., p. 530) as the Master affectionately called them) found in Ramakrishna's room at Dakshineswar a blessed refuge from the world, a place apart where the dream of life could awaken into the greater Dream of God.

The revelation of the spiritual world, however, was only one side of Ramakrishna's activity as a teacher. As evidenced in his training of Sarada, he could be thoroughly down-to-earth when the situation demanded it. But Ramakrishna would have been the last one to have drawn any distinction between the spiritual and the earthly. To give a man a taste of higher things, to whet his appetite, is necessary. But if you don't at the same time strengthen his character and reinforce his discipline, then you run the risk that the nourishing food of the spirit that you have given him will simply slip through his fingers and never be ingested or assimilated.

Therefore, Sri Ramakrishna concerned himself with all aspects of his disciples' lives—with their family affairs, diet, and choice of friends quite as much as with their practice of meditation and prayer. In evaluating those who came to him, he laid great stress on sound physical health and mental purity, both of which he viewed as necessary prerequisites if the practitioner were to bear up successfully under the tremendous forces unleashed during the inward journey to the source of consciousness. And as a preparation for that journey, he never tired of emphasizing the need for practicing the cardinal virtues of truthfulness, humility, and nonattachment. Only the strong of character are fit to undergo the rigors of the spiritual path. Only the strong can mount the wild colt of bliss. And only the strongest can ride it for long without being thrown painfully to the ground.

The inexperienced seeker often romantically pictures the spiritual path as consisting of the pursuit of strange states of consciousness and supernatural experiences. Bewitched by a surface glamour, it is all too easy to forget that the path to that "other world"—that spiritual realm which Ramakrishna and other divinely inspired souls inhabit—leads directly through this world. It is even more difficult to appreciate that that "other world" is not, in fact, different from our own. Indeed, the sages affirm that what is usually called "the other world" is, in reality, our familiar world as it is perceived through the eyes of wisdom, rather than through the distorting lens of our hopes and fears, as ordinarily happens.

This is not to deny that within creation there are different planes of manifestation. Certainly the mystic experiences of Sri Ramakrishna and of saints throughout history testify to the existence of alternate worlds, heavens, spheres of the Gods, and realms of pure form which are every bit as real as our own. Christ reflected on this multiplicity when he stated: "In my Father's mansion there are many rooms." However, it is important to remember that these different rooms, or realms of consciousness, do not appear to the holy seer as exclusive compartments. The walls demarcating the various realms are transparent to his enlightened vision. He takes in the entire mansion in one glance, and regards it as a single world. Ramakrishna once compared himself to a fish swimming joyously through the sea of consciousness. Like the fish in his fluid world, the seer is able to dart without hindrance from one level to next, ranging freely from the most obscure depths to the glittering surface. But what he finally realizes is that no particular level, no particular psychic state, has any priority over another. Whatever he sees, however spectacular, however mundane, are just permutations of the Mother's waters of consciousness—modes of consciousness within an undivided sea of consciousness.

This crowning realization distinguishes Sri Ramakrishna from the ordinary yogi who craves to attain and then to inhabit indefinitely a particular state of expanded awareness which he regards as Ultimate. Ramakrishna's universal vision made him equally at home in all states of consciousness, since he perceived the Divine Presence interpenetrating them all like the ever-present background drone which supports the melody line in Indian classical music. From every level of experience, as much in ordinary social intercourse as in the exultation of *nirvikalpa samadhi*, the clear note of the Divine resounded for Ramakrishna. This extremely rare state is referred to as *sahaja samadhi* (literally, "the natural *samadhi*," or *samadhi* become natural). For the sage who attains the permanent condition of *sahaja samadhi*, the universe has become completely transparent to the Divine. He no longer depends on extraordinary spiritual states in order to perceive God. Though ecstasies, visions, and other phenomena often continue to occur, as they did in Ramakrishna's case, all modes of consciousness are now recognized to be different notes of the same Divine *Raga*, none intrinsically superior to any other.

The recognition of Divinity in the everyday world is, of course, the last word in spirituality, the fruit of a long pilgrimage which, like a great arc, ends by curving back toward its own starting point. For a beginner, on the other hand, the distinction between sacred and profane, God and world, is real enough. It is a useful, even an inevitable, starting point for the spiritual search. This dualistic separation between God and world, seeker and sought, stimulates the flow of spiritual yearning just as surely as the positive and negative electrical poles within a battery create a flow of electricity. Paradoxically, the illusion that God is separate from ourselves and from all that is familiar to us sets up the vital tension by which we are driven to seek Him, and eventually to discover Him as indistinguishable from our own being. But even in the early stages of *sadhana*, the sharp dualism between God and world is best tempered by the mature wisdom that affirms that the two are ultimately One.

The dangers for those who would ignore this truth are substantial. Narrow zealotry, dogmatism, rigidity, and even madness may result for the seeker intoxicated with the heady new experiences and ideas associated with the spiritual path who goes overboard in his rejection of the physical plane. Blind enthusiasm for God can all too easily spawn hatred for the world.

In correcting those aspirants who had become overzealous and unbalanced, Ramakrishna's true art as a spiritual guide came to the fore. Ever careful to temper the immature excesses of his devotees, he urged those who had turned grimly stern with earnestness to smile, and those who tortured themselves with austerities to relax their rigid hold on things. If a devotee had too much trust in his own unaided efforts, Ramakrishna would remind him to have more faith in God. For he was keenly aware that the one who tries to race to God on his own two feet, ends up panting toward an ever-receding mirage on the horizon. He knew that the God that we set before ourselves as a goal is an imaginary God. And he knew that the only shortcut on the spiritual path is the one that God takes on his way toward us—the one God takes as an act of pure unearned grace when we finally surrender our self-willed efforts to reach Him.

If it is foolish to try to take the Kingdom of Heaven by storm, then it is equally misguided, in the Master's view, to attempt to flee the realm of nature. For one thing, it is quite impossible to do so. Nature is the lap of the Divine Mother. Wherever we Her children may wander in either body or spirit, we can never fall from that all-encompassing lap. The aspirant motivated by the urge to escape finds himself being pursued by the very *maya* he so urgently flees. The problem is not with nature or *maya*, but with our attitudes toward it. Generally, we tend toward one of two extreme positions. Either we accept the natural order uncritically as a value in and of itself, without making any effort to discover its source, or we may reject the creation in the expectation that we will thereby attain the Creator.

Ramakrishna's way was different. He didn't reject *maya*, because he never regarded it as separate from God. The immanent and the transcendent are two aspects of the same Divine Reality, like fire and its burning power or a diamond and its luster, to use Ramakrishna's analogies. Nature is revealed to be the blissful play of the Mother in Her infinite playground of space and time.

"My Mother, the Primal Divine Energy, is both within and without this phenomenal world. Having given birth to the world, She lives within it. . . . She is the spider and the world is the web that She has woven. The spider brings the phenomenal web out of herself and then lives on it. My Mother is both the Container and the Contained."[1]

The archetypal image of the Indian holy man is that of the wizened sage sitting atop a Himalayan peak, proclaiming the world of phenomena to be a dream. Ramakrishna might not have disagreed with our sage's characterization in principle. But he probably would have asked the question: Whose dream? For the Master, the answer would have been obvious—the world is God's dream. The implication that he always drew from this is that what God has dreamt cannot be unreal in its fundamental nature. What God has dreamt is a projection of God Himself; the Dreamer is one with His Dream.

This view of the radical unity of nature and God had wide-ranging practical implications for Ramakrishna's guidance of his devotees. Recognizing the sacredness of the world, the Master taught that even the most material levels of reality deserve our reverence. His ideal was to avoid becoming ensnared by *Maya*, not to despise Her. For Mother *Maya* is a Janus-faced Goddess; those who view Her as a terrible ogre binding man to illusion and to death have grasped only a part of Her reality. The one who binds also unties the knot; the one who slays also grants life everlasting. It is true that the seductive drama of nature can divert us from undertaking a deep inquiry into the underlying Reality. It can enslave us to the superficial appearance of things. But the same natural order contains within itself tremendously powerful forces that are able to sweep us in a moment to the far shore of Wisdom. The same wave that drowns one man carries another who knows how to ride it triumphantly to safety. So the task is neither to reject nature, nor to abandon ourselves uncritically to its treacherous waters, but to learn how to surf it home to freedom.

This delicate balancing act is an art form, exacting and hard to master. Generally, when we first become attracted to the spiritual life, we have only a very crude conception of what is required of us. We see our efforts as a race and a struggle. We view ourselves as crusaders, and arm ourselves with an avenging sword when a scalpel would have been more appropriate. We view things simplistically in black-and-white terms, and feel called upon either to accept or reject. If *x* is right, then *y* must be wrong. It has not yet occurred to us that the cold dualism of logic and the alienating logic of zealotry are inappropriate to the life of the spirit, which is less a triumphal march to a preconceived goal than an exquisitely undulating dance in which we step now this way, now that, now forcefully, now gently. Fortunately, the guru is there to point out to us where we have strayed from the middle way, and to direct us back to a more balanced and healthy approach.

When the austere Hari asked Ramakrishna how to free oneself from lust, the Master surprised him by asserting that his attitude was all wrong. Lust is life manifest, the creative force of existence; to kill lust is to destroy the life force in oneself. The proper course, Ramakrishna insisted, was not to crush desire, but to harness it to the Spirit. When the same young devotee bragged that he was repelled by women and shunned them like the plague, Sri Ramakrishna admonished: "You talk like a fool. You must never look down on women. They are manifestations of the Divine Mother. Bow down before them with reverence. That's the only way to avoid becoming sensually ensnared by them. If you hate them, you will fall into the snare" (R.D., p. 229).

As Ramakrishna's skillful handling of the drinker Surendra revealed, the Master saw nothing to be gained in the suppression of desire. It was his great Tantric intuition that even the darker impulses of the personality are at base wholesome desires for a greater joy and fullness, desires that have been diverted from their natural course by the distorting power of illusion. These impulses embody a powerful current that needs to be transformed into momentum for the spiritual journey. Rather than trying to swim against the stream of matter, Ramakrishna advised, "Direct the six passions to God. The impulse of *lust* should be turned into the desire to have intercourse with the Supreme Self. Feel *angry* at those who stand in your way of God. Feel *greedy* for Him. If you must have the feeling of *I* and *mine*, then associate it with God.

Say, for instance, 'My Rama, my Krishna.' If you must have *pride*, then feel like Bibhishina, who said, 'I have touched the feet of Rama with my head; I will not bow this head before anyone else' " (G.S., p. 220).

Even the thoroughly human attachment to kith and kin can be fruitfully enlisted to the spiritual quest. Once a young woman came to Ramakrishna and complained that she could not focus her mind on God. The Master asked her what she cherished most, and she answered that she adored her young nephew more than anything. Taking this attachment as a base, Ramakrishna counseled her to regard the child as Krishna, and to serve him with all of the love and reverence in her heart. Surprisingly, when she acted on the Master's unconventional advice, it had the effect of releasing the spirituality within her. Attached to a dearly beloved element in her own daily life, the devotion, which she had once struggled dryly to achieve, flowed freely along its own natural channel of least resistance and filled her with a wonderful consolation.

To some it may appear wrongheaded to mix devotion with human affection in this way. But Ramakrishna was more practical. He believed in making use of whatever lay at hand. In his advice to the young woman, he had acted on the perception that affection and devotion are not ultimately separable, but are actually points on a continuum, stages in a journey of the ever-widening expansion of love. And on that sacred journey, we must start from the square foot of ground on which we stand. We can't leap in a single death-defying bound to embrace the Universal Spirit. We approach on a series of rungs leading by degrees from the familiar to the Mystery without name or form. Since he knew that God pulses within all beings as love in the heart, it was never Ramakrishna's way to renounce natural affection. Instead, he aimed to gradually expand affection beyond measure until, purified of all selfishness and narrowness, it penetrates to the immaculate boundlessness of that Love which is God.

It is precisely here that Ramakrishna's genius as spiritual friend and guide lies. There was about him a sublime practicality, a divine craftsman's profound respect for his medium—the subtle grain of human nature as it manifested in the endless patterns of the lives of his devotees. Lesser craftsmen might try to cut away the distinctive knots and swirls in the lumber that comes to their workshops; Ramakrishna preferred to make good use of these features in the final design. His special art consisted in the unfailing recognition that each individual has a constellation of affections and aversions, qualities of head and heart, that are absolutely unique, like the grain of a particular piece of wood, and need to be respected. The Tantric path which Ramakrishna embodied does not call for rejecting these individualistic elements, but for engaging them as powerful allies on the way. Consequently, the path will be subtly different for each man and woman who treads it. Only a fully illumined Master with the divine spontaneity and flexibility of a Ramakrishna can possibly react appropriately to all of the diverse spiritual needs in those who come to him, and give each one a push along his or her natural path to unfoldment.

As a result of his own practice of many different spiritual disciplines, Ramakrishna graphically realized that there is no particular strategy superior to all others for approaching the Divine. God has assumed all forms, as well as formlessness. He is not restricted to any particular form or modality of manifestation. But He is not absent from any form either. Therefore, He can be pursued and realized through any form, through any technique that one chooses, or through the form of formlessness. What makes a given mode of approach better than another is not its objective "superiority," but the subjective predilection of the seeker himself. We picture God in any of a number of ways—as Love, as Beauty, as Purity, as Luminous Void, as Impersonal Wisdom, as Mother, as Lover, or as Friend. God is all these things, and infinitely more besides. The particular image that someone chooses is his own unique window on God. For, if it truly corresponds to the deepest archetypal levels of his own unique being, then it has the potential to lead him beyond itself into the Clear Light of the One.

Because Ramakrishna stood in that Clear Light and had practiced such a variety of spiritual disciplines to get there, he was in a unique position to guide the diverse *sadhakas* who came to Dakshineswar. He who had tread so many different paths, however, never imposed a particular path on anyone. The crusading spirit that drives one man to convert another to his own mode of thought and action was altogether absent in Sri Ramakrishna. Trusting fully in the innate wisdom of the soul to choose its own most congenial way, the Master yearned to nurture all, but to mold none. As a result, the Christian who visited him became a better Christian, the Brahmo a more sincere Brahmo, the worshiper of Kali a more zealous devotee.

What is crucial, in Sri Ramakrishna's view, is not the particular spiritual ideal that a man chooses to follow, but the depth and sincerity of the faith that he brings to bear on it. True faith renders spiritually potent any object which it takes up. The Master illustrated this principle with a story:

> Let me tell you how powerful faith is. A man was about to cross the sea from Ceylon to India. Bibhishina said to him: "Tie this thing in a corner of your wearing-cloth, and you will be able to cross the sea safely. You will be able to walk on the water. But be sure not to examine it, or you will sink." The man was walking easily on the water of the sea—such is the strength of faith—when, having gone part of the way, he thought, "What is this wonderful thing Bibhishina has given me, that I can walk on the water?" He untied the knot and found only a leaf with the name of Rama written on it. "Oh, just this!" he thought, and instantly he sank. (T.S., p. 60)

According to Sri Ramakrishna, the devotee should have the unwavering conviction that the Name of God is the same as God Himself. This faith will empower the chosen Name, forging it into a concrete link for joining one's ordinary consciousness to the Divine Reality which the Name embodies. By chanting and singing the Name, and repeating it silently at all times (*japa* yoga), the devotee becomes powerfully focused on God. As Sri Ramakrishna assured his followers: "When you chant His Name with single-minded devotion you can see God's form and realize Him. Suppose there is a piece of timber sunk in the water of the Ganges and fastened with a chain to the bank. You proceed link by link, holding to the chain, and you dive into the water and follow the chain. Finally you are able to reach the timber. In the same way, by repeating God's Name you become absorbed in Him and finally realize Him" (G.S., pp. 878–79).

As we have seen, a large variety of Divine Names were chanted at Dakshineswar. Ramakrishna honored all of the many forms of God which his devotees worshiped. This catholicity had a broadening influence. While few gave up their chosen deities, many were led to view them in an entirely new light. Gradually the limited and limiting attachment to a narrowly defined ideal of Divinity would give way to a truer understanding of the universality of that ideal as it expresses its sacredness in innumerable guises. The devotee of Rama, for example, wouldn't renounce Rama, but would come to see Rama reflected in Krishna and Kali, in Allah and Christ. He would realize how he had been, perhaps unconsciously, limiting Rama within the bounds of his own all-too-human conception. Moreover, he might be inspired to recognize in Sri Ramakrishna himself an embodiment of the God which he had been following.

One who did so was the widow Gopala Ma. Gopala Ma had lost her husband while still a child. Observing Hindu custom, she never remarried, but instead dedicated her life to the spiritual quest. Initiated by a guru of the Vaishnava sect, the young woman took up the worship of the child Krishna, known as Gopala; hence, she came to be known as Gopala Ma, or Gopala's Mother. By regarding Gopala with intense attachment and nurturing love, just as if He were her own child, Gopala Ma channeled her unfulfilled motherly longing to the pursuit of spirituality. Her tender feelings for the child Krishna opened out wonderfully, and, though she lived alone in the most austere surroundings, her life was sweetened with a radiant love.

In the year 1884, Gopala Ma visited Sri Ramakrishna in the company of another woman devotee. (Sri Ramakrishna had a number of female followers, though they were usually not present during the general gatherings of the devotees.) Uplifted by this contact with the Master, her devotion of three decades was greatly stimulated. So much so in fact that shortly thereafter, as she prayed in her home, Gopala Ma was blessed for the first time with a waking vision of Gopala. Enthralled by the palpable presence of her God, she cradled Gopala lovingly in her arms and rushed on foot to Dakshineswar. Gopala Ma must have been quite a spectacle with her hair disheveled and her widow's white sari dragging carelessly in the dirt, but Ramakrishna immediately recognized her exalted state. Remarkably, he also shared her vision as it was taking place. Sitting together in rapt communion, the two God-intoxicates watched the Divine Child crawling playfully between them. Now and again, Gopala seemed to disappear into the Master's body, only to reappear moments later.

For several months, Gopala Ma frequently enjoyed similar visionary episodes. Gradually, however, they became rarer. And simultaneously, she opened to the realization that they were, in any case, superfluous, since Sri Ramakrishna was himself one with the Divine Child who had been appearing before her. Soon this awareness widened still further and she came to regard other holy persons—and eventually all beings—as the living forms of her beloved Gopala.

Gopala Ma's experience was not unique. Many other aspirants had found, through the quickening touch of Sri Ramakrishna, their initial spiritual ideals expanding beyond measure. The seed of dogma and narrowness exists as part and parcel of all merely human ideals; Sri Ramakrishna's approach was not to throw this seed away, however, but to painstakingly nourish it with the waters of his own spirit of boundless liberality until it burst its own limitations and developed into a towering and many-tiered tree—a tolerant tree of the spirit, sheltering every possible species of bird and beast in its welcoming branches.

This image of the tree, which Sri Ramakrishna himself used at times as a symbol for spiritual maturity, evokes the qualities which he sought to foster at other levels as well. If he desired that his devotees become wide as a banyan tree, he demanded that they remain as firm as one. And while it was important that the branches of understanding reach tolerantly out in all directions as well as soar upward toward the heavens, it was equally essential, in his view, that the tree remain rooted in everyday experience. In order to be effective, the Master knew that the heady ideals of a God-dedicated life have to be anchored in the here and now, lest they loose their stabilizing base. He was careful, therefore, to discourage any tendency toward unworldliness in his young students. It was his lifelong conviction that a devotee must remain with his head in the clouds of God-consciousness at the same time that his feet are firmly planted in the soil of a shrewd practicality and common sense.

An incident involving the young devotee Yogen bears this out. When Yogen returned one day from the bazaar with a cracked iron vessel which he had purchased at Sri Ramakrishna's request, the Master rebuked him sharply: "What! You bought a pot and didn't examine it first. The shopkeeper was there to do business, not to practice religion. . . . Just because you are a devotee, that's no reason to be a fool" (R.D., p. 222).

Ramakrishna took every opportunity to strengthen the mettle of the dreamy and unassertive Yogen. One day, the boy was in a dory on the Ganges when he overheard some passengers slandering Ramakrishna. The words were painful to hear, but Yogen reasoned that the men were really more to be pitied than despised for passing judgment without any first hand knowledge of the situation. So he swallowed his resentment and remained stoically silent. Later Yogen narrated the incident in a light way to Ramakrishna, probably expecting that he would be amused by it. But the Master surprised him. "They spoke ill of me without any reason, and you sat in silence and did nothing!" Ramakrishna exclaimed. "Do you know what the scriptures say? A devotee should cut the head off of anyone who speaks ill of his guru!" (R.D., p. 222).

Ramakrishna's reaction at first glance seems curiously out of character. But it is revealing to compare it to something the Master told his disciple Niranjan (the future Swami Niranjanananda) in nearly identical circumstances. Niranjan, too, had overheard fellow passengers maliciously abusing Ramakrishna on a Ganges ferry. Unlike Yogen, however, the excitable Niranjan became enraged. He demanded that the slanderers stop at once. When they ignored him, he sprang to his feet and started rocking the vessel violently, threatening to capsize it on the spot. This had the effect of bringing the erring commuters speedily to their senses (they couldn't swim, Niranjan could), and they judiciously pleaded for forgiveness.

If Niranjan had acted with the confidence that the Master would approve of his act of manly loyalty and devotion to the guru, he had miscalculated as badly as Yogen had; for when Ramakrishna became aware of the incident, he sternly admonished the devotee:

> Anger is a deadly sin. You should never let it carry you away. The seeming anger of a good man is something different. It is no more than a mark made on water. It vanishes as soon as it's made. As for those mean-minded people who talked against me, they weren't worth getting into a quarrel with—you could waste your whole life in such quarreling. Think of them as no more than insects. Be indifferent to what they say. See what a great crime you were about to commit under the influence of anger! Think of the poor helmsman and the oarsmen in that boat—you were ready to drown them too, and they had done nothing! (R.D., p. 221)

Some might read these vastly different reactions to such similar situations as evidence of an ambivalence on Ramakrishna's part. But the ambivalence is not Ramakrishna's. It is the ambivalence of human nature that, depending on the individual, strays either to one side or to the other of the golden mean and needs to be balanced with its complement. The timid Yogen required more manly fiber and strength, and the temperamental Niranjan needed to develop restraint. But neither strength nor restraint are ends in themselves. Ramakrishna was very particular to point out that holiness should not be confused with some static list of ideal qualities. Holiness is a process. Holiness is the growth to wholeness. And what one man needs in order to be whole is often just the opposite of what his neighbor needs.

Religions like to bisect the world with "Thou shalt" and "Thou shalt nots." No doubt it is reassuring to do so. But the saints have always known how much of true morality slips through the warp and woof of that jerry-built net of right and wrong. Morality is without a doubt the very foundation of spiritual life. But prefabricated rules are never adequate. Each man, in a sense, has his own personalized set of God-ordained commandments, his own *swadharma*, the law of his individual nature which needs to be realized. And for each of us, these "commandments," this *swadharma*, is subtly adjusting itself moment to moment to the particular situation and to the stage of our growth in Truth.

Ramakrishna always insisted on two inviolable principles—to love God and not to harm His creatures. But even these principles were not intended to be carried out blindly as inflexible dogmas. When we do the right thing for the wrong reason (out of a stern sense of duty, for instance, or a rigid psychic compulsion), it is like a plastic flower—admirable, perhaps, in an abstract way, but lifeless. There is no enduring merit in such an act, and because it is performed without love, it fails to bring us closer to the God who is all Love. That is why Sri Ramakrishna put so little stock in philanthropy and public works. To share with the poor and aid the indigent he regarded as a sacred privilege, not as a duty to be fulfilled, still less as a favor to be bestowed on one's inferiors.

Ramakrishna spoke forcefully to his disciples of the attitude that needs to be fostered: "This universe belongs to Krishna. Know this in the depths of your being and be kind to all creatures." Overwhelmed with emotion, he softly repeated, "Kind to all creatures," and fell into reverie. After some time, he picked up the thread once more: "Kind too all creatures. . . . Kind? . . . Aren't you ashamed, insignificant insect? How can you show pity to God's creatures? Who are you to show mercy. . . . No! No! Mercy is impossible. Serve them as if they were Shiva!" (T.L.R., p. 213).

Ramakrishna's conviction in the divinity of life—the oneness of all life in God—was not a matter of idle speculation, but had arisen directly out of his own experience. Those who treat religion as if it were a collection of pleasantly vague and virtuous sentiments may well be shocked by the literal way in which Ramakrishna experienced his unity with all that lives. Watching a man trampling a field of recently sprouted grass, for example, he actually felt a searing pain in his chest. On another occasion, seeing a bull cruelly whipped, Ramakrishna cried out in agony, and his own back became streaked and enflamed with the marks of the scourge.

But such stunning empathy for the suffering of other beings didn't blind Sri Ramakrishna to the fact that absolute *ahimsa,* the textbook nonviolence of certain Indian sects such as the Jains, is a matter more of theory than of life as it exists in the world. Life lives on other life, life treads on other life—that is the way the Mother's game had been set up. And even the most committed vegetarian, or the Jain monk who wears a gauze mask over his face to avoid breathing in small airborne creatures, does not finally have it in his power to change those rules, even for himself.

That Sri Ramakrishna was not inflexibly opposed to the taking of life in all cases can be seen from an incident involving Balaram Bose. Balaram was a strict *brahmin* householder devotee of Sri Ramakrishna. Influenced by his orthodox beliefs, he had always considered it a grave sin to kill. One day during his meditation, he was so disturbed by mosquitoes that he couldn't focus his mind on God. This set into motion a novel train of thoughts. For the first time, he was struck by the moral ambiguity involved in such a situation. Which would be the greater evil, he wondered, swatting a few mosquitoes or failing in his sacred duty of meditation?

The very thought of killing (even in such a seemingly justified cause) proved jarring to Balaram's orthodox sensibilities. Deeply disturbed, he hurried straight away to Dakshineswar with the intention of asking Sri Ramakrishna for his guidance on the matter. When he arrived, however, he was stunned to see Ramakrishna calmly removing the bedbugs from his pillow and killing them one after another. The Master gazed up at his devotee long enough to explain matter-of-factly: "They've been breeding in my pillow. They bite me day and night, and keep me from sleeping. So I am killing them" (R.D., p. 241). Balaram's question had been answered before it could be asked.

Ramakrishna's unusual demonstration to Balaram was, nevertheless, entirely in character. The Master disapproved of rigidity in action, whatever form it might take. It was his conviction that the principles of spiritual life have to be applied sensitively and with a keen, discriminating intelligence. It is never enough just to follow a set of conventional laws. The orthodox prescriptions of tradition are little more than fetters to the soul if they are obeyed in a knee-jerk way without the flexibility that comes from a true understanding of their inward meaning. As Sri Ramak-rishna observed, "Too much concentration on orthodox purity becomes a plague. People afflicted with this disease have no time to think of God or man." (T.L.R., p. 252)

Even the priceless words of the guru, which have the power to liberate the one who follows them faithfully, are only effective if the disciple has fully digested them and thereby made them his own. To merely obey without assimilating can lead to a sterile fanaticism. It can also lead to comically, or even tragically, inap-propriate responses, as can be seen from one of Sri Ramakrishna's favorite stories.

In this parable, a holy man comes upon a notorious cobra that had wreaked havoc upon all who had unwittingly strayed within its territory. Seeing the saint, the serpent immediately raises its hood in menace and races toward him. But just as it is about to strike, the holy man chants a mantra which renders the snake harmless as an earthworm. He then preaches to the serpent, admonishing him to give up his evil ways, to recite God's name, and to refrain from harming anyone in the future. By following these injunctions, the holy man assures him, the sins of his past will be purified and salvation attained. So the cobra sets about repeating the sacred name the holy man has given him. But, no sooner do the village boys discover that the erstwhile scourge of the neighborhood has turned meek as a kitten than they turn to torturing him cruelly. Pelting the hapless snake with stones, they wheel him around by the tail, dashing him against a boulder and leaving him for dead. But, by the grace of the powerful mantra which he had received, the shattered cobra manages to survive. A few days later, when the holy man returns to find his devotee pathetically broken and in pain, he asks him how he has come to such a sorry state. Whereupon the serpent relates the tale of his cruel persecution at the hand of the urchins. Shocked, the holy man exclaims, "You fool! I told you not to bite. But that didn't mean that you shouldn't hiss."

Ramakrishna drew out the moral as follows: "So raise your hood. . . . But do not bite! . . . A man living in society, particularly if he is a citizen and the father of a family, ought to pretend to resist evil in order to defend himself. But he must at the same time be very careful not to return evil for evil" (T.L.R., p. 212).

It is significant that Ramakrishna specifically directs this advice toward householders with families to protect and support. In practice, the Master always differentiated between the conduct appropriate to a citizen of the world and that which is proper for the renunciate. Traditionally in India, the renunciate has been expected to follow a course of nonresistance in keeping with Christ's admonition to "turn the other cheek," because the whole point of his life is that, having surrendered all to God, he no longer has anything of his own to maintain or protect.

This distinction between householders and monks is a key to reconciling many of the seeming contradictions to be found in Ramakrishna's wide spectrum of teachings. While the householder is urged to engage in a delicate balancing act between the contradictory claims of Spirit and matter, God and Caesar, the monk is encouraged to go straight to God without so much as a sidelong glance at standards of the world. The Master felt so keenly the contrasting *dharmas* of these two groups that he set aside certain days exclusively for the instruction of his monastic disciples, his "inner circle," as he liked to call them. He knew that the level of detachment appropriate for a renunciate was neither advisable nor even possible for those caught in the web of worldly responsibilities. The chronicler "M" was a married man who didn't take part in the gatherings of the inner circle. Therefore, most of what we have available to us of Sri Ramakrishna's teachings was spoken to the householders, or to mixed gatherings of householders and future monks.

What we do know of the Master's teachings to his inner circle is that he spurred them on to the strictest renunciation, and emphasized the unreality and delusive nature of the world in the strongest terms. The objects of the senses which men prize so highly and dedicate their best years to pursuing and enjoying are really insubstantial, like images in a dream, the Master told them. The joy men vainly seek in phantom pleasures of a moment's duration can be found truly only in God, who alone is real because He is abiding. All else is illusion.

In later years, Swami Vivekananda related that when Ramakrishna used to instruct his young disciples he would rise up from his bed and look to see if any householders were approaching. If none were in sight, he launched into a fiery discourse on the glories of dispassion and a life of asceticism. Urging the disciples to safeguard their precious freedom at all costs, he would admonish them never to be a slave to anyone or anything—not to wife, honor, money, or comfort. So strongly did Sri Ramakrishna cherish the independence of his young disciples that he once declared that he would rather hear that one of them had died than that he had bartered away his priceless freedom to accept paid service under another man. Only when such employment was absolutely essential for the support of family members who would otherwise be unprovided for, and only when it was clearly of a temporary stopgap nature, would he countenance it. Clearly, Sri Ramakrishna had a far higher vocation in mind for his young disciples.

Besides spurring them to the highest standards of renunciation, the Master shared with a chosen few the Vedantic vision in which the devotee and the object of devotion are revealed to be one. Swami Vivekananda has stated that Ramakrishna, while outwardly playing the role of the *bhakta*, was inwardly a *jnani*, a man of austere knowledge. And he further revealed that in the private teachings that Ramakrishna gave to him personally the Master taught nondualism rather than worship of the forms of God which he usually emphasized in the public gatherings of his followers.

Since Sri Ramakrishna felt that devotion to the Personal God, the God with attributes, brings Divinity within easy access of men and women everywhere, he regarded it as the most suitable practice for the great majority. However, despite this advocacy of devotion, and his own lifelong love affair with the forms of God, the Master never lost sight of the fact that the Absolute is far beyond mere human standards of knowledge and judgment. On occasion, he would offer glimpses of a transcendent vision of the Godhead without attributes—the vision of the Highest as it is perceived from the standpoint of wisdom rather than love.

"The Absolute is without attachment to the good as well as the evil," he once declared. "It is like the light of a lamp. You can read the Holy Scriptures with its help, but you can equally well commit forgery by the same light. . . . Whatever the sin, the evil, the misery we find in the world, they are only misery, evil, or sin in relation to us. The Absolute is above and beyond. Its sun lights the evil as well as the good. I am afraid that you must accept the facts of the universe as they are. It is not given to man to penetrate clearly the ways of the Lord" (T.L.R., p. 204).

Sri Ramakrishna never encouraged metaphysical speculation among his followers. The great enigmas that theologians in all religions have spent millennia puzzling over without finally solving to anyone's satisfaction save, perhaps, their own—the purpose of creation, the meaning of evil, and similar problems—did not interest Ramakrishna. He assumed that the solutions to such questions (if it is valid to speak of "solutions" relative to issues that transcend rational analysis) exist in a different realm of experience entirely from the one in which the questions are asked. The intellect only knows things secondhand, as it were, through reasoning, whereas all true spiritual knowledge comes directly, as an unmediated revelation. Whatever anyone might say, therefore, the Master knew that God is inscrutable to the mind; what we can know of Him comes to us via the heart, that is to say, through the direct intuitive capacities awakened by selfless love.

"Is it possible to understand God's actions and motives?" He once asked rhetorically. "He creates, He preserves, He destroys. Can we understand why He destroys? I say to the Divine Mother: 'Oh Mother, I do not need to understand. Please give me love for your Lotus Feet.' The aim of human life is to attain *bhakti*. As for other things, the Mother knows best. I have come to the orchard to eat mangoes. What is the use of calculating the number of trees, branches and leaves?" (G.S., p. 161)

Nevertheless, Sri Ramakrishna did not discount the role the dedicated intellect could play when harnessed to the spiritual search. It may not be capable of approaching the Absolute directly; it can never determine in a positive way what God *is*. But it can approach Him indirectly, through the rear door as it were, by telling us what He *is not*. In fact everything that the intellect can conceive of or name is automatically not God, since God, by definition, is inconceivable. Therefore, by a reverse path of negation, a *via negativa*—saying of all phenomena, all objects, all states of consciousness, all beings and forms as they arise in our awareness, *"neti, neti"* ("not this, not this") one is finally led, by a process of sheer intellectual exhaustion similar to that created by a Zen koan, to step beyond the mind and all its limited expressions into the realm of pure Essence, the realm of the ineffable Brahman.

This method is best suited to sharp, discriminating, and skeptical temperaments like Naren's, aspirants whose natural bent of mind is to ceaselessly cut away at all sham and conventional illusions in the relentless pursuit of Truth. These qualities—which unchecked could easily lead to excessive negativity, faultfinding, and argumentativeness—are guided by the subtle hand of the Tantric Master toward the creative outlet of *vichara*, or inquiry into the fundamental nature of things.

Vichara can proceed along either of two generalized lines of questioning. Either the practitioner can ask, "Who am I?" or he can inquire, "What is the nature of Reality or God?" In both cases, he proceeds by rejecting all the incidental qualities, saying for example: "I am not this ever-changing mass of flesh and bones that I call my body, nor this kaleidoscope of shifting thoughts and states of consciousness that I call my mind; God is not these shapes and colors that my eye perceives, nor any of these qualities or attributes which my imagination posits."

The practitioner of *vichara* goes on reasoning in this way until it becomes second nature to him and no longer an intellectual exercise but a vivid perception. Having eliminated the unreal, the Real shines through unobstructed. Spontaneously, he realizes that what he has called "I" and what he has called "God" are at root the same primal purity in which events and qualities of various sorts arise and disappear, but which itself remains unaffected by that arising and disappearing, just as a movie screen is unaffected by the images projected upon it. The questions "Who am I?" and "What is God?" have, paradoxically, led to the identical realization. And the practitioner repeats with the great sages of the Upanishads, *"Aham Brahmasmi,"* which translates literally as "I am Brahman," or "I am God."

According to Sri Ramakrishna, there are two equally valid attitudes which the aspirant can adopt toward God. Either he can say, "I am He" or "I am His devotee." These radically different premises are not actually inconsistent. As Sri Ramakrishna affirmed:

There is no difference whether you call Him "Thou" or call Him "I am He." Men who realize Him through "Thou" have a very lovely relation with Him. It is very much like that of an old trusted servant with his Master. As they both grow old, the Master leans and depends on his friend the servant more and more. . . . The Master consults his servant regarding every serious matter that he wishes to undertake. One day . . . the Master takes him by the hand, then seats him on his own august seat. The servant is embarrassed and says, "What are you doing, my Lord?" But the Master holds him next to himself saying, "You are the same as I, my Beloved." (T.L.R., pp. 205–6)

It is clear that Sri Ramakrishna considered the "I-Thou" relationship as a gentle and graceful flowering into Oneness. In contrast, the Master regarded the path of wisdom, with its affirmation "I am He," as steep and abrupt, suitable only for a born spiritual warrior like Naren. For most, it is an inappropriate, even a dangerous, path. To repeat "I am God," while still to some degree falsely identifying that "I," with the limited body and personality through which it expresses itself, easily leads to the very egotism spirituality aims to undermine. At the very least, it can produce a crippling confusion in those lacking the discriminating sharpness of intellect to distinguish in practice between the larger Self, which is identical with God, and the smaller self, which is a barrier to God-consciousness.

The Master did not deny the utility of the *jnana marga* for those who are temperamentally suited to its rigors. But he remained keenly aware that both the path of love and the path of wisdom follow their own unique logic. While they certainly meet in the end, they lead up to the goal by very different angles of approach, and are suitable to vastly different natures. It is therefore unwise to try to mix them during the early stages. Consequently, Ramakrishna was very particular that the uncomplicated devotion of the majority of his young disciples not be disturbed by a premature exposure to nondualistic philosophy. He went so far as to forbid Naren and a few others to discuss these ideas with other devotees, or to read to them from the Vedantic scriptures.

What the Master emphasized for both the *bhaktas* and the *jnanis* was the need for withdrawing the mind from its preoccupation with sense objects. He told them: "If the matches are dry, you get a spark by striking only one of them. But if they are damp, you don't get a spark even if you strike fifty. You only waste matches. Similarly if your mind is soaked in the pleasures of worldly things . . . then God-consciousness will not be kindled in you. You may try a thousand times, but all your efforts will be futile. But no sooner does attachment to worldly pleasures dry up then the spark of God flashes forth." (G.S., p. 629)

To dry the mind of all worldliness and thereby prepare it for God's all-consuming flame, a rigorous mental discipline is required. Ramakrishna compared this discipline to constructing a sheltering fence around a vulnerable young sapling (an absolute necessity in India where scavenging cattle are everywhere.) A man who struggles to live a spiritual life in the midst of the temptations of the world is like an unprotected sapling. He runs the risk that his still unformed resolve will be prematurely cropped by the passions that roam uncontrolled in the world around him. It is far wiser to shelter one's growing ardor behind the fence of restraining discipline, Ramakrishna argued. That way, the sapling of devotion has an opportunity to grow into a mighty tree of unshakable faith—a huge banyan, which no longer requires protection, but which itself offers shade and shelter to countless others.

Ironically, it is just this fence of strict discipline that gives the renunciate a freedom undreamt of by men whose hearts are bound to the world. The worldly man, the Master once revealed, while outwardly free, is inwardly like a silk worm bound up in a tightly formed cocoon woven from the tangled threads of his own desires, hopes and schemes. Like the silk worm, he is fated to live and to die encapsulated within the all-too-precious dwelling that he has fashioned himself.

On the other hand, the man of renunciation has, through a strict discipline, restrained his own natural impulse to seek security in a self-woven prison of hopes and fears, of likes and dislikes. By laboriously cutting through all the strands of attachment that still bind him to his view of himself, he finally succeeds in standing free, dramatically metamorphized. The crawling earthbound caterpillar of ordinary human nature emerges as a brilliant butterfly floating free on the wings of Divinity.

In the Bhagavad Gita, Sri Krishna states poetically: "What is daytime for the ordinary man is darkness for the sage who sees." We might expand this and say that what is freedom for the ordinary man is bondage to the sage. The freedom which most men seek is the freedom of the marketplace, the freedom to choose at whim from among the many voices jostling simultaneously for one's attention—the strident voice of ambition, the seductive voice of the senses, the clamorous call to duty, the voices of vanity and shame and pride. And amid that dinning babble of tongues, there is the whisper of the soul, at first barely audible. Sri Krishna's incomparable flute, easily drowned out by the more insistent calls of the ego-self, calls us gently to the only real freedom that there is—the boundless freedom of God-realization, which is not a barren choosing among false options, but a surrender to the infinite potentiality of the choiceless ground of Being.

Naturally, to follow the call of Sri Krishna's flute, you have to hear it first. And to hear that exquisitely subtle melody, you must tune out all of the discordant voices of attachment; the smallest clamor of desire will easily drown out the delicacy of the soul's call. Therefore, an iron-willed renunciation—which says no to all the distracting voices—is required. Renunciation, as Sri Ramakrishna conceived of it, must be the solid rock on which spiritual life rests. But the renunciation has to be an inward one. It is not enough to put on the robes of a monk while at the same time mulling over the pleasures of the world in one's mind. The Master bluntly compared such *sadhus* to men who, having spit out impurities, take them up and swallow them again. Nevertheless, as we have already seen, he regarded external renunciation, when it was sincere, as an invaluable aid to fostering mental detachment. The earnest monk who strips himself of outer ties and dons the ochre robe of the renunciate has a built-in head start over those who are constrained to carry the heavy burden of worldly responsibilities.

Ramakrishna was always careful to insist, however, that one

can attain the goal whatever one's station in life; the handicaps under which the householder must operate can be overcome, because the only real prerequisite for finding God is to want Him unconditionally. But one's determination must be absolutely uncompromising and intense. The Master illustrated this with the following story:

> A disciple asked his teacher, "Sir, please tell me how I can see God." "Come with me," said the guru, "and I shall show you." He took the disciple to a lake, and both of them got into the water. Suddenly the teacher pressed the disciple's head under water. After a few moments he released him and the disciple raised his head and stood up. The guru asked him, "How did you feel?" The disciple said, "Oh! I thought I would die; I was panting for breath." The teacher said, "When you pant like that for God, then you will know that you haven't long to wait for His vision." (T.S., pp. 29–30)

Given the need for this degree of intensity, it is hardly surprising that Ramakrishna felt that the householder devotee, whose mind must be split among so many outward concerns and worries, would have a difficult time in attaining it. As an aid in cultivating that one-pointed yearning, the Master advised that his married devotees periodically spend some days alone praying with a longing heart. That way, they would return again to their worldly duties fortified against the tendency toward mental dispersion by the peace and inner strength acquired in solitude.

Sri Ramakrishna gave the following analogy: "Before you break open a jack fruit you must rub your hands with oil, otherwise the gummy juice of the fruit will stick to them. Anoint yourself with love for God, and then you can attend to the duties of the world." (G.S., p. 82)

To one and all, Ramakrishna offered a vision of hope. God is not only for the chosen few who become *sannyasis,* but for anyone who cries out to Him with sincere longing. "Wherein is the strength of a devotee?" he once asked rhetorically. "He is a child of God, and his devotional tears are his mightiest weapon." (T.S., p. 47)

They are also a sure sign that God is near at hand:

> Yearning for God is like the coming of dawn. Dawn comes before the sun itself rises. When yearning for God comes, the vision of God Himself must follow.
>
> The worldly man loves his wealth; the mother loves her child; the chaste wife loves her husband. If your love for God is as intense as all these attachments put together, then you will see Him.
>
> Call on God with a longing heart. The kitten simply calls its mother, crying "meow, meow." It stays wherever the mother cat puts it. It doesn't know what else to do. And when the mother cat hears its cry, no matter where she may be, she rushes to it. (R.D., p. 267)

In words such as these, simple and touching, Ramakrishna conveyed his message of hope to the world, a message repeated a thousand times in a thousand different ways. But always the import was the same: God is not deaf; He hears. But men are deaf who no longer hear His call in the soul. God is not dumb; He speaks. But men are dumb who no longer cry out to Him. God is not dead; He lives. But men are a living dead who have consigned Him to entombment in their dim temples, while they remain outside obsessed by the glittering surface of things. As proof of these assertions, Ramakrishna offered his own experiences. And as evidence of those experiences, he offered himself. But he offered himself not as an object of worship, not as a teacher of Truth. He offered Himself in all simplicity as a child of God; and he offered a child's untainted vision, and a child's abiding hope to those weighted down by the burdens of the world.

To those who flocked to him for spiritual guidance, the Master proclaimed, "Do not speak of love for your brother! Realize it! Do not argue about doctrines and religions. There is only one. All rivers flow to the Ocean. Flow and let others flow too! The great stream carves out for itself according to the slope of its journey—according to race, time, and temperament—its own distinct bed. But it is all the same water. . . . Go . . . Flow on towards the Ocean!" (T.L.R., p. 257)

Chapter 14

Final Days

W HILE KESHAB CHANDRA SEN WAS IN THE THROES OF HIS LAST illness, Sri Ramakrishna had said to him: "Many spiritual emotions have passed through your body. . . . I've seen big steamers going by along the Ganges. While they're passing, you hardly notice anything. But, oh my goodness, what a tremendous noise there is, when the waves they make start to splash against the bank!" (R.D., pp. 243–44). In a similar manner, the Master explained, the upheaval caused by a great spiritual struggle is not immediately apparent. Only many years later do the psychic waves dash against the physical body, tearing down in their fury whole chunks of the "bank."

What the Master said of Keshab applies equally well to Ramakrishna himself. The spiritual whirlwind through which he had passed took an invisible toll. Added to this was his life long habit of ignoring the body's needs, including, in his last years, following a grueling routine which often required spending twenty hours out of the twenty-four sharing himself physically, emotionally, and spiritually with an ever-increasing number of visitors. Clearly, there was a price to be paid.

For most of his life, Ramakrishna had driven his flesh-and-blood organism with the good-natured tyranny of one who knows that flesh and blood are but a vesture for the Spirit. As had

Saint Francis of Assisi, Ramakrishna looked upon the body as "brother ass"—stubborn, ornery, self-willed, and best taken strongly in hand and guided with a no-nonsense firmness. Brother ass is not here to range freely, or to pursue his own fancies; he has no other purpose than hauling the soul, his master, to God, and then guiding others along the same mountain path of spiritual attainment. It did not occur to Ramakrishna to try to preserve the beast for its own sake, or to pamper it like an indolent pet.

For Ramakrishna, the body was like a log of wood, and the spirit a flame. Life was an offering to the sacred flame, an offering to God, an offering to the God in man; it fulfilled itself in being consumed, and not by being hoarded away. "I will give up a thousand such bodies to help one man," he had proclaimed. "It is glorious to help even one man!" (T.L.R., p. 258)

Ramakrishna would soon make good on his desire to sacrifice for the sake of others. The first harbinger of the storm that lay ahead came in January of 1884. The Master was walking alone out of doors when he suddenly swooned from an excess of spiritual emotion. With nobody to support him, he fell to the ground and dislocated a bone in his left arm. The injury proved extremely painful and slow to heal. Like a wide-eyed child surprised at his own metamorphosis, Ramakrishna showed off the splinted arm to one and all, sometimes naively asking whether it was going to get better. At other times he would pout to Kali: "Why did you do this to me, Mother? Just look at my arm—how badly it's hurt!" (G.S., p. 383) But a few moments later—joking, singing, chatting, as convivial as ever—he seemed to have forgotten all about it.

Curiously, Ramakrishna's injury sparked both a sense of detachment from his own bodily form, and a heightened attachment to the devotees. Seeing the broken doll of his body, the Master became ever more conscious of himself as a plaything of the Divine Mother. "As a child builds up his toy house and then breaks it down, so God acts when creating, preserving and destroying the universe," (G.S., p. 176) Ramakrishna had once remarked. The injury graphically exposed life in all its fragility and evanescence. But the Master wasn't depressed by this vision of life's transience. Rather, it intensified his perception of the world as *lila,* as inscrutable play—the play of Eternity in time, the play of God in man. With his consciousness now compelled to dwell at painful length on the physical plane, Ramakrishna was more than ever a captive audience for the poignant drama of humanity being played out before him. And it touched him with an aching and bittersweet compassion as never before. Increasingly, he came to cherish the company of his devotees; perhaps he sensed that the play of his earthly love for them was, even then, swiftly coming to a close.

Less than a year after Ramakrishna finally recovered from the injury, his health took a second, more troubling, turn. What commenced innocently enough as a persistent irritation—"clergyman's sore throat," the doctors called it, blaming the condition on Ramakrishna's unstinting instruction of his devotees—soon progressed to something far more ominous. By July of that year, after all attempts at treatment had failed and the wound had hemorrhaged badly, the dread diagnosis "cancer" was heard for the first time.

The seriousness of his illness now clear, Sri Ramakrishna was persuaded to leave Dakshineswar for Calcutta, where the best possible medical care could be arranged. A house was rented, and several of the young disciples took up full-time residence to serve their ailing Master in shifts throughout the day and night. Sarada Devi came a short time later to cook for Ramakrishna and his attendants, and to assist with the nursing. Doctors trained in both Indian and Western traditions of medicine were consulted. Finally, Doctor Mahendra Lal Sarkar was chosen to treat the Master. While Doctor Sarkar, a homeopath, was aware of the gravity of Ramakrishna's condition, he did not at first despair of a cure. Prescribing a regimen of medicines and a strict diet, he urged Ramakrishna to avoid talking, as far as possible, and not to enter into *samadhi,* which invariably resulted in an irritating flow of blood to the throat. The Master made a half-hearted attempt to comply. But his expansive nature rebelled. When people came hungry for spiritual sustenance, how could he remain silent?

Even Doctor Sarkar couldn't restrain himself from engaging the Master in conversation. The doctor was a rationalist with little sympathy for religion. Nevertheless, he was taken in by

Ramakrishna's vibrant personality, and, as a scientific man, he warmed quickly to the Master's uncompromising devotion to Truth. Doctor Sarkar offered his treatments free of charge. His frequent house calls, to the neglect of paying patients, often lasted for hours at a stretch as he listened spellbound while his patient discoursed on Spiritual Truth. Whenever the Master fell into *samadhi* (which inevitably happened when he spoke of the Divine), the doctor was ready with stethoscope in hand to confirm what his medical training told him was impossible—Ramakrishna's heartbeat and other vital signs had completely disappeared.

One of the ironies of Ramakrishna's move to Calcutta is that, far from encouraging the orderly treatment and rest which the doctor had ordered, it made them all but impossible. Word spread quickly throughout the city of the Master's presence there, and daily the number of people who flocked for his blessings multiplied. Ramakrishna himself complained to the Mother: "Why do you bring so many people here? There's such a crowd I don't have time to wash or eat. This body's nothing but a drum with holes in it; how long can it last if it's played day and night?" (R.D., pp. 285–286) But when the disciples tried to restrict the flow of visitors, Ramakrishna offered them no support. On the contrary, weary and in nearly constant pain though he was, the Master refused to send away anyone who came to him for guidance. Without regard to his own pain, he busied himself relieving the spiritual suffering of others. He only prayed that each and every day the Mother grant at least one person solace through the instrumentality of his broken body.

Just how much of the Master's suffering had come about through years of such ungrudging sharing of himself with others was made clear in a vision. As he walked about his room one day, Sri Ramakrishna saw an etheric double of light detach itself from his body. He was shocked to see the back of the double marred by a welter of dark sores which were most concentrated around the area of the throat. As he gazed in silence, the Mother explained that prolonged physical contact with those who had committed evil deeds had caused their negative karma to be transferred to his body so that it could be worked out there as physical illness.

Final Days

In the light of this revelation, it became painfully obvious why, throughout his life, Ramakrishna had cried out in anguish whenever he was touched by a person of impure habits during one of his ecstasies. Other Indian saints, cognizant of the price of mixing freely with their less evolved contemporaries, have chosen to live in jungles or mountain caves far from society, or have severely limited their contact to a few carefully chosen disciples. Even those leading highly public lives often forbade others from touching them. Ramakrishna, on the other hand, lived fully exposed by choice. Preternaturally sensitive though he was, the Master surrendered himself to all of the currents of joy and sorrow, craving and delusion, eddying around him. Like Jesus, he called to himself the poor and the heavily laden. And like Jesus, he suffered the martyrdom of their sins in his own body.

As Ramakrishna daily grew weaker and more infirm, his devotees looked on with a growing sense of their own helplessness. But the tragic course of events worked to bind them ever more closely to one another, and to their Master, in the intimacy of shared suffering. While the casual devotees drifted away to the sidelines, the dedicated core was welded into a conscious unit as never before. Under Naren's guidance, the young disciples gave themselves selflessly in cooperative service to their guru. Several had moved full-time into the house in Calcutta, where they were living away from the family home for the first time—in some cases in the face of considerable opposition from parents and kinsmen. The structured routine of service and meditation which they followed became, with time, almost monastic. The seeds of renunciation which Ramakrishna had planted were, in this hour of crisis, visibly taking root.

Meanwhile, the householder devotees were rallying to their stricken Master with supplies of food for the growing corps of young attendants, and with funds for renting the Calcutta house. The spectre of imminent loss made Ramakrishna appear now suddenly more precious than ever before. Not only were the devotees realizing just how important the Master was to each of them personally, but they were gaining an appreciation for the full measure of his spiritual stature. There was an awesome quality in the spectacle of the child of God wasting away before them,

SRI RAMAKRISHNA

but with his spirit intact and shining with redoubled intensity, broadcasting joy and good cheer and a subtle power which seemed to flare up in reverse measure to his failing health. The broken figure appeared all the more ethereal, disembodied, divine. What had previously been hidden was now, with the falling away of the physical form, becoming openly manifest for all to see.

Several years earlier, the Master had predicted, "Before I go, I'll cast my whole secret to the winds" (R.D., p. 196). Now, as the devotees looked on at their frail but incandescent Master on his sick bed, the prophecy was fulfilling itself before their eyes. On occasion, Ramakrishna confirmed explicitly what they had come to perceive viscerally. "There are two persons in this body," the Master revealed. "One is the Divine Mother . . . the other is Her devotee. It is the devotee who broke his arm. It is the devotee who is now sick" (R.D., p. 299).

On occasion, the growing awareness of Ramakrishna's Divinity crystallized into acts of spontaneous homage. During the annual festival of the Divine Mother, a ceremony for the worship of an image of Kali was arranged in Ramakrishna's room. As the devotees assembled, Girish Ghosh suddenly began showering the Master with flowers and anointing his feet with sandal paste. He had realized that Kali was fully manifest in Ramakrishna, and that idol worship was superfluous in that living presence. The contagion rapidly spread. Rakhal, "M," and the others followed Girish's lead, and the room filled with exultant shouts of "Victory to the Divine Mother! Victory to Her!" Ramakrishna was jolted as if by an electric shock. His body stiffened; his arms spontaneously assumed the gesture of Kali offering blessings to Her devotees. Transfigured, the Master's countenance became radiant with a luminosity and power that few had seen there before.

Elated by such thrilling moments of transcendence, the faith that Sri Ramakrishna was not merely a God-realized saint, but a Divine Incarnation bearing a message of love to the struggling humanity of the present age, took on new life. While this belief had first been expounded by the Brahmani decades earlier, it had rapidly gained adherents since the onset of the Master's illness; Girish, with his passionate temperament and dramatist's flair for publicity, became its leading advocate. Ironically, Girish's good news about the Avatarhood of Ramakrishna was, at the same time, a harbinger of his imminent departure. Several years earlier, the Master had uttered the grave prophecy: "When many people have discovered who I really am, and start to whisper about it, then this body will cease to exist, by the Mother's will." (R.D., p. 296)

The burgeoning faith in Ramakrishna's divinity was a mixed blessing. Undoubtedly, it greatly stimulated the zeal of many. But for the more volatile, it sometimes had the effect of stirring up emotion instead of genuine devotion, and hollow sentimentality, even hysteria, at the expense of true feeling. Naren felt a deep mistrust of the growing tendency toward making an outward show of devotion. The very manifestations which had so beautifully revealed the spirituality of Sri Ramakrishna—the shedding of tears, dancing in ecstasy, and falling into trances—were less than edifying when acted out for the appreciation of an audience, as some misguided devotees were now doing, or merely to burn off steam.

And even when they were not consciously being "faked," there was still a world of difference, in Naren's view, between tears that flow out of the depths of one's being and represent, as they did for Sri Ramakrishna, a whole-souled heaving after Divinity, and those tears that glance superficially off a momentary "overexcitement of the nerves," (V.B., p. 30) as Naren termed it—just as there was a world of difference between the morbid unconsciousness of the hysteric and the dazzling superconsciousness of the mystic. To mimic the Master's actions without acting from his deeply blissful awareness of the omnipresent Divine is to grotesquely caricature the very state of consciousness one wishes to attain. And it is to run the risk of real madness, rather than the benign and blessed state of God-madness of the genuine ecstatic.

As Naren warned somewhat melodramatically: "When people try to practice religion, eighty percent of them turn into cheats, and about fifteen percent go mad. It is only the remaining five percent who get some direct knowledge of the Truth and so become blessed. Therefore beware!" (R.D., p. 290). When

Naren's attempts at persuasion were less than completely effective, he turned to mimicking those who would mimic Ramakrishna, and thereby successfully shamed them into a measure of self-control.

Given their belief in the Master's divine nature, it is not surprising that many of the devotees regarded Sri Ramakrishna's illness as essentially unreal, a drama that the Mother had staged for a particular purpose (perhaps of uniting the devotees, and strengthening them in their resolve). It was a drama, moreover, which She would surely throw off as soon as that purpose was served. Most of the young Western-educated disciples, however, tended to look for a less supernatural explanation. Naren especially was careful to make the distinction between the indwelling divinity, on the one hand, and the body of Ramakrishna, on the other hand—a body, he reasoned, which was as susceptible to the same natural forces of growth, decay, and death as were other bodies. Despite these divergent views on the nature of Sri Ramakrishna's illness, all were united in hoping against hope that somehow it might be cured. With the prospects rapidly fading for a medical solution, the focus turned to prayer.

In December of 1885, on the doctor's recommendation, Sri Ramakrishna was moved to a more spacious garden house at Cossipore on the rural outskirts of Calcutta. Shortly thereafter, a well-known pundit, voicing the silent thoughts of many, asked Ramakrishna: "The scriptures tell us that a *paramahamsa* like yourself can cure his physical illness by his own will power. Why don't you try it, sir?" (R.D., p. 295).

The Master responded sharply: "You call yourself a pundit, and you can make such a suggestion! This mind has been given to God, once and for all. How can I withdraw it from Him and make it dwell on this worthless body?" (R.D., p. 295).

But a short time later, Naren and others pursued the Master on this point. If not for his own sake, then at least for their sake, Ramakrishna must cure himself, they demanded.

"Do you think I'm suffering like this because I want to? Of course I want to get better! But it all depends on the Mother," he responded.

"Then pray to Her," Naren urged.

"That's easy for you to say, but I cannot speak the words," Ramakrishna replied. But after continued pleading, he reluctantly agreed to try. A few hours later, however, when Naren asked him if he had prayed yet to the Mother, Sri Ramakrishna responded: "I said to Mother, 'I can't eat anything because of this pain—please let me eat a little!' But She pointed to all of you and said, 'Why, you're eating through so many mouths already!' So then I felt ashamed and couldn't utter another word" (R.D., p. 295).

Sri Ramakrishna's last months at Cossipore were a torture of evermore excruciating pain. The cancer's advance was relentless, a slow motion crucifixion. But the Master's smile and habitual good cheer never left him. The evanescent bloom of life was being crushed. And the more it was crushed, the more it gave out its subtle fragrance to the air. "Let the body and its sufferings busy themselves with each other," he said. "Thou, my mind, remain in bliss. Now I and my Divine Mother are one forever" (T.L.R., p. 273). A serene detachment gripped Ramakrishna. At times he seemed very far away, suspended in a mighty, imperturbable calm. The knots of the body and of the mind were unraveling, and the Master was floating free on the Ganges of the Spirit, within sight of the luminous Sea. When he brought himself back, by an act of will, to the devotees gathered at his feet, his every word and act was redolent with a strange tenderness. He held their hands and touched them softly on their chins and cheeks, and gazed with a fathomless maternal gaze into their questioning eyes. Everywhere, the rich and swelling stream of love overflowed its bank, fertilizing the thirsty soil on all sides.

One afternoon, Sri Ramakrishna was feeling somewhat stronger than usual. It was a public holiday and the gardens were filled with his lay devotees. So he strolled out among them, smiling, pausing to greet each of them in turn. Coming to Girish Ghosh, he said, "Well, Girish, I hear you're saying all these things about me to everyone, wherever you go. What is it that you see in me that you can say such things?"

The playwright devotee fell to his knees and pressed together his palms in fervent salutation. "Who am *I* to speak of

Him?" he said. "Even the great sages could find no words to measure His glory." (R.D., p. 296)

The Master was deeply touched. "What more do I need to tell you?" he said. "Be illumined!" (R.D., p. 297) With these words, a thrill passed through Ramakrishna's body; he seemed to swell with divine power. Simultaneously, a great wave of exultation rippled through the gathering. The devotees rushed in from all sides. Overwhelmed with emotion, they prostrated before him one after another. For each one, Ramakrishna had a few choice words of personal blessing. Then he tapped each in turn lightly on the head or shoulders. The effect was electric. Some fell into ecstasy. Others perceived divine forms. Still others shuddered uncontrollably, or passed into states of profound meditation. Many found the lifelong and secret wish of their hearts fulfilled in a moment by Ramakrishna's liquid touch of bliss. All felt themselves to be in the presence of Divinity. But there was a sadness at the very core of the ecstasy—the sadness of knowing that Ramakrishna was making his last gift, the farewell gesture of a deathless love.

Of all the disciples, perhaps none recognized so clearly as the unflinching Naren that the Master had resigned himself to giving up the body, that there would be no last-minute divine reprieve. It was a difficult time for Naren. He was torn more than ever by the conflict between the financial needs of his family, and the inner call of the Spirit, the call of his dying Master. Studying for the bar examination one evening, he became suddenly nauseated at the thought of the life for which he was preparing himself, and he burst into bitter tears. He left his law books scattered on the floor in disarray, and ran impulsively into the night. Blindly he fled through Calcutta. His shoes flew off; he collided with a haystack. Covered with hay and dust, bruised and crazed with grief, he ran and didn't stop until he reached Cossipore.

Naren had finally made his decision; there could no longer be any turning back. But often he tortured himself with the thought that neither could there be any forward movement. Spiritually, all was dry and unavailing. Like so many aspirants before him, Naren could not help but wonder if his dark night would ever end. For all the breathtaking experiences that Ramakrishna had bestowed upon him, Naren had yet to attain the highest of them all, the *nirvikalpa samadhi*. As his hunger for the trackless vastness of the Absolute grew daily, his failure to reach it seemed daily more inexcusable. Now, with his guru fading visibly before his eyes, he began to despair of ever reaching this spiritual consummation of all his desires.

Full of anguish, the young disciple begged Sri Ramakrishna to grant him the nondual state. But the Master scolded him sharply; he was surprised, he said, that Naren should entertain such a small-spirited and selfish desire, just like other men. There was a state much higher than *samadhi*. To realize God in trance is one thing. But how much greater it is to recognize His presence in all that exists. To see Him in His Universal Form, to serve Him in all beings with love and reverence—that alone was a goal worthy of Naren's compassionate and all-embracing spirit, Ramakrishna insisted.

For the moment, however, Naren remained unconvinced. He only knew that he yearned mightily to experience the Infinite. The craving gnawed inside him like an illness. Then one evening it happened. He was sitting absorbed in meditation when a brilliant lamp seemed to burst above him. The light rapidly enveloped his physical form; everything disappeared in the unutterable radiance beyond the world. After some time, as Naren gradually came to himself, he was alarmed by the sensation of his own incorporeality. "Where's my body? . . . Where's my body?" (N.p., n.d.) he cried out. Gopal Ghosh, an elderly devotee who had been meditating nearby, tried to calm him. But Naren continued to call out, and Gopal rushed off in a panic to tell Ramakrishna. The Master, however, was unperturbed. "Let him stay that way for a while," he remarked with a knowing smile. "He's been bothering me long enough to put him into that state!" (R.D., p. 301)

A few minutes later, bathed in an unearthly peace, Naren entered Sri Ramakrishna's room. The Master regarded him tenderly, and then spoke softly: "Now the Mother has shown you everything. But what She has shown will be hidden from you. It will be shut up in a box, like a jewel—and I'll keep the key. When you're finished doing the Mother's work on earth, then the box will be unlocked and you'll know everything you knew just now." (R.D., p. 301)

In the days and weeks that followed, Sri Ramakrishna spoke often to Naren of what lay in store for him. Once, unable to speak, he scrawled on a slip of paper: "Naren will teach others." (R.D., p. 301) Naren, who envisioned a future as a world-renouncing monk, objected strenuously to Ramakrishna's suggestion. But the Master was adamant: "You will have to. Your very bones will make you do it." (R.D., p. 301) On another occasion, Sri Ramakrishna was even more explicit. "Very soon Naren is going to shake the world with his intellect and his spiritual power," he predicted. Again, he told Naren: "I am leaving these boys in your hands. See that they practice meditation and worship. Don't let them go back home." (R.D., p. 298) With such hints, Ramakrishna was preparing him, by degrees, for the great task which lay ahead.

Naren was not the only one who was being prepared for a future role. When Gopal Ghosh returned from pilgrimage with twelve ochre robes for distribution to *sannyasis*, Sri Ramakrishna pointed to his disciples: "Why don't you give them to these boys. They are full of the spirit of renunciation. You won't find better monks anywhere." (R.D., p. 300) So Gopal handed the robes to Ramakrishna, and the Master distributed them to his disciples. On another occasion, the Master told the young men to go out and beg their food from all castes without distinction. When they returned from the streets of Calcutta with their modest offerings, Ramakrishna was beaming. He ate a few grains of rice, and exclaimed proudly: "Well done! This food is very pure." (R.D., p. 298)

With his last ounce of energy, Ramakrishna whispered precious words of encouragement and guidance to the disciples. The illness had cruelly wasted him; he was little more than a framework of skin and bones, with deep sunken eyes and grotesquely protruding cheekbones. But still he called his disciples to him. Naren sat at his feet every night. And every night, Ramakrishna poured out his counsel on the training of the young men who were being left in Naren's charge. One evening as they were alone together, Sri Ramakrishna gazed lovingly at his spiritual heir and went into *samadhi*. Naren felt a subtle power enveloping him. Gradually, he lost consciousness. When he returned to outward awareness, he was surprised to see Sri Ramakrishna weeping.

"Oh Naren, I've just given you everything that I have—and now I'm as poor as a beggar!" the Master exclaimed. "But these powers I've handed over to you will make you able to do great things in the world. When all is accomplished, you can go back from where you came from" (R.D., p. 303).

A few days later, just after midnight, August 16, 1886, Ramakrishna spoke hoarsely to Naren: "Take care of these boys," (T.L.R., p. 274) he urged him again and again in barely perceptible tones. Then, miraculously, his voice returned. Thrice, in a full-throated voice that was ringing and firm, as it had not been for months, he repeated the name of Kali. A thrill of joy ignited his sallow features. The hair on Ramakrishna's body stood on end. A beatific smile appeared like the mellow globe of the sun at dawn—the smile of Spirit's final victory over matter. The devotees thought that the Master had gone into *samadhi*. But this was no ordinary *samadhi*. It was the *mahasamadhi*, the great ecstasy beyond recovery.

As the hours passed, hope gradually faded. The following noon, Doctor Sarkar confirmed that Sri Ramakrishna was no more.

That evening, as the dying sun ignited the high clouds over the Ganges, the devotees carried the body to the shore of the sacred river and, placing it upon the pyre, set it aflame. Oddly enough, when they returned from the cremation ground carrying the ashes of their Master, there were no tears, only a strange sense of euphoria, of the unreality of all that had transpired. "Jai Sri Ramakrishna, Jai, Jai!" they cried out their chant of victory and of hope.

Some weeks before, the Master had said, "A band of Bauls descends upon a house. They chant the name of the Lord and dance with joy. Then suddenly they leave. As abrupt in going as in coming! And the people know them not" (T.L.R., p. 271).

He was referring to himself, to the Incarnation who comes

to the world with his disciples and leaves the world unknown and unsung. Now Ramakrishna had come and gone like the Baul. But he had left behind him a band of young followers on fire with God. The fire that had flared in Ramakrishna, the fire that had engulfed his personality, like a burning bush, without consuming it, that same flame that had finally consumed his body on the bank of the Ganges, destroying forever the dark cage of the Spirit— that fire now burned in a handful of young souls who were bent on igniting the world.

The Baul had come and gone. But his band would continue to dance their way through nearly half of the twentieth century. Through most of the nations of the earth, through India, through the alien lands of Europe and America and the Far East, they would dance their heady dance—unsung, unknown perhaps to the great mass of men, but not without sowing the flaming seeds of Love on the winds of the dark age of untruth.

Notes

Chapter 3

1. Sri Ramakrishna Math, 1972. *Thus Spake SriRamakrishna* (T.S.), Madras, India. P. 48.
2. Sri Ramakrishna Math, 1965. *Sayings of Sri Ramakrishna* (S.R.), Madras, India. P. 315.
3. Advaita Ashrama, 1948. *Life of Sri Ramakrishna* (L.R.), Calcutta. P. 69.
4. Sri Ramakrishna Math, 1974. *Sri Ramakrishna as Swamiji Saw Him* (R.S.), Madras, India. P. 75.
5. Gupta, Mahendranath. *The Gospel of Sri Ramakrishna* (G.S.), New York: Ramakrishna-Vivekananda Center, 1942. P. 138.

Chapter 4

1. Isherwood, Christopher. *Ramakrishna and His Disciples* (R.D.), Hollywood, California: Vedanta Press, 1980. P. 85.
2. Rolland, Romain. *The Life of Ramakrishna* (T.L.R.), Calcutta: Advaita Ashrama, 1930. P. 197.

Chapter 6

1. Ramdas, Swami. *In the Vision of God,* Kanhangad, India: Anandashram, 1985. P. 154.

Chapter 7

1. Nikhilananda, Swami. *Holy Mother*, London: George Allen and Unwin, 1962. P. 30.

Chapter 8

1. Mukerji, Dhan Gopal. *The Face of Silence*, New York: E. P. Dutton and Company, 1962. P. 92.

Chapter 10

1. Prabhavananda, Swami. *The Eternal Companion* (E.C.), Hollywood, California: Vedanta Press, 1974. P. 13.
2. Nikhilananda, Swami. *Vivekananda, A Biography* (V.B.), New York: Ramakrishna-Vedanta Center, 1953. P. 9.

Chapter 11

1. Tapasyananda, Swami. *Swami Vivekananda, His Life and Legacy*, Madras, India: Sri Ramakrishna Math, 1952. P. 42.

Chapter 13

1. Abhedananda, Swami. *Gospel of Sri Ramakrishna* (short version), New York: The Vedanta Society, 1947. P. 154.

Glossary

advaita   Nonduality, the philosophy which teaches the unity of God, the individual soul, and the cosmos. Also referred to as *Advaita* Vedanta.

ahimsa   The doctrine of nonviolence.

ananda   Bliss; see also *Sat Chit Ananda.*

ashram   A retreat dedicated to the cultivation of spirituality, similar to a monastery, but including lay practitioners.

Atman   The indwelling Spirit, the true Self of all beings.

Aum   The sacred seed syllable out of which creation is said to have arisen.

Avatar   An incarnation of God.

Bala Krishna   The playful and mischievious form of Krishna as a child.

Baul   A sect, centered in Bengal, preaching ecstatic devotion for God.

Bhagavad Gita   The "Song of God." The Hindu scripture in which Lord Krishna instructs his disciple Arjuna in spirituality.

bhairavi   A nun of the Tantric sect.

bhajan   Devotional songs.

bhakta   A follower of the path of love.

bhakti yoga   The path of loving devotion to God.

Brahma Muhurta   The sacred hour just before sunrise, considered especially suited for meditation.

Brahman   The name given to the Absolute when it is considered in its transcendent aspect, beyond creation.

brahmin   A caste of Hindus, the members of which are supposed to dedicate their lives to the cultivation of spirituality and to spiritual study.

chakra   Psychophysical centers arrayed along the spine through which the kundalini power rises.

chapati   Indian flat bread.

chit   Pure Consciousness; see also *Sat Chit Ananda.*

dasya bhava   The attitude of being a servant of God.

dharma   One's duty, or God-ordained role, in life.

dhoti   A piece of cloth worn as a lower garment.

dhuni   Sacred fire.

diksha   Spiritual initiation imparted by the guru.

Ganga   The Ganges.

ghat   Flight of steps leading to a riverbank.

Gita   See Bhagavad Gita.

gopis   The milkmaid companions of Sri Krishna. Symbols of one-pointed devotion.

guru   Spiritual master.

gurukulu   The ancient system of education in India, whereby students would live with and serve their teacher in small *ashrams,* usually located in the countryside.

Hanuman   The monkey devotee of Lord Rama who regarded himself as a servant of God.

Hari Aum   A sacred mantra.

hookah   A water pipe.

Ishta Daiva   The form of God or spiritual ideal which the devotee chooses to follow.

Jai   A chant meaning victory.

japa yoga   The path of union with the Divine attained through the repetition of God's Name, or a sacred mantra.

jiva   An embodied being.

jnana   The highest divine knowledge; wisdom.

jnana yoga   The path for attaining *jnana* in which one discriminates in the mind between the real and the unreal.

jnani   One who has attained *jnana,* or one who practices *jnana* yoga.

Kali   A name for the Divine Mother of the universe.

kali yuga   The dark age of unbelief in which we are now living.

karma   Can simply mean activity in general, or it can refer to the good or bad destiny which one has earned through past actions.

karma yoga   The path of working without attachment to the fruits of one's efforts, while remaining conscious that God impels all activity. Work as an offering to the Divine.

karma yogi   A follower of the path of dedicated work.

koan   A Zen Buddhist technique wherein the practitioner focuses on an illogical or unanswerable question in an attempt to propel the consciousness beyond the limits of the intellect.

kirtana   Devotional singing, often accompanied by dance.

Krishna   The eighth Hindu Avatar, sage of the Bhagavad Gita, and divine lover of the gopis.

kshatriya   The Hindu caste of warriors.

kumkum   Sacred red powder, often placed on the forehead, which symbolizes the Divine Mother.

kundalini   The serpent power which is said to rest at the base of the spine and to rise upward through the various *chakras* during the awakening of spiritual consciousness.

kuthi   A bungalow in the temple gardens at Dakshineswar.

lila   The divine play of God. The manifest world is regarded by Hindus as the *lila* of God.

madhura bhava   The most intimate attitude which the devotee can adopt whereby he looks upon God as a lover looks upon the beloved.

mahabhava   The highest range of ecstatic love for the Divine.

mahasamadhi   Literally, "the great *samadhi,*" the final merging of a saint's consciousness into the Absolute at the time of his passing.

mantra   A sacred formula repeated during *japa* in order to cultivate spiritual consciousness.

Math   Monastery.

maya   The obscuring ignorance which renders beings unaware of their true divine nature, and which makes the One appear as many. *Maya* is regarded as a creation of the Divine Mother.

mouna diksha   The highest form of spiritual initiation through silence.

muni   A silent sage.

Naga   A sect of renunciates who remain naked as a reminder of their utter detachment from the world.

neti   Literally, "not this." The process of rejecting the relative in the search for the Absolute.

nirvana   The Buddhist term for absorption in the Absolute.

nirvikalpa Samadhi   The highest state, in which consciousness is no longer divided into subject and object.

nityasiddha   The "ever-free" soul who is full of spiritual knowledge from birth, having attained it in previous lifetimes.

paramahamsa   An honorific title, literally, "great swan." One who floats upon the waves of the world without being stained by them.

pooja   Ritualistic worship.

prasada   Food or drink that has been offered to God or guru.

prema   The most exalted love for God, free from desire or attachment.

pundit   A teacher.

Puranas   The mythological scriptures of Hinduism.

Radha   The greatest of the gopis. Sri Krishna's consort, an embodiment of the most intense love for God.

raga   An Indian musical composition based on a set scale of notes.

Rama   One of the Hindu Avatars. The hero of the Ramayana.

Rani   Literally, "queen." An honorific title.

rishi   Ancient sage of India.

sadhaka   A spiritual practitioner.

sadhana   The practice of a particular spiritual discipline for the attainment of enlightenment.

sadhu   A monk.

sahaja samadhi   The natural *samadhi*, or *samadhi* become continuous and natural, no longer dependent on trance. The highest spiritual state of uninterupted communion with God.

Glossary

sahasra padma   The highest *chakra*, the thousand-petalled lotus at the top of the skull where the *kundalini* force ends its journey, merging the consciousness into the infinite.

sakhya bhava   The attitude of being a friend of God.

samadhi   Absorption in the Spirit, a trance-like state.

samsara   Life in the world of illusion.

sanatana dharma   The eternal teachings of India.

sannyasi   One who has renounced the world; a monk.

sat   Being, reality; see also *Sat Chit Ananda.*

Sat Chit Ananda   Literally, "Being, Consciousness, Bliss." Used as a name for the ultimate divine state.

Sat Guru   The highest type of guru; the teacher of Truth.

satya yuga   The golden age in which all beings will live in the awareness of spiritual Truth.

savikalpa samadhi   The samadhi in which the form of God is perceived.

Shakti   The energy of the Divine as it manifests in the material world. Shakti is regarded as feminine.

shanta bhava   The attitude of adoration of the tranquil devotee before the transcendent Godhead.

Shiva   One of the Gods, the destroyer in the Hindu trinity. Shiva is worshiped by those who practice the path of discrimination.

siddhi   An occult power developed through spiritual discipline.

Sita   The wife of Rama.

sloka   Sanskrit verses from the Hindu scriptures.

swadharma   The uniquely personal duty or destiny of an individual, in contrast to *dharma*, which usually refers to the more general duties that fall to one as a member of a certain caste or social group.

Swami   A title of respect for a renunciate or spiritual teacher.

Sri   Literally, "blessed." An honorific originally used to designate a saint, but now much more widely applied as a rough equivilant of "Mr."

sruti   The background tone played during Hindustani classical music.

sudra   The Hindu caste of laborers.

Tantra   The path associated with the Divine Mother that uses

235

the ordinary energies of the world as tools for spiritual attainment.

Upanishads   Philosophical scriptures of Hinduism.

Vaishnava   A devotional sect which worships the Avataric forms of Vishnu.

vaishya   The Hindu caste of merchants.

vatsalya bhava   The attitude which looks upon God as Mother. Also the attitude in which the devotee experiences himself or herself as the mother of God.

Vedanta   The philosophy of nondualism. See *Advaita*.

Vedas   The most ancient core scriptures of India.

vichara   The path of inquiry into the nature of Truth.

Vishnu   The preserver of the Hindu trinity and seed of all the Avatars.

visudha chakra   The psychospiritual center at the throat. Fifth of the seven *chakras*.

wallah   A person who performs a specific duty or service.

Yashoda   Mother of Krishna.

yoga   Literally, to yoke or to join. The different paths leading to union with God are referred to as yogas.

yogi   A practitioner of one of the yogas.

yuga   According to Hindu thought, the world cycle is divided into four ages, or *yugas*. We are presently in the *kali yuga*, the least enlightened of the great ages.

Suggested Reading

Works on Sri Ramakrishna

Advaita Ashram. *Life of Sri Ramakrishna.* Calcutta: Advaita Ashrama, 1948. This is the highly readable official biography of Sri Ramakrishna by the monks of the Ramakrishna order in India. An excellent sourcebook of over seven hundred pages for serious students.

Isherwood, Christopher. *Ramakrishna and His Disciples* 2nd ed. Hollywood, California: Vedanta Press, 1980. An elegant and somewhat detached narrative by one of the great authors of the twentieth century, himself a devotee of Sri Ramakrishna.

"M" [Mahendra Nath Gupta]. *The Gospel of Sri Ramakrishna.* Translated by Swami Nikhilananda. New York: Ramakrishna-Vivekananda Center, 1942. These faithful transcripts of the Master's discussions with his followers at Dakshineswar (over a thousand pages long) offer a unequaled sense of the ardent spiritual atmosphere around Sri Ramakrishna as well as a full record of his teachings. This inspiring work is highly recommended.

――――. *The Gospel of Sri Ramakrishna,* rev. ed. Revised by Swami Abhedananda. New York: Vedanta Society, 1947. This short edition, revised from the original English text, provides excerpts from the *Gospel*, offering an introduction to Sri Ramakrishna's teachings.

Mukerji, Dhan Gopal. *The Face of Silence*. New York: E. P. Dutton and Company, 1926. This short, poetic book, more a work of art than of accurate biography, nevertheless offers some inspired passages on the life and teachings of Sri Ramakrishna.

Rolland, Romain. *The Life of Ramakrishna*. Calcutta: Advaita Ashram, 1930. This passionate biography, while far from exhaustive, does offer a lively and moving portrait of Sri Ramakrishna.

Saradananda, Swami. *Sri Ramakrishna The Great Master*. Translated by Swami Jagadananda. Madras: Sri Ramakrishna Math, 1952. The seminal work on the life of Ramakrishna by one of his direct disciples, including extensive theological explanations by the author. This exhaustive work will be of most interest to the scholar.

Works on the Disciples of Sri Ramakrishna

Advaita Ashram. *The Disciples of Sri Ramakrishna*. Calcutta: Advaita Ashram, 1943.

Nikhilananda, Swami. *Holy Mother*. London: George Allen and Unwin Ltd., 1963. A full-scale biography of Sarada Devi, the wife and one of the leading spiritual disciples of Sri Ramakrishna.

———. *Vivekananda*. New York: Ramakrishna-Vivekananda Center, 1953.

Prabhavananda, Swami. *The Eternal Companion*. Hollywood, California: Vedanta Press, 1947. The life and teachings of Swami Brahmananda.

Rolland, Romain. *The Life of Vivekananda and the Universal Gospel*. Calcutta: Advaita Ashram, 1931.

Sri Ramakrishna Math. *The Gospel of the Holy Mother*. Madras: Sri Ramakrishna Math, 1984. A collection of spiritual discussions of the Holy Mother.

Index

Index

Haladhari, 48–49
Hanuman, 30; Ramakrishna
  imitates, 54
Hari, 195
Hari Aum, 64
Hari Nath Chaterjee, 159
Hari Prassana Chaterjee, 162–163
Hinduism: influence of on Brahmo
  rituals, 110–111; on secret task of
  life, 90; spiritual culture of, 4–5;
  spread of, 5
holiness, 202
holy men, ritual of visit to, 163
homa bird, 129
householders, vs. monks, 206
Hriday, 22; as protector, 47

idolatry: Keshab on, 105–106;
  Ramakrishna on, 108–109
image worship, 107–110, 157
"inner circle," Ramakrishna's, 206
integrity, Ramakrishna's, 166
intellect, spiritual search and,
  208–209
inward purity, Ramakrishna
  teaches, 134
Isa, Sri (Christ, Jesus), 77
Ishta Daiva, discarded, 51–52
Islam, 76–77, 100
I-Thou relationship, 210

Jains, 204
Jamuna, 81
Janaka, King, 127–128
japa yoga, 198
Jayrambati, 43
Jillellamudi Mother, 171
jiva, 70
jnana marga. See jnana yoga
jnana yoga, 29; blind spot of, 67

Kali, 163; as Bewitcher of Worlds,
  128; the Divine Mother, 19;
  identity of, 24; miracles of, 185;
  as Mother Maya, 32–33; Naren's

acceptance of, 157–158;
  Ramakrishna and, 126, 132,
  165–166, 220; songs to, 177; two
  faces of, 33–35. *See also* Divine
  Mother; Maya
kali yuga, 25, 189
Kali's arms, meaning of, 34
Kali's sword, purpose of, 34
Kamarpukar, 7–12; Ramakrishna
  and Sarada at, 91–92
Kanyakumari, 4
karma, transfer of negative to
  Ramakrishna, 218
karma yoga, 29–30
Keshab Chandra Sen, 73, 215;
  Brahmo Samaj and, 99–103;
  death of, 115; profile of, 102–103;
  Ramakrishna and, 100, 104,
  105–106, 113–115
Khudiram, 11, 13, 19
kirtana, 84
kith and kin, attachment to, 88–89,
  196
koan, 209
Krishna, 130, 131, 160;
  Ramakrishna's love for, 85
Krishna, Avatar, 182
kshatriya, 15, 137
kumbha mela festivals, 81
kumkum powder, 164
Kuan Yin, 31
kundalini, 52, 173–174

Latu, 135–137, 181
lila, world as, 216–217
Lord of the Gopis, 54
love: as disinterested, 91; God as,
  30–31
lust, Ramakrishna on, 126, 195

"M", 165, 169, 206
madhura, 53
magnet, God as, 186–187
mahabhava, state of, 51
mahasamadhi, 227

241

Index

Index

women, Samaj on education of, 100

words, as Naren's element, 152

Yashoda, 52, 131

Yogas, 29, 60

Yogananda, Swami. *See* Yogen

Yogen, 180–181, 201

"young souls", 27, 73–74, 120

yugas, 25

Zen, 84, 90, 209